MY JEET KUNE DO UNLIMITED ADVENTURE

The "Burt Offerings" Columns and More!

BURTON RICHARDSON

EMPIRE BOOK/AWP LLC
Los Angeles, CA.

DISCLAIMER

Please note that the author and publisher of this book are NOT RESPONSIBLE in any manner whatsoever for any injury that may result from practicing the techniques and/or following the instructions given within. Since the physical activities described herein may be too strenuous in nature for some readers to engage in safely, it is essential that a physician be consulted prior to training.

First Edition published in 2024 by AWP LLC/Empire Books. Copyright (c) 2024 by Burton Richardson and AWP LLC/Empire Books.

All rights reserved. No part of this publication may be reproduced or utilized in any form or by any means, electronic or mechanical, including photo- copying, recording, or by any information storage and retrieval system, without prior written permission from AWP LLC/Empire Books.

First edition Library of Congress Catalog Number:

ISBN-13: 978-1-949753-64-6

24 23 22 21 20 19 18 17 16 15 14 13 12

Library of Congress Cataloging-in-Publication Data

My Jeet Kune Do Unlimited Adventure by Burton Richardson -- Compiled & Arranged ed. p. cm.

ISBN 978-1-949753-64-6 (pbk. : alk. paper) 1. Martial arts-- philosophy. 3. Large type books. I. Title. GV1114.3.F715

20711161.815'3--dc22

20060166325

Printed in the United States of America.

TABLE OF CONTENTS

DEDICATION 4

ACKNOWLEDGMENTS 5

INTRODUCTION 7

BURT OFFERINGS (1 - 60) 10

BURT RICHARDSON:
AN UNLIMITED JOURNEY 243

DEDICATION

To my exceptional wife Sarah, for always being supportive of my massive amounts of training and teaching, all the way back to the "Burt Offerings" days.

To my daughter Talina for being an inspiration for everything I do.

To Guro Dan Inosanto for being the absolute best mentor a person could have. All the joys and accomplishments in my life spring from his guidance

ACKNOWLEDGMENTS

Thanks to publisher Jose M. Fraguas, my long time friend and fellow martial artist for suggesting this project and seeing it through.

Thanks to all my teachers who have put up with my many errors and endless questions.

Thanks to all of my students past and present who allow me to share my knowledge, and who actually end up teaching me.

Thanks to all my sparring partners who have shown me my weaknesses.

INTRODUCTION

In 1991, I was asked by Curtis F. Wong (owner of the very popular "Inside Kung Fu" magazine and its parent company Unique Publications) to make a video series on JKD Concepts. This was at the very beginning of the instructional video revolution. I made the series and I was quite pleased that it was very well received. Since I had a writing background, (I completed a 4-year writing and literature honors program at USC in addition to biological sciences) I told Curtis that I was interested in writing a column for the magazine. He said that he would introduce me to the IKF editor, but the decision would be up to him.

Although reluctant, the editor-in-chief at that time, agreed to read one offering. I wrote a piece on Indonesian Silat and turned it in. The editor called a few days later and said, "If you keep writing like this, you'll have a place here for a long time."

When the first piece was published, the heading above the title read "Burt Offerings". The magazine editor had come up with that. I proceeded to write the "Burt Offerings" monthly column for the next decade. It was quite a privilege to share my thoughts, ideas, and evolution with a wide audience. And, I earned a whopping $50 per month, which actually made a difference at that era of my life!

As I reread each piece that made it into the book, I had a many precious memories flow back into my consciousness along with flashbacks of so many pivotal moments in my development. I remembered particular moments training with Guro Dan Inosanto at the original Kali Academy, at the IMB Academy, and at his old Marina Del Rey Academy. So much kindness and wisdom while imparting JKD, FMA, and other arts. There were tough fighting lessons from Sifu Richard Bustillo, along with his cheerful stories and local boy Hawaiian humor. Arduous Muay Thai training with Master Chai Sirisute. Hitting the deck thousands of times assisting Pendekar Paul DeThouars at his home, in group Silat classes and on seminars. My first night fighting Eric Knaus years before our group became known as the Dog Brothers. Starting BJJ with Rigan Machado, training with Chris Haueter, and then beginning my journey into the world of "No Holds Barred" fighting with Egan and Enson Inoue before the sport evolved into modern day MMA. Phenomenal experiences training with Zulu warriors in their combat methods in the hills of South Africa and when learning from the sword master Tatang Ilustrisimo in Manila. So many valuable lessons earned in the crucible of combat.

When Jose M. Fraguas suggested that we do a book on my "Burt Offerings" columns and other additional articles, my concern was that the information contained within those essays would not be valuable to martial artists today. So much has changed in the last thirty years, and I wanted to be sure that the pieces are still relevant and useful today. Thankfully, at least in my assessment, they are. For me, much of it was like restudying notes taken years prior. I got a lot out of that process and it actually prompted me to change a few things in my current modes of practice. I hope the insights and advice that I garnered from training with many of the very best martial artists in the world will help you to be better than ever in your endeavors.

I want to express my profound thanks to all of my instructors. I don't know what I would be doing if it weren't for them. I wish to also give my deep appreciation to all the training partners I've had the pleasure of working with through the decades. I thank my students who allowed me to teach them and better hone my craft. And of course I want to thank my wife Sarah for always being incredibly supportive of my training, even when it is costly and time consuming. And I thank her for being a very tough sparring partner! Thank you to our dear daughter Talina for being such a light in this world and for being another tough training partner! Lastly, thanks to my longtime friend and fellow Kali Academy student Jose M. Fraguas for the idea and for realizing this book.

To each of you reading this book, please enjoy and I hope you can put many of the ideas to work to better your training and life. I hope to see you at one of my seminars or here in Hawaii if you come for a visit. You can contact me through jkdunlimited.com or through social media. I am here to help.

Enjoy your training!

Aloha,
Burton Richardson

Waimanalo, O'ahu, Hawaii

1. ACHIEVING SELF-DISCIPLINE

One of the great benefits of martial arts training is that students are supposed to develop the kind of self-discipline that can be used to succeed in any area of their life. Just like the techniques that are practiced so that a student can defend himself, self-discipline must be consciously practiced to become ingrained. Unless this is taught specifically, the student will probably end up like the average person who goes through life without making the tough choices. Let's take a look at what self-discipline is, and how it is related to our martial arts training and the rest of our lives.

Here is my definition: self-discipline is the ability (learned skill) to choose to take the course of action that is best for you, even though you would prefer to do something else that is easier. If you have ever been on a diet you will understand this definition. It takes self-discipline to stay on that diet. You know what to avoid eating, but often you will find yourself eating the food that is easier or more fun for the moment. People do this with their savings. They know that they should save money every month, but often opportunities arise that give instant gratification, so the money is spent on that instead of being saved or invested. Many people will try to eat differently, start a running program, or work on their flexibility daily, only to fall into back into their previous bad habits. Why? Because you don't need to think about those old habits. They are automatic responses that come very easily for you. When a person realizes that they are back to their old habits, they will often say that they just have no will power, and begin to feel bad about themselves. Acquiring self-discipline does require will power, but it isn't as hard as it seems when we understand just how your will is involved in becoming disciplined.

The trick to becoming self-disciplined is to develop new habits that are more in line with your goals than your present habits. That is all you have to do! But there are three vital ingredients that you

must gather: First, you must have a specific goal. Second, you must decide what actions you must take to reach that goal. Third, you must commit to reaching that goal by consistently taking those actions. This is when the will power comes into play. You must use your resolve, to take the new, beneficial actions consistently until those new actions become automatic. Once these actions becomes a habit, they will be a part of you. You can then use your will power to focus on creating new habits in another area of your life. Here's an example.

Let's say that you have a habit of eating late at night. This habit tends to lead to unwanted weight gain. You know that you should change this way of eating, but the habit is so ingrained that it is difficult to change. What should you do? First, set a goal. Maybe it is to lose 10 pounds. Now decide on your new habit. The new habit will be to have a cup of herbal tea (no sugar or caffeine) before bed instead of eating something heavy with lots of calories. Think of your goal and resolve that each night, no matter how tired you are, regardless of how your day went, you will have your cup of tea and be satisfied with that. You absolutely refuse to eat late at night under any circumstances. Now comes the will power part.

You must realize that there will be nights that you really feel like eating. Maybe you worked out extra hard that day. Maybe you didn't eat enough that day. Maybe you have a friend over who wants to eat. You have to absolutely refuse to give in to those old habits. You must use your will power for the first couple of months to overcome those cravings. After a few months, your new habit will take over and you don't have to worry about it anymore.

How does martial arts training relate to increasing discipline? It has to do with will power and being tough. When your instructor pushes you farther than you thought you could go, you should realize that you are tougher than you thought you were. You may have felt like quitting, but you kept going because your teacher prodded you to do so. How did you feel after that experience? You felt great because you found out that you were better than you thought. The key is that you did something that you didn't feel like doing, that you were glad you did later. You felt better and you reaped more benefits for a little extra effort and discipline.

Every chance you get in your martial arts training, try to go beyond what you feel is comfortable. That is how you grow. Try to think of the long term benefits rather than a temporary, short term gratification of stopping. The same applies in your life goals. Be tough and make the choices that will propel you toward your goal. It may be more difficult now, but you will soon create a habit that runs without thought or effort. I do this with my training, my eating, and writing. It may be hard at first, but the long term rewards are well worth a little temporary suffering.

2. WISDOM OF THE AGES

Quotations that survive through the years are often gems of inspiration that can shape and point lives. Martial artists who constantly strive to better themselves can peruse these bits of wisdom just as they ponder the words of the sifu or sensei. Here are a few for you to think about.

Mark Twain is always good for a sage quote, so how about this one. "There is nothing that training cannot do, nothing is beyond its reach." This is a great affirmation of the belief that we all have the power to change. We don't have to remain at our present level. If you want to kick better, train your legs. If you want to be a great puncher, train with a striking coach. If you want a better job, get the training that will qualify you. All it takes is direction and hard work.

I used to feel that success was so far away that it was highly improbable if not altogether impossible. One of the things that changed my mind was a particular definition of success. "You are successful when you are actively progressing toward your goal." If you are actively progressing toward a goal, you will certainly reach it. The only variable is time. It also helps to have a good plan. In the martial arts, we develop tactics to handle different types of opponents. Do the same for any goal you want to reach. Figure out a good method of attacking any problems that occur and always flow around the resistance. Each time you take action toward the goal you should feel a glow of accomplishment. Success is as sure as your focused actions.

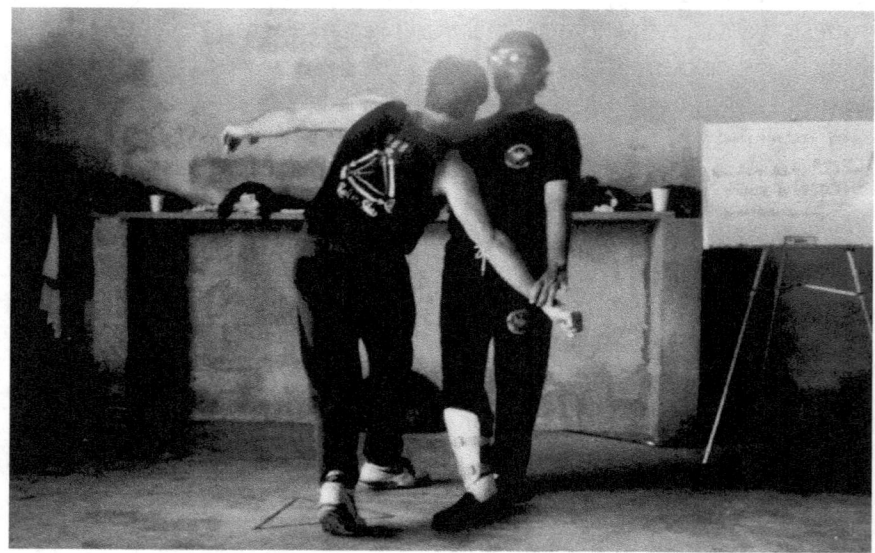

Pendekar Paul de Thouars, grandmaster of pentjak silat serak and creator of bukti negara, often says, " When in a fight, you are the director and he (the opponent) is the directee. You must take charge in a fight and make the enemy conform to your wishes. Otherwise, you will be at the mercy of the bad guy." We can apply that same sentiment to life. You can't wait for good things to happen to you, you must create them. Take charge and do the things that you want to do. It's your life so live it in the way you wish. Want to go to Hawaii? Can't afford it? Figure out a way to swing it. Use your brain. If nothing else, put away a dollar a day for a couple of years. You can do anything you want as long as you take charge and make it happen.

One of my favorite sayings is, "You only see the obstacles when you take your eyes off the goal." This quote reminds me of when I was learning the trapping hands of wing chun kung-fu and jeet kune do. I became so obsessed with which trap to use and which trap comes next and which hand goes where that I forgot that the object was to hit the opponent. I was focusing on the obstacles. Once I began to concentrate on the goal, I could trap spontaneously to remove the obstacle between my fist and the target. Avoid dwelling on the difficulties that lay before you. Concentrate on the goal and you will find a way to reach it.

The Filipino martial arts gives us the saying, "Tira ng tira hangang matapos." This means, "Hit and hit until it is finished." Great advice for a physical altercation but also an allegory for getting through tough times in life. Persistence is a very important quality to develop if you want to succeed. Well-meaning people who want to "save you" from pain will tell you that you've set your sights too high or that your goal is unreachable. Don't listen. Setbacks will occur, but if you push on and on you will eventually break through the resistance. Keep plugging away and don't stop until you get the results you desire. At bare minimum you will be better off than you are now. As Norman Vincent Peale said, "Shoot for the moon. If you miss, you'll land amongst the stars."

Here is one more quote from a highly accomplished Hollywood stuntman Jon Epstein. He and fellow stuntman extraordinaire Bob Brown travel the world doing the things that famous actors can't. How is it that after years of success both of these men are constantly doing bigger and better stunts? Jon likes to say, "It's not what you were, it's what you are now." This is great advice for the martial artist who has achieved a significant goal such as a black belt or an instructor credentials. A certificate of accomplishment is great, but it only describes one point in time. Sifu Dan Inosanto points out that plenty of guys could bench press 300 pounds in college, but very few maintained that strength over the years. Relish your accomplishments, then move ahead. You'll make better progress by keeping your eyes on the road in front instead of in the rearview mirror.

Memorize the positive quotes that you find and use them for

motivation or guidance. You can change your life and every single one of you can move towards your goal. Make a plan, keep a positive focus, and never, ever give up!

3. SOLO TRAINING

The secret to proficiency in any endeavor is to practice consistently and correctly over a long period of time. We martial arts know this well. Only those practitioners who follow this natural law of improvement reach the highest levels in the arts. To practice correctly, you need good instruction. To practice consistently, a dedicated training partner is invaluable. This is also one of the hardest things to find. Your schedules must match up, you must share the same drive toward perfection, you have to live near one another, and it helps to be about the same size. You should also have a good training rapport and be interested in developing in the same areas of the martial arts. The fact that we will have limited time with training partners leads we dedicated martial artists down the path toward solo training; practicing alone.

There are obvious disadvantages to training by yourself. You don't get to interact with the energy of a live human being. It is easier to get bored. You don't have someone there to motivate you when you are feeling a little sluggish. Nonetheless, solo training is crucial to the martial artist and you can insert solo training wherever it fits in your schedule. There are many ways to get around these drawbacks and fly down that road of constant and never-ending improvement.

First, you should make a schedule that you promise to follow. If you had a partner to work with, you would have to set dates and times to train. Do the same with yourself so that your workouts are done on a regular basis. Use music to keep your energy upbeat. Play something that will really get you in the mood for the training at hand. You will progress faster and you train more often.

It is a good idea to vary your training. This will keep your workouts fresh and interesting. Better yet, train your mind to really enjoy the repetition of the most basic of movements. I love to practice, and I find great joy in performing fundamentals over and over again. I will never get that jab to be absolutely perfect, but each jab thrown with a concentrated effort to improve takes me nearer to that goal. If I am moving toward perfection then I am happy even though I will never reach it in my lifetime. Cultivate this attitude and you will have a great time working the basics.

Remember, the basics are the most important part of you training, for without a good foundation you can only build your house so high. Now that you are ready to train solo, let's look at some different things that you can do to get the most out of each session.

When training solo you are either going to practice in the air or on a piece of equipment. As you train alone, you will either do a set pattern, or you will do spontaneous movements that we often refer to as shadowboxing or flowing. You should also train standing up, on the ground, and with various weapon combinations both standing or on the ground. Working in all the ranges and in different environments will give you a complete sense of the arts.

Your standing fighting can be practiced slowly in a routine, as in tai chi chuan or pentjak silat dance, or at full speed as when applying these arts or others on the bag or in the air. Regardless of whether you train in shotokan karate, kali, or muay Thai, fast practice is essential. This can be a set pattern or you can just let yourself go and see what happens.

Some people will say that kickboxing has no set patterns to follow, but if you jab, cross, hook, rear roundhouse kick over and over, then you are practicing a set pattern. Training in this manner to memorize the moves is very important to ingrain the art into your being.

The great martial fighters utilized mindful solo training to increase their practice time and further hone their skills. Add this to your repertoire and you too will find that your skills improve at a faster rate. Be precise, and enjoy the process!

4. FACE YOUR FEARS

What is it that keeps people from really living their lives and pursuing their dreams? What is the element that causes so much anxiety and feelings of failure in people all over the world? By the title of this column you have probably figured out that it is fear. Fear can be an ugly word that holds connotations of the worst that life has to offer. But what is it that we really fear? Pain.

We all want to avoid pain in our lives. We want to feel good and skip the bad altogether, so we avoid pain by throwing different situations onto the fear pile. Whether we group it as fear of physical injury, humiliation, loss of money, or loss of time, the truth is that we are just trying to avoid pain. We are afraid to do certain things because the results of those actions will be very painful to us. But we all know that this attitude holds us back and stifles our dreams. So how can we get past this fear?

The first step in achievement of any goal is honesty. This is true in martial arts or learning to play the piano. Before we start on the journey of self-improvement, it is vital that we take the time for introspection and self-analysis. This means taking a good long look in the mirror to take note of where you really are right now, and to determine how you are going to get to where you want to go. For example, let's say that you are taking martial arts, and you decided that you want to be a complete martial artist. You took the time to check your progress in the different areas of conflict, and you determined that your greatest weakness was in ground fighting. You aren't totally helpless, as you know a few techniques on the ground, but you have seen enough no holds barred competitions to realize that you have serious limitations in that range. Great. You were honest enough with yourself to find a limitation in your training, and have decided to get some training to improve yourself.

Time goes by, and one day you notice that you have not taken any steps toward actually starting your training. This is strange, since you were pretty excited about the thought of becoming a good ground fighter. In truth, you didn't even take the time to look for a school. As you ponder the situation, you notice that you are still hesitating. What is keeping you from making a simple telephone call? Of course, it is our constant nemesis, fear! You are avoiding taking action towards your goal because somewhere inside of you, possibly deep within your subconscious, you believe that starting you ground fighting classes will somehow be a painful experience. This is where honesty comes in again. First you must be honest with yourself about your weaknesses, and second you must be honest about the fears associated with overcoming the weakness. If you do not take this step to recognize the fears, you will never be able to take action and move towards your goal.

So you stop and think about this logically. What are you afraid of? What could it be? Are you afraid of the new environment? That doesn't make sense. You find yourself in new environments all the time. Maybe the training is physically painful. It must hurt to have people putting you in locks, and laying on top of you. But your current training involves contact, so it can't be that. Let's say that after some soul searching, you decide that it is your ego that is keeping you from starting up. You have been doing martial arts for quite a few years now, and you enjoy the feeling of being one of the top students at your school. You realize that you are actually afraid of being humiliated. You fear that you will look bad in front of all the students at the new school. You are afraid to be a beginner because the other students may laugh at you or make fun of your lack of skill. Worse yet, you might feel like a failure. After more introspection, you decide that this is no way to live your life. You do not want your life to be directed by fear, so you decide that you have to do something about the situation. Now! You pick up the phone and call that jiu-jitsu school to make an appointment for your first class.

Congratulations. You have just done what very few will do in this life. You took the time to honestly recognize your fears, and then decided to overcome that fear. Now comes the hard part. You must take the final step, and face your fear. Identifying and deciding to do away with your fear is easy compared to actually physically confronting the situation that you are afraid of. This will require courage and commitment. You must commit to going to the class, and have the courage to follow through regardless of how much anxiety you feel in the process. Remember that courage is not the absence of fear, but the ability to act in spite of your fears. Be courageous, face your fears, take action, and an amazing thing will happen.

You made the phone call, got the information, and went to that first class. You walked into the small school that was basically a wrestling mat and a phone. You see students in sweaty, tangled knots of arms, legs, and uniforms. You realize at this point that you really know nothing at all about this ground fighting. It is worse than you had imagined! Your heart is pounding and you are looking for a way to leave when the instructor approaches you. He greets you with a smile and a handshake and invites you to get changed and try your first class. Even though you have your workout bag in your hand, you hear yourself say that you just came to watch. Boy, that fear has some power! It spoke up for you! The instructor kindly coaxes you to just try, and that you will have fun. It is difficult to say no, so you walk to the bathroom to change.

You do so, but very slowly, somehow hoping that you will be late for the class and that you can just sit and observe. You finally emerge from your temporary sanctuary to see that the room has been filled with even more students. What will they think of me? Will I have to spar? Are they all out to get the new guy? You have not even started your warm-ups, but the sweat is already trickling down your forehead.

Class starts, you do the calisthenics, and immediately begin to feel better. I can do this part, you tell yourself. The instructor goes into a technique, which for you is complicated. Again, you feel the fear that you will look bad because you don't understand what the instructor wants you to do. He tells the students to pair up, and then brings a student to work with you. The instructor says to start just with the position they are working from and to forget the arm bar. You work through class, and become lost in the learning process. You do some sparring at the end of class, and even though you were pretty much helpless, your partner gave you some tips and you now understand the game a bit better. With class over, you feel great that you have learned many things that you never knew about before. You have faced your fears, and feel a great relief with the knowledge that you are now progressing towards your goal - and you are enjoying it!

So what took so long to try the class? Fear, right? Yes, but if we look a little deeper, we will have a better insight into the fear process, and will be able to short-circuit it more easily. Remember that what we call fear is the association of a great deal of pain with an action or situation. If you are avoiding something, it is because you are afraid of it, which means that you somehow associate pain with that situation. There are two ways that we associate pain with different situations. One is through a painful experience that we have had in the past in a similar situation, and the second is through imagination. Negative imagination kills more dreams than anything else. We often imagine severe pain although we've never experienced the particular situation. Those negative images create a fear that stifles our ability to act. This is a good thing in the proper situation. You should be afraid of jumping off of a tall building, even though you have never done this before. The problem is that we can imagine all sorts of negative scenarios about situations that would be highly beneficial for our lives. If we focus on the negative rather than the positive, we will become slaves to the evil master named fear.

After finally facing your fears, you will probably wonder why you were so deathly afraid in the first place. In the case of the ground fighting school, tens of thousands of people train on the mat every day, so it can't be that bad. Look at your fear logically, and it will diminish. Face your fears up close and personal and they will shrink substantially.

Be honest with yourself. Recognize your weak points, and identify your fears. Have the courage to face those fears, and you will be unstoppable. Remember that most fears are just negative visualization, and that changing that vision to a positive one may be all you need to take steps towards living the life you have always dreamed of living!

Note - I wrote this in the mid 1996. Decades later, having the courage to face my fear has resulted in tremendous personal growth. It is a habit that can be acquired. The biggest decisions in my life were also the scariest, but they pushed me forward to an exceptional quality of life. I wish the same for you.

5. FUN FUNDAMENTALS

What do all great fighters have in common? Physical fitness is a common trait, but how about technically? What does boxing champ Evander Holyfield have in common with jiu-jitsu champ Rickson Gracie? What secret does sumo grand champion Akebono share with kickboxing champion Maurice Smith? It is the same quality that puts basketball great Michael Jordan and football star John Elway at the top of their respective fields. The secret is strong basics.

Basics are the key. When two people compete in any arena, the one with the strongest basics pertaining to the parameters of that event will usually come out on top. If this is true, then we martial artists should spend a large percentage of our time honing those basics. Otherwise we could end up being a person who knows a lot, but can't apply any of our knowledge during a stressful encounter.

The guiding principle in Bruce Lee's Jeet Kune Do concept is that each individual should strive to become his or her very best at the art of fighting. That means being able to perform your art against a skilled, aggressive, unwilling opponent. Not just looking good when your partner throws a punch out and holds it there for you while you go through a barrage of blows, throws, and locks, but actually being able to handle someone who doesn't want to be handled. The surest way to accomplish this to work your basics until they are at a high level.

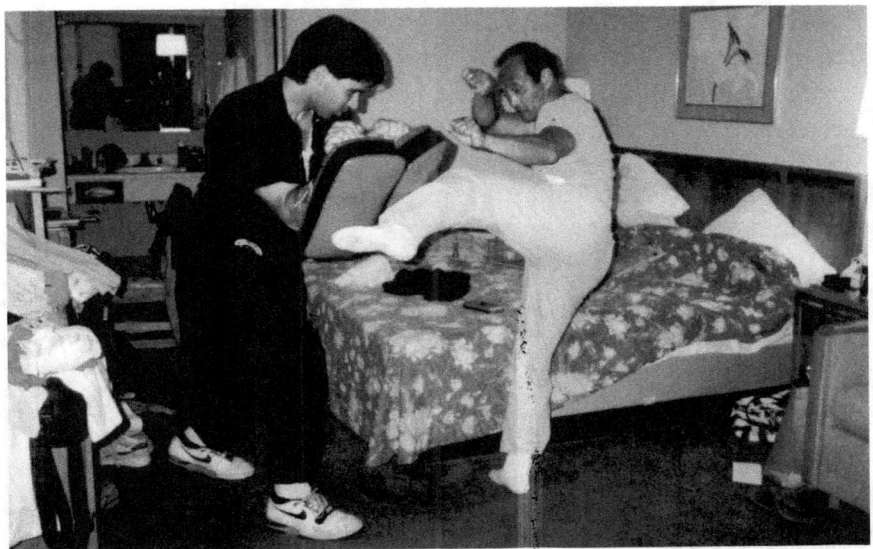

Let's talk about why these fundamentals are so important in fighting. There is a common attitude amongst martial artists (including many JKD practitioners) that whoever knows the most techniques is the best. Let's think of this logically. Say two men were about to fight. Fighter one knows 500 techniques against a straight punch. He also knows 25 forms which he can perform flawlessly. He has 15 lock flows down pat, and 30 knife disarms that he can perform blindfolded, provided that his training partner feeds him the right "energy". Fighter number two knows 6 counters for a straight right hand. He doesn't know any forms or lock flows, and would probably try to run away if someone pulled a knife on him.

So these two decide to go at it. Number two feints and fires a right cross with all his power. Number one starts his block. At the moment of impact, that one millisecond in time, does the number of techniques that each person knows determine the outcome? Not in that unique moment of time. All that really matters is whether the particular defense fighter one puts up will counter that powerful right hand. Now questions of attributes arise. Is the defense powerful? Is it performed efficiently with suitable precision? Is it on time? Was the punch thrown accurately? Was the offense faster than the defense? These are the things that will determine the outcome of the first engagement. If fighter one has not honed the one particular block he needs in the moment, there is a good chance that fighter two's punch is going to land.

I think that it is important, over time, to learn as many functional defenses and attacks as possible so that you have a large pool to draw your basics from. Your basics should be those techniques that work best under pressure against an uncooperative opponent. The best way to find out which basics work for you is to spar in the different ranges. You should have a few core basics in each range against each of the most common attacks. These are the fundamentals that must be drilled and drilled and drilled some more. These must become automatic reactions when the pressure is on, when there is no time to think.

But isn't that boring? It doesn't have to be. We have to outsmart the boredom factor. Because repetition of the core techniques can become tedious, it is vitally important to develop training methods that keep this sort of repetition enjoyable. This is what I call the "fun fundamentals". If I just want to work on my lead leg roundhouse kick to the groin, I can practice in the air 1000 time (and never want to do it again!), or I can devise methods of practicing the kick that will keep the training fun. Maybe I'll do 50 kicks in the air to warm up. Then I can do rounds on the focus mitts, kicking shield the heavy bag, and kicking towards my partner's groin (without hitting). I can do focus mitt rounds where I start with the kick then go into a hand combination. I can start hands and end with the kick. Maybe I block a kick then return the kick, or vice versa. I can start with the kick, move into different ranges, then finish with the kick. After various rounds, I can do some sparring. We can start with kicks only. We can try kicks versus punching, or full sparring. I will see how often and in how many ways I can land that kick. I will analyze the session afterwards, see what I need to work on, and practice those aspects during the next session of fun fundamentals.

Train your basics well in an enjoyable manner and they will be there for you when the pressure is on. Play with the different techniques, but always remember to drill your basics first!

6. THE KEY TO SUCCESS

Success has been defined as "actively progressing toward one's goal." So, how do you progress toward your goal? First, you must have a goal. As motivational speaker Zig Zigler says, "The greatest archer in the world will have trouble hitting a target if he is blindfolded and can't see where it is. How can you expect to reach a goal if you don't even have one?" Once you have a goal, you should formulate a plan to get from where you are now to where you want to be. With that accomplished there is just one more small task to fulfill to reach your goal; you must take action by following your plan until the objective is reached. This is where we get to the key ingredient that will make all of this planning actually work: DISCIPLINE. Without discipline you will find it very difficult to reach a lofty goal.

Discipline is a word that is thrown around freely in most martial arts circles. It is one of the selling points in the majority of advertisements for the local schools. Many people begin studying the arts because they crave the ability to discipline themselves in many facets of their lives. But what exactly is this magic entity that so many yearn for? What is it that we all want to be able to do consistently?

I like to define discipline as simply doing what is best for your long term aspirations instead of succumbing to whatever feels good in the moment. Not the easy choice, or the best tasting choice, or the choice of habit. Discipline is simply making the choice that is in line with your plan to reach your goal. Training in the martial arts can give you the feel for self-discipline that you need to succeed in other endeavors.

Discipline is really the battle of mind vs. body. Dr. Paul Bragg, the man who inspired Jack LaLanne to follow a healthy regimen and opened the first health food stores, wrote often about this battle. In his book about weight reduction Dr. Bragg says: "You must use your mental power to win over the cravings of the body. In other words, it is mind over matter. Flesh is dumb. There is no intelligence in flesh. You must recognize that there is a lifelong running battle between the mind and the flesh. Flesh is weak and must be controlled by the mind."

This conscious control by your mind is what discipline is all about. You know what to do to lose body fat. Simple to know but much tougher to follow through on. You must make the right choice every time you face the choice between moving in a positive or negative direction.

Luckily, improving your discipline is a lot like improving your martial art skill. The more you practice the correct way the more it becomes ingrained in your subconscious. Unfortunately, the opposite is just as true. Each wrong decision will become just as ingrained until if forms the all too familiar bad habit. I am sure you have heard that practice makes perfect. You may have heard that only perfect practice makes perfect. Dr. Michael Colgan, a top expert on sports performance and nutrition, has a more concise saying. He states that, "Practice makes permanent." Whatever you practice will become a permanent part of you. This is why it is crucial to take control of your cravings and make an intelligent decision regarding the important choices we make every day. Remember that our lives are the sum total of our choices--be they good or bad.

One of the factors that hampers our ability to consistently make the best decision is fear. There are many types of fear, but two success killers are the fear of failure and the fear of the unknown. Fear of failure manifests itself through negative thinking. "What if I make this big sacrifice and nothing comes of it. That will be a waste of time." You must get negative thoughts out of your head. If you plan well, you will know that success is certain as long as you follow the plan. Don't let negative thoughts from yourself or others keep you from the joy of accomplishing your goal.

Fear of the unknown creeps up when we start saying, "What if it hurts to run that five-mile course. What if I can't make it and my friends find out. What if I start lifting weights and I injure myself. What if I start that new kickboxing class and I find out that I'm not as good as I thought." These are the types of ridiculous arguments that we have with ourselves when we are afraid of trying something new. Who cares what others think? Who says you have to start with five miles?

A few years ago I finally conjured up the discipline to begin a running program. Guess how many miles I start with. A couple? Three? Try four blocks. I am glad I did. I started very slow and now I can whip out a five-mile run in under 40 minutes with no problem. If I thought that I had to prove my manhood by starting with a long run I would have gotten so sore that quitting would have come easily.

Don't worry about what others think of you or your plan. Put your mind in charge and you can reach your objective.

Styles that have a ranking system are very good for developing discipline in attaining a goal. The student who starts as a white belt knows that he is going to have to attend class and practice certain things to attain the next rank. This is the all-important plan. Reaching short-term goals will culminate in reaching the long-term goal of the black belt. Other ways of developing discipline can be seen as well. Just as there are many wonderful ways of training self-defense, there are countless ways of practicing discipline.

One method used in some Japanese and Korean systems involves having the students sit on the floor with their eyes closed. An instructor will walk around with a shinai, a bamboo practice sword, and without warning strike the ground next to a student. The body's natural reaction is to flinch, but a person with a calm, disciplined mind can keep the body from following its natural urges. When you spar you must resist flinching and closing your eyes as strong blows come in. A good Thai boxer will stand strong and firm in the face of oncoming fists, feet, knees, and elbows. Such discipline is indeed impressive, but I guarantee that it was cultivated through years of practice.

If you want to better your discipline do what you are doing now: read. Get books on the subject or audio tapes. The Neuropsychology of Self-Discipline in an excellent course. Set your goal, form a good plan, and then discipline yourself to take consistent, disciplined action toward that goal. You will be so glad you did.

7. GROUND FIGHTING PRINCIPLES VERSUS STANDING

Many martial artists ask me why I spend nearly half of my class working on ground fighting. Real fights often go to the ground, and if you have trained well on the ground you will greatly enhance your chances of finishing the fight in your favor. The fact is that in most self-defense situations, we prefer to avoid going to the ground. It is easier to escape from a standing position and you have a better chance (although it is still very difficult) to deal with multiple attackers successfully. Being on the ground, especially on your back, in a real fight is very, very dangerous. And that is exactly why we spend so much time practicing from that position. Another fact is that there are times when a fight is a one on one situation. This can be a challenge fight or a backyard brawl where some type of street etiquette is imposed. (This seems to be more common these days, where a group of people will encircle the two fighters and let them fight, almost like a mixed martial arts match in the street.) In these situations, the ability to fight on the ground can give you a huge advantage, even over someone much larger than yourself. Here are a few tips to help you with your ground fighting.

The key to winning a ground fight is to get to and maintain a dominant position. From there, you can control the opponent while you work to finish the fight. In order to do this you must have good fighting skill on the ground. The all-important key to developing fighting skill, whether in kickboxing range, clinch range, or on the ground, is to actually practice applying your techniques against a partner who is fighting back. Just practicing techniques with a partner who offers no resistance will not prepare you for a real fight. A real attacker will fight your every attempt to subdue him, so you must practice your techniques against an uncooperative partner. It is much more fun too. You will learn how to get to that dominant position, hold the position, and finish the fight from there.

There are many different positions in a ground fight. Each of the positions can be a Top or Bottom position. This makes the ground range different than kickboxing or clinch fighting. If you are kickboxing, both of you are trying to apply similar techniques. You both try to strike, get to the clinch, or shoot for a takedown. If you are in the clinch, you both try for similar moves, such as working for superior position, striking, and hitting takedowns. But on the ground, the person on top is going for different techniques than the person on the bottom. If you have achieved a dominant position like the mount (sitting on your downed opponent's chest) you can strike hard, work for chokes, arm bars, arm locks, or move to his back. The person on the bottom has none of these options. He must try to get to a more favorable position. So while we categorize kickboxing and clinch as distinct ranges, ground fighting has to actually be looked at as two entities: ground game top and ground game bottom. Being on top is almost always better than being on the Bottom. (The only exception is if you are on your opponent's back while your back is to the ground. He is on top, but you have a huge advantage.) You can strike harder from the top and you usually have better control over your opponent because you can use your weight to limit his movements. If you are on Top, you usually try to eliminate space to keep the opponent from moving to a better Position. If you are on the Bottom, you usually want to create space so that you can maneuver. If you want to effectively defend yourself, you must train to fight in all of the different ground positions.

Ground fighting with striking is very different than just grappling. It is very tempting to only do submission grappling in your training without any strikes. This leads to bad habits. I highly encourage you to almost always allow strikes in your ground fighting practice. Do it safely with proper protective equipment, but make sure that striking is almost always part of your ground fighting training. In a real fight, a student who has trained ground fighting with striking for six months will almost always beat a person who has grappled for a year without adding strikes. In the street, the opponent will surely strike.

If your primary goal is street self-defense, be sure to make ground fighting part of your practice. It will raise your confidence to a new level.

8. CARLSON GRACIE'S VALE TUDO TRAINING

Brazilian jiu-jitsu has taken the world by storm. Limited rules fighting matches have been dominated by the grappling expert, especially those trained in the Brazilian brand of jiu-jitsu. Terms like "the guard" or "mount position" which were uncommon a few short years ago are now common knowledge to most martial arts practitioners. Much of the popularity of the art has come through events such as the "Ultimate Fighting Championship", "Extreme Fighting", and "The World Combat Championships". While very new to western audiences, "Vale Tudo" (everything goes) no time limit matches that include bare knuckle punches, kicks, elbows, knees, and head butts standing, in the clinch, and on the ground have been held in Brazil for over seventy years. Preparing for such intense fighting involves very serious training.

One of the most famous trainers of tournament jiu-jitsu champions

and Vale Tudo champions in Brazil is Carlson Gracie. Now 62 years old, Carlson was himself the undefeated Vale Tudo champ of Brazil for 25 years, defending the Gracie family name against all opponents. It is indeed rare to find a great champion who also becomes a great trainer and mentor of champions. Now, Carlson is located in West Hollywood, California producing more future champions at his Carlson Gracie Academy. Here are nine principles that Carlson Gracie uses to take students of jiu-jitsu and make them into Vale Tudo champions.

1. Brazilian Jiu-Jitsu with a Gi. The base of the Carlson Gracie vale tudo fighter is Brazilian jiu-jitsu. Each fighter must first come up through the ranks training in jiu-jitsu. This develops the devastating ground game that the Brazilians are known for. The student learns how to move on the ground, learns the positions, and the techniques for escape, control, or submission from each position. Besides years of learning, practicing, and sparring in the school, competitions with other jiu-jitsu schools keep the skill level high. Training for a tournament always motivates students to give the extra effort during practice sessions. The competition itself allows participants to test themselves and discover weaknesses, while learning how to deal

with the pressures that accompany big tournaments. Most vale tudo fighters have been in many tournaments before they ever step into the bare-knuckle arena.

One of the greatest benefits of training in tournament jiu-jitsu is that the gi is worn. When your opponent can grab your sleeves, collar, and pants, movement becomes much more difficult. Learning the art of jiu-jitsu with the gi makes fighting without any handles for the opponent to grab much easier.

2. Cardiovascular Conditioning. This is an important part of jiu-jitsu training, but it carries over to the vale tudo practice. Running, skipping rope, and long sessions of drilling or sparring on the mat bring the fighter's stamina to a very high level. Vale tudo matches routinely go fifteen minutes, and often continue for over an hour until one fighter submits the other. Cardiovascular conditioning should not play a part in the fight if the combatant has trained properly.

3. Strength Training Calisthenics and weight lifting go hand in hand to develop the strength of the fighter. Weight training is used to condition the athlete to handle strong, heavy opponents. Nothing builds muscle mass faster than heavy resistance training. Along with weights and weight machines come calisthenics exercises. Pull-ups, push-ups, ab work, and other weight-free movements develop stamina in the muscle by making the athlete put a large strain on the muscle for a long period of time. Combining cardiovascular and strength training make a fighter with great short burst strength along with the long term strength needed to hold an opponent throughout a lengthy match.

4. Vale Tudo Technical Training. This is where Carlson Gracie teaches the fighters the fine points of grappling without a gi when striking is involved. There are many techniques that work in jiu-jitsu tournaments that are dangerous in the ring. The fighters learn how to get to the position they want without taking too many blows. They learn techniques specific to fighting without a gi where there is no material to grab onto. They practice holds that will put them into position to throw punches, elbows, head butts, and knees effectively. New innovations are also perfected so they can be put to use in a vale

tudo match.

5. Vale Tudo Grappling Training. This is the same as tournament jiu-jitsu, but no gi is used. The fighters are also aware of the positions that they need to get to in the free-fight. Sometimes the fighters will just practice passing the guard against each other, or work from one particular position over and over again to hone the skills. Other times they will just grapple. They will start standing, work for a takedown, then continue on the ground.

6. Boxing All of Carlson Gracie's fighters practice boxing. Some put in more time than others, but every fighter must spend time with a boxing coach to develop offensive and defensive skills in the punching range. Carlson knows that being able to punch is a great asset standing and on the ground, and being familiar with boxing hand work helps the fighter to enter into grappling range safely against a good puncher, or dole out punishment before going to the ground.

7. Vale Tudo Drills These are similar to the vale tudo grappling, but punches are added to the drill. One fighter may practice punching from the guard while the other works on defending against the punching and working to a better position. One fighter may start across the side of the partner and practice punching, elbows, and knees while the other tries to defend and escape the position. The two may play "pass the guard", but with the striking elements added.

8. Vale Tudo Sparring This is simply sparring where everything that is allowed in a vale tudo fight is used. The two start standing, punch, kick, elbow, and knee, enter, throw, and go to the ground. The sparring continues until the round is over, or until one of the partners submits the other. If this happens, the two stand up and start again. Of course, control is used with all the strikes to maintain the health of the fighters. Carlson doesn't want to send an athlete into a match whose body is beaten up from training.

9. Vale Tudo Fights- This is where the fighter is taken out of the classroom and put into the laboratory. Everything is full power, and often no protective equipment is used at all. No gloves, no padding,

nothing but skill to protect the combatants. The attitude of the fighter is that he will go in and do his very best to win the fight. He will fight hard and never give up. He expects to win, but if he comes out on the losing end, it is just another experience that will motivate him to train even harder than ever, so that he too will become one of Carlson Gracie's team of champions.

This is how Carlson Gracie trains his fighters. Of course there are the intangible aspects of the training such as the environment of being amongst a group of great fighters. And there is no substitute for having the experience and knowledge of Carlson Gracie available at a moment's notice.

The recent debut of Vitor Belfort, a Carlson Gracie protégé, in the Ultimate Fighting Championship was a great example of what happens when a gifted athlete with a good mind trains for years under the tutelage of one of the best fighters and teachers in Brazilian history. Vitor, at the age of 19, dominated the heavyweight class to win the Ultimate Fighting Championship in his very first attempt. Other famous fighters from the stable such as Mario Sperry, Wallid Ismael, Carlos Barrera, and Murillo Bustamante have shown their prowess in fights around the world. The question that arises is, "Who will be Carlson Gracie's next champion? I am sure that we will all know soon.

9. THE BURTON RICHARDSON INTERVIEW

When and how did you first start your training in martial arts?

- My first introduction to the arts was when I was about 7 years old. A classmate in elementary school showed me some his "secret" karate moves on the playground. I remember being captivated by the notion that there was an actual method to fighting. When I was about 10, I heard a loud sound coming from the gymnasium at a local park. I peeked in and saw fifty people in karate uniforms standing in horse stances, throwing punches. They all did their "kiais", which resonated throughout the building. It was very impressive to a young guy in a pretty tough neighborhood. I didn't start any actual martial arts training until I was 17.

How did you first hear about Bruce Lee and his art of Jeet Kune Do?

- I first saw Bruce Lee in the Green Hornet television series. I just loved Kato, and I loved that car. I didn't know that it was Bruce Lee until many years later. I first learned of Bruce Lee when I was about 11 years old. I spent many afternoons and evenings in the local parks in Carson, California, the city where I was raised. After a basketball practice on the blacktop, a friend took out a small booklet that had photos of Bruce Lee in Enter The Dragon. I remember being mesmerized by the photos, but I still didn't know anything about Jeet Kune Do.

Years later, my first girlfriend was taking lessons with Sifu Dan Inosanto and Sifu Richard Bustillo at the original Kali Academy in Torrance, California. I was 17 when she asked me out on our first date- a matinee showing of Enter The Dragon. I became very interested in training, and she took me to the Kali Academy. Because I was too busy with studies and baseball to sign up, she taught me some of the basics. For my 18th birthday (January of 1980), she bought me the Tao of Jeet Kune Do and the Bruce Lee's Fighting Methods series. I began training at the Academy that summer, and have been hooked ever since.

What was it about JKD that led you away from traditional martial arts?

- I hadn't actually trained in traditional arts, but my first trip to the Academy was a great relief for me. I really didn't like those uniforms that I saw in karate. Since I was a baseball player, the fact that the guys and girls at the academy worked out in sweatpants and t-shirts was very appealing to me. It looked like an athletic training session rather than a ritualized routine. It suited my taste very well..

JKD has gone through a lot of phases over the years due to different theories on how the art should be taught. What is your take on the "Concepts" vs. "Original" controversy?

- First off, there are many, many different incarnations of "concepts" and of "original". Watch two original instructors teach and you will usually see two very different approaches. Even more so with concepts. I agree with the original mindset that we must really hone our basics until they are very, very strong. It is true that some concepts practitioners have gotten into the "more is better" approach. If you keep accumulating knowledge without honing the basics, you will not be very functional. It is like owning seven Ferraris, but none of them have an engine. They look nice, but they aren't very useful.

That said, I see that many of the original people have not continued with their education, and are now behind the times. Yes, a finger jab will still work. Yes, a straight blast can still be functional, but there are many, many other useful elements that can be added to make the fighter more well-rounded than ever before. Arts like Brazilian Jiu-Jitsu were simply not available in Bruce Lee's day, but aspects of the art are very important for those striving to become a well-rounded fighter.

My personal emphasis is on well-rounded, street-effective training. I believe that is what Bruce Lee was after, and he showed us the way to reach this goal. The one vitally important aspect of training that I see lacking in many (not all) original and concepts classes is sparring. Bruce Lee emphasized that in order to be skillful in fighting, you must put on the protective gear and go nearly all-out against a partner who is resisting you one hundred percent. This principle was so important that he chose to show this kind of sparring as part of his famous demonstration at the Long Beach Internationals. But, many JKD instructors and students shy away from hard sparring, as it is very rough. I understand this point. It is not for everyone, and we don't want to only offer the art to hard core athletes. The problem is that many of these schools throw out sparring altogether. It has been proven over and over again that without sparring, you will not be able to develop a high level of fighting skill. As Bruce Lee emphasized, one must "get in the water" if they want to learn how to swim. JKD is experiential, meaning that each individual must experience combat for himself or herself. It isn't a spectator sport. JKD practitioners must live it. The only way to become good at fighting is to actually fight from time to time. That may sound scary, but it does not have to be an all-out slugfest. Students who don't want to go hard can spar lightly by using what I call "progressive resistance" or "variable intensity" methods. Each person puts on protective gear and spars at his or her own skill and comfort level, in a safe, fun environment. This way, EVERYBODY can spar and improve actual fighting skills, which is exactly what I believe that our Sigung was after.

You have trained with several original Bruce Lee students. Please list your instructors in JKD and what you have learned from each of them and some of the differences in their teaching styles and their application and interpretations of Jeet Kune Do.

- I have learned many important lessons from each of my JKD instructors, but I will just list one major element for each.

My first instructor was Sifu Dan Inosanto. He is incredibly generous with his knowledge, and is a magnificent example of someone who spends more time training and researching than standing in front of the class teaching. I think that this quality has been the most important for me and my students. It is very easy to get into the "Sifu" mode, teaching classes and tending to students. But I don't want to just be a professor. I am first and foremost a martial artist, which means that I am constantly engaging in training and learning from others. Teaching improves our understanding of the art, but training and sparring with top martial artists in various disciplines is where we expand and improve our skills. Bruce Lee sparred with the top fighters of his time. That improved him. I follow his example and spar with the top fighters of our time. I seek out MMA champions, kickboxing champions, BJJ champions, and submission wrestling champions to spar with and exchange knowledge with. I seek out instructors from various fighting methods all over the world for my research. I have trained in the Philippines, Brazil, China, Japan, France, and have even made several trips to South Africa to train in Zulu stick fighting. I then take the techniques, tactics, and training methods that prove most useful and spar with them under street self-defense conditions. (Allowing simulated groin, eye, and throat strikes.) I then add the most effective methods to our daily training. If I tried to make everything up myself through trial and error it would take me ten thousand years. It is best to utilize the experience of the very best fighters in order to improve more quickly. Sifu Inosanto showed me how to train with many different instructors, and would even take me to other instructors so that I could train with them. That is a generous mentor!

I have trained extensively with Sifu Richard Bustillo. He was very influential in getting me to think critically about the combat effectiveness of various techniques. I remember a lesson at the Kali Academy when he asked us how to counter a jab to the stomach. It was a phase 2 class, and we came up with a few responses. "Block with the lead hand, parry the punch, move out of the way", etc. After letting us go on, Sifu Bustillo finally had someone demonstrate with him. As the jab came in to his midsection, Sifu ignored the jab as he turned and dropped a right cross on his partner's jaw. "Just take it and hit him hard. If you're in shape, that jab is not going to hurt you, but you can land a knockout blow." That sort of instruction can change your understanding of real fighting.

I have also spent a great amount of time with Sifu Larry Hartsell. Sifu Hartsell taught me a great deal, but one conceptual lesson sticks out. He taught me about immediately taking control of a situation. I still remember the first time he did a pak sao on me. He didn't just knock my arm out of the way; he crushed my forearm into my ribs and totally shut me down for a split second. He immediately took charge, which then gave him a window of opportunity where he could follow up and end the situation before the opponent could recover from the initial contact. Each time he did the pak sao it was with full force, moving my body. Each time he punched it was with his whole body behind it. Each time he grabbed me, I knew I was being grabbed! On the ground, he applied tremendous pressure. Whatever the range was, he put the opponent on the defensive and kept him there by constantly pressuring with physical force and psychological intent. This attitude helped me tremendously in hard sparring, and especially in a challenge matches that I have had. A key aspect of my success came from Sifu Hartsell.

Sifu Tim Tackett has also had a big influence on me. One big lesson was his concise explanation and demonstration of the principle of intercepting. I knew what it was to intercept, but he broke it down completely, going beyond techniques to the underlying principles of fighting measure, footwork, and reading. Nearly twenty years later, I still use this lesson when I spar in kickboxing, boxing, stick fighting, knife sparring, and even when grappling. He has a great deal to offer.

I have spent time with Sifu Taky Kimura, and I have had brief sessions with James DeMille, Bob Bremer, and Steve Golden. But I didn't actually study with them. Each generously shared interesting aspects of JKD with me, and I appreciate their help, but to claim to be their students would be an exaggeration of the truth.

It is difficult to comment on the particular approaches of my instructors because they have all shifted directions over time. Not one of them has kept to the same curriculum, focus, or method of imparting the knowledge. These are living, breathing men, and as their knowledge and perspective changes, so will their expression of the art.

Haven't you also trained with "The Dog Brothers"? Please describe your training under them.

I am actually one of the original "Dog Brothers". It wasn't called "Dog Brothers" when I started. In the beginning, it was a pure situation, very "JKD" in my eyes. Eric Knaus started it all. Here is a guy who loves the art of stick and knife fighting. He came up with a very simple question which guided his training. That question was, "What happens in a real stick fight when you go all out and wear very little protective equipment?" To answer that, he donned strong headgear and good hand protection, picked up a heavy rattan stick, and looked for others who would fight him at 100% intensity. Now that is a martial scientist dedicated to searching for the truth! A student of mine named Marc had fought with Eric, and thought that I would want to do the same. At that time, I would drive eight hours one way to enter a stick fighting tournament, so having someone come to the Marina Del Rey Inosanto Academy was a real treat. Now, when we sparred with sticks, we either used lots of body armor with very light rattan, or used minimal armor with heavily padded sticks. If we ever used light rattan with minimal armor, we "sparred" at a very slow pace and with great control to be sure that we didn't accidentally ding each other. So, I put on the headgear and hockey glove to face Eric. He comes up, presents a heavy rattan stick, and says, "Mind if I use this?" I look at it and say "No problem." In my mind I'm thinking, "Boy, with that size stick and almost no protective equipment, we are going to have to go super slow and light." I was incredibly wrong.

Eric moved around, stepped in, and unleashed a tremendous two-handed backhand blow toward my head. I was able to somehow deflect it, but I was now wide awake! After a few more extremely powerful strikes to the head, he dropped down and ripped a shot with that heavy rattan at my bare, unprotected knee. I evaded the blow, but now I was a little angry. He was trying to smash my knee! This guy was obviously evil, coming at me with malicious intent. He tried three or four more knee shots throughout the round, and (due to lots of sparring with the soft sticks) I was able to evade those blows. The buzzer rang, ending the round. I remember glaring through my helmet at this 6'5" beast. He pulled off his helmet, walked up with a big smile on his face, gave me a hug and said, "I was really trying to hit your leg, but I couldn't get it!" He was genuinely happy, and I was genuinely dumbfounded. Eric's only intent was to go all out with little protective equipment to see what works and what doesn't. He wasn't there to hurt anybody, only to improve. Very "JKD" in my eyes.

That night, when I sparred with the threat of serious injury, I found that my defense was pretty good. But, I mounted no offense at all. I just hadn't prepared myself well enough, and I was not used to that scary environment. I wouldn't just step in to attack because I was afraid of getting smashed. I fought with Eric and others many times after that, and improved each time. This was a huge step in my progress toward my focus on functionality, and I am thankful to Eric for his profound influence.

What do you think is the biggest misconception that people have about Jeet Kune Do as Bruce Lee taught it?

- Since I wasn't there to see Bruce Lee teach, I can only go by what I have been told. With that in mind, it seems that the biggest misconception is that there was a structured curriculum that Bruce Lee followed. It sounds to me like he was very spontaneous, working on those things that he wanted to work on. He changed often, as new and better ideas emerged. For example, I was told that for awhile in Chinatown, he taught lots of trapping, and also added some kickboxing. But he noticed that guys with a kickboxing background were dominating the trappers in sparring. So, he switched and started teaching the

kickboxing first, then trapping second. So as he evolved, what he taught and how he taught it also evolved. But again, I wasn't there so I can't speak from first hand knowledge.

Do you accept the claims by Dan Inosanto that Bruce Lee taught three different arts as opposed to the idea that Lee called his art different things at different times?

- Again, I wasn't there, and I have not ever heard Sifu Inosanto make that claim. Any answer that I could give would be utter speculation.

A lot of emphasis has been put on whom Bruce Lee actually certified and what art he certified them in. Your thoughts?

- My thought is that it really doesn't matter. What matters is whether or not the instructors are now helping students to become better people. That is what is most important.

How has Bruce Lee's philosophy affected you?

- It has affected every area of my life. The concept of looking for the truth,

being honest with the findings, always improving, not being set on one thing, using what works, testing theories (sparring) to find out what works, etc, etc. This is in action every day of my life. I work on improving myself each day. I have lots to improve, (laughing) so I'll be using Bruce Lee's philosophy for a lifetime!

Do you think The Tao Of Jeet Kune Do is a good representation of Lee's art?

- I believe that it is a great representative of the thinking behind the art. Since it is a compilation of notes, there are contradictions in the book. But overall, you see a "success" philosophy that can be used to improve skill in martial arts, or in any other area of endeavor. It is about working on yourself, and practicing correctly, and it is an effective philosophical treatise.

I had an acquaintance while I attended the University of Southern California who was the on the swim team. In practice, he was a good swimmer, but not great. The night before a meet, he would read the Tao of Jeet Kune Do. The mental edge that he got from reviewing the mental aspects from the book propelled him to win actual events over and over again. And he didn't even train in the martial arts! I believe that the way we think determines the actions that we take, which in term determine our destinies. The Tao of Jeet Kune Do is a great primer to get people thinking in a positive and productive manner.

What most bothers you about the JKD community?

- Too much complaining, not enough training. Anytime you see that kind of bickering, it means that the people doing it are thinking about politics and not about self-improvement. There are two ways to "elevate" yourself. The first is to spread rumors in an attempt to tear down the reputation of your rivals. But that isn't real. The honest approach is to improve yourself daily. When you get in the gym and spar with really great fighters, you will be so busy thinking about how to improve your performance that you won't have time for petty jealousies.

Dan Inosanto has been ridiculed over the years for his somewhat abstract way to teach Jeet Kune Do. Your thoughts?

- Honestly, I believe this comes from people who resent his success. My first question to such a complainer would be "How many JKD classes have you taken with Sifu Inosanto?" When he teaches JKD, also called Jun Fan, he focuses on what Bruce Lee did and taught. That's it. Sifu Inosanto also teaches Filipino martial arts, Indonesian, Thai, Brazilian, Japanese, French, Western, and other martial arts. Since first meeting him in 1979, I have never seen him teach something from other disciplines and call it JKD. He may say that the

JKD concept is about research and development, and should therefore include many, many influences. But I personally have never heard him refer to the blend as "JKD".

When teaching JKD do you give credit to arts that Lee himself did not practice or do you simply lump all styles into one "concept" that make up your personal version of JKD without distinction as to where a move may have come from?

- I call what I do JKD Unlimited, which immediately implies that it is not solely the JKD that Sigung Lee had developed during his lifetime. I believe in giving credit, which is why I use the term JKD. Bruce Lee's philosophy is the basis of what I do. I train in lots of combat sports, but I don't teach sport unless a student specifically asks to train for a competition. We train for practical, efficient street self-defense, which is what Bruce Lee espoused training for.

In class, I don't give the history lesson on the origins of each technique every single time I teach. But, students know that the straight kick to the groin, our primary kick, is from JKD. They know that when we punch to the groin during a grappling session that we are mixing in the JKD attitude with Brazilian Jiu-Jitsu. They know if we do a neck clinch that it is from Thai Boxing, and they know that when we knee to the groin instead of the body that it is because of Bruce Lee's influence. I do not just throw things together and say "This is JKD." That would be dishonest, and disrespectful to JKD and to the other arts from which we draw techniques, tactics, and training methods.

In your opinion, was Bruce Lee a Kali or Silat practitioner?

- This is just an opinion, because I wasn't there to ask him about this. Here is my opinion. If I were to go talk to a ballet teacher about strengthening my legs, that would not make me a ballet practitioner. To be a practitioner, you have to spend time actually practicing that art diligently. If a new student starts in a JKD class somewhere, I don't think that they are really a practitioner until they have at least a year of training. From what I understand, Bruce Lee was exposed to Kali and Silat, but didn't actually undergo training in those systems.

Have you ever met or trained with Ted Wong and if so, do you see any differences in his application of JKD as compared to Dan Inosanto and Larry Hartsell?

- Unfortunately, I have never had the pleasure of training with Sifu Wong. I would certainly like to see him in person. I hear that he is fantastic.

How often do you teach and how many students do you have?

- I teach classes Tuesday and Thursday nights here in Honolulu. I teach a weapons class, followed by a beginning JKDU class, then an intermediate/advanced JKDU class. We are fortunate to have a very large space which could accommodate sixty, but we don't sign up more than eighteen people per class. That means that most classes consist of about ten to twelve students. I like keeping the classes small so that I can coach each individual in every class. I only teach group classes twice per week because I want to look forward to each training session, rather than making it like work. I make less money, but I am happier. I also have a few private students that I teach each week. In addition, I have many students around the world, thanks to seminars and my distance learning program. I actually make a DVD every single month to send out to JKDU instructors and students so that they can be up to date on the latest technological and training advances. I am very pleased with all of this, especially because my students are good, fun-loving people who train very hard. They are great representatives of the martial arts.

What do you look for in prospective students?

- Attitude comes first and foremost. It is difficult to change an aggressive, abusive person into a kind and giving soul. So good attitude is first and foremost, and we turn people away who don't fit into our group. That is really the only criteria. I don't care about athletic ability or previous experience. As long as it is a friendly person who is willing to train honestly and safely, he or she will be welcome in our classes.

Have you ever had to use JKD in real life encounters and if so, how effective was the art?

- My first encounter after training was in college. A good-sized guy was bullying people in our dorm. People would walk down the hall, and he would come out of his doorway and punch them for no reason whatsoever. I was walking down this hall and saw it happen to a couple guys ahead of me. He hit them pretty hard, and they ran off. As I approached, the bully came out of his room throwing a punch. I stepped to the side and delivered a right hook kick to the groin. He doubled over, turned around, and stumbled back into his room. He never bothered anyone again.

After college, I lived in a very bad part of Los Angeles for many years. The confidence that I gained through training allowed me to avoid many situations.

I encountered guys many times who were obviously sizing me up. Because I didn't show fear, they went along their way. I had one situation in particular where a very large guy in a black trench coat approached me after nightfall. I was walking down an alley to close a gate. He appeared suddenly, and just stood there watching me, hands in his pockets, as I walked toward him and the gate. I never took my eyes off him, never got nervous. I got to the gate, slowly closed it, eyes still on him. He turned and left. I can't be sure, but I think if I had gotten flustered that he would have done something crazy.

I've also had to fight other martial artists, and I am happy to say that my training has worked well for me.

Who do you respect in JKD in regards to second-generation instructors?

- There are many, but I will just mention a few. The first that come to mind are Erik Paulson, Greg Nelson, Frank Cucci, and Rick Young. They are truly outstanding, and I believe that they have achieved a high level of fighting skill because they continue to train with top level fighters and coaches. They constantly strive to improve themselves and their students. There are many others who deserve recognition, but these were the first to enter my mind. The

only thing I don't respect is when instructors, regardless of style, feel that they need to start gossiping and casting aspersions on other instructors to make themselves look better. If you want to look better, train harder.

What are your goals in your training and teaching of JKD?

- My general goal is to improve my fighting skills in each of the ranges every week. That means that I need to train and spar in each range every week. This encourages me to keep a strict training schedule in order to meet my goal. Time goes by whether we train or not. Ten years ago I was absolutely horrible on the ground. Now I am a black belt in Brazilian Jiu-Jitsu. That is just because I trained and sparred in the art consistently over time.

As I train and improve, I take note of new insights and understanding in order to better teach my students. I believe that my students should improve much more quickly than I have, because I can give them all the shortcuts that I have found over the last 27 years of training. Part of this training method includes introspection in order to determine where my weaknesses are. Then I can formulate a plan to transform the weakness into a strength. I apply the same method to myself as a person, so that I can constantly take small steps to improve who I am. One example here would be with language. Years ago I started doing seminars in Europe, and I found it difficult to work with people because I couldn't communicate well. I like to explain philosophy and tactics, which is mainly a verbal endeavor. It takes a large chunk of the seminar to do this when everything I say must be broken down and translated step by step. So, I started working on improving my language skills. By working a little at a time over nine years, I can now speak Italian and French, and can get by in Spanish and Portuguese. I give a much better seminar in Italy, France, or Switzerland, as I can teach in the native language. Introspection is humbling, though, because if you look at yourself honestly you will find a lot there to improve upon! But, the little victories are fulfilling.

For the future, I will continue to make my findings in martial arts available to the public through my classes in Honolulu and world wide seminars, and through my books, DVDs, website (jkdunlimited.com), seminars, and distance learning programs. Above all, we make sure that we have a great time training and improving in a very realistic manner.

10. STOP COMPLAINING AND START TRAINING

Why did you join the martial arts? Was it initially for fitness? Did you want to be able to defend yourself, or did you just think that it was a fun activity where you could meet other people? Whatever your initial reasons for stepping into the martial arts world, I'll bet that sitting around and talking negatively about other martial artists was not one of them. If you have been in a school for any time, you will probably find that this activity is very popular. In fact, it often takes up more time than the actual skill training does. There was a time when I was as guilty of this meaningless banter as anyone.

I was training at the Inosanto Academy in Marina del Rey, CA back in 1986. There were some Saturday morning classes which ended somewhere around noon. After classes were over, the instructor (not

Sifu Inosanto) and a small group of the "senior" students would walk to the local Del Taco (another marvelous idea) to have lunch and talk. I should actually say to sit for over an hour and gossip. The topic was always the same. "Did you hear what this guy said about so and so?" "Everyone thinks that instructor is good, but he actually can't fight a lick. Have you ever noticed how he doesn't spar?" "I don't know why that guy got promoted. I think it is political." What a colossal waste of time. We would sit there pumping each other up by putting everyone else down. For me, this ritual went on for nearly a year. Luckily, one day I had a change of heart.

I spend a lot of time reading self-improvement and philosophy books, and the idea of speaking negatively is often addressed. You can easily find one hundred authors on successful living who have devoted countless pages to the ravages of negative thinking. Everything starts with your mind. From the way you stretch to the way you fight to the way you live your life each day is a result of your thought processes. The way you think should be analyzed often and steps should be taken to improve your methods of thought. It is the same as your martial arts skill. Work on it, check your results, find your weak areas, and spend time strengthening those aspects that are holding you back.

As I was improving my way of thinking about life and its obstacles, I came to realize that what all of the authors were saying was true. My perception of events was the key determining factor in the quality of my life! If my car was broken into, (and, thanks to living in a terrible part of town, it was often) I could either rant and rave and spread the misery to others, or I could just take care of what needed to be replaced and be happy that they didn't take the whole car. There was a stimulus in front of me, and I got to choose how to respond to it. This is where the word "responsibility" comes from; you have the ability to respond to whatever conflicts should arise. Understanding this put the responsibility for my happiness and enjoyment of life squarely on my own shoulders. Others will do what they will, but I have the power to choose how to respond to those actions. The question is, will I have a "normal" reaction or will I consciously choose the response that best serves me?

The same responsibility carries over to pursuing your goals. You choose whether you want to work toward your goal each day. If your dream is to own your own martial arts school, but you don't have enough money, use your head to figure out some ways of earning extra money. Save for as long as you need to and you will one day have enough to open that school. You make the choices that determine whether or not you will reach your goals. It is not just fate. Every time you take action toward your goals, fate steps in behind you and gives you a little extra push. "If it is to be, it is up to me!"

So one fine Saturday morning I went off to the Inosanto Academy to take the classes, and ended up at that bastion of health and nutrition, Del Taco. We sat down and before we even got our food, the negativity began. This time, though, I didn't join in. I was more of an observer than a participant as the conversation moved from bashing one person to the next. Here was one instructor talking trash about another Inosanto Academy instructor. It became very apparent to me that the main motivation for these discussions was fear. Fear that the other guy was better, or fear that the other instructor might get more recognition. They were talking about a guy who had trained hard for years and was a good fighter, but they would find little things about him to pick on. Amazing. As though we were all perfect. I thought about this all week, and was determined to change my destiny.

After classes had ended the next week, the crew packed up and started the short walk to the cholesterol palace. When I said that I was going to stay and train some more on the heavy bag, they were all surprised. As a matter of fact, they actually tried to convince me to skip the extra training and come down to talk with them! I am so glad that I refused their persuasions and practiced. What a difference. I spent over an hour practicing basic moves while they were practicing verbal battery. With that one distinction my skills started to improve faster than ever. It motivated me to practice more at home, and my rate of progress had increased to new levels. I believe that making the choice that day to stay in a positive environment and train rather than miring myself in the quicksand of negativity was one of the turning points that lead me to a career as a martial artist. I am thankful that I made the right choice in the face of peer pressure.

I often have people ask me questions that are purely political in nature. I get asked about this JKD guy or that jiu-jitsu instructor, or am asked to give my opinion on some teacher of the Filipino martial arts. I can often hear that what they want is some dirt on the person. There is often a surprised look on their face when I say "I think that he is very good." We all know that there are people in the martial arts that aren't well meaning or whose skills are not what they claim, but often people want to deride someone simply because he or she is not part of "the group." I think it is because people often build their self-esteem by associating themselves with a group of people who have a good reputation. The person starts to think that his group is the best group, and therefore he must be one of the best. If someone in another group shows promise, the easiest way to retain the feeling of being superior is to knock the other group down, even if it is solely through negative talk. This way the first group retains the feeling of being the best. As silly as this sounds, it happens every day.

I have a saying within my group, Jeet Kune Do Unlimited. "While they are complaining, we are training!" Naturally, I get a lot of negativity thrown my way because I have worked hard and have had the good fortune to be able to have my views heard. When it is time for me to sit down and write this column or an article, my goal is to provide the reader with something that will help him or her to become a better person and martial artist. When I state my viewpoint about being a complete martial artist, or learning from different instructors, or not being struck to tradition, other will invariably take that as an attack on their method and lash out against me. It doesn't matter. I just want what is best for my students and for martial artists everywhere who want to be the best they can be.

11. GET IN THE WATER

I am one of the instructors who answers questions on Tim Mousel's JKD Discussion Forum on the internet. I was recently asked if most JKD concepts practitioners also train in "Original" Jeet Kune Do, the particular techniques and tactics that Bruce Lee did himself at the end of his life. I want to repeat here what I wrote in the forum, and add some other things to think about in regards to the value of combat sports competitions. Most "concepts" practitioners that I know have been trained extensively in Jun Fan Gung Fu (Bruce Lee's earlier expression before adding hard sparring) and Jeet Kune Do. The reason for this is that these are great arts. The kicking, punching, throwing, and some of the trapping techniques still work very well in today's environment. Why is it, then, that these fighters don't just stick to the Jun Fan/JKD curriculum? Because the truth of the matter is that, while Original JKD is a great style, it is by no means a complete art. We must go out and seek better ways of doing things; just as Bruce Lee did to go from Wing Chun to Jun Fan Gung Fu and then to Jun Fan JKD.

If our mindset is that our current methods are perfect methods, then we will be left behind as the fighting arts develop. And they will become better and better with or without JKD fighters. If we focus on fighting efficiency, we will get past bias and "use whatever works". As Bruce Lee said in one of his movies, which he wrote, "It doesn't matter where a technique comes from. If it can help you in a fight, you should use it!" I think that a lot of JKD people forget that being an effective, complete fighter should be the guiding force in our training. If you want to be a good fighter, you must think like a fighter and train like a fighter.

A real fighter, one who actually spars hard in all of the ranges, is always going to be looking for a better way of doing things. Those who think that there is only one style that works hasn't done enough sparring outside of his own group. Spar a good Thai boxer and see if Jun Fan totally nullifies his method. Spar a good BJJ practitioner and see what happens. Take it up several notches and fight a Vale Tudo fighter and get even more feedback. If you stick to one style, there is going to be another style that can counter you.

Let's talk about combat sports competitions. No, they are not the same as street fights. But they are extremely valuable to combat effectiveness. Most athletes, be it in baseball, football, basketball, soccer, etc., go through rigorous training, then actually play the game. After the game, they analyze their weaknesses, and make adjustments in the training. Many martial artists train, but never play the game against an uncooperative opponent. They end up theorizing extensively without testing their theories. Over time, the techniques devolve until they can become ridiculous to an experienced fighter. I think this is the main problem with the "original" group, and also with many of the "concepts" people who think that any technique that they learn from any style can work against anyone at any time. If we want to be good at the fighting arts, we must fight. To paraphrase Bruce Lee's advice, don't be a dry land swimmer, get into the water and see what it is like when you get wet, the water is cold, and there are waves pounding on you. This is the JKD ideal; wisdom from experience is greater than theoretical knowledge.

This brings up the competition aspect. If you really want experience, you must go all out against an unfamiliar, uncooperative, aggressive, skillful opponent. The best way to do this is to enter competitions. There are so many to choose from. You can get experience in point fighting, grappling, stick fighting, or no holds barred events. You will be able to get into the ring with someone and go for it under pressure. The experience you gain will be invaluable, and you will surely find ways to change your training for the better. My own competition experience was invaluable in my development. Some types of competition aren't very realistic, but just getting through the nervousness and having to face someone you have never seen before will give you the seasoning you need to keep your cool in a street encounter.

I emphasize to my students that there is only one thing worse than having no victories on your competition record, and that is having no victories, no defeats, and no ties because you never even tried. And please don't badmouth competitions unless you have actually tried yourself. They aren't street fighting, but it takes courage to get in there and risk your body and, especially, your ego.

Please don't be someone who just talks about martial arts. Get in the water and get wet!!! As BJJ and MMA world champion Egan Inoue has printed on his t-shirts, "Only a fighter knows the feeling!" I don't want people to look at JKD as a bunch of hypothetical techniques taught by teachers with no experience. Competition is a part of the puzzle that will bring out your best!!!

12. THE STICKY SUBJECT OF WEAPONRY TRAINING

There was a recent debate about the art of stick fighting that disclosed a number of combat myths. Let's take a look at what it takes to become a good fighter with weapons. Before we can talk about techniques, strategies, and training methods, we have to know exactly what type of scenario we are training for.

To keep things simple, let's just limit our scope to single stick against single stick, in a squared off situation. Basically, dueling. In a street fight, you don't know where a weaponry attack will come from because often these sorts of attacks are ambushes. One guy sneaks up behind another, and WHAM, the fight is just about over. Awareness, luck, and a very thick skull are the only things that will save you from an ambush, so we will start one on one, like a sparring match. The main point of the match is that you are going to try to hit your opponent as hard as you can, as often as you can, without getting hit yourself. You nemesis will be attempting the same. Everything will be moving at full speed and full power, and strikes can be targeted anywhere on the body. Thrusts and butt strikes are allowed with the stick, as well as any other striking such as punches, kicks, knees, and elbows. Throws are allowed, along with the grappling that often follows. Now let's imagine that you are going to have this match in four weeks. What should you do to get ready and how are you going to approach the fight?

In many cultures around the world, this has been a real question posed on a consistent basis. Many cultures have and/or still do fight regularly with sticks or blades. In western culture, however, the notion of having a full-contact stick fight in a month is indeed rare. It just doesn't happen very often. From a fighter's point of view this would seem odd. There are probably tens of thousands of people in the U.S. alone who train with sticks, but for most there is not even an inkling of a thought of actually using the skills. Boxers, wrestlers, kickboxers, and free-fight athletes train to use their skills at full speed and power against an opponent who is trying to do accomplish the same goal. The competition guides the training, and gives motivation to get in the gym and work hard. This is what it will take for you to become an accomplished stick fighter.

In order to train for a fight, you simply must practice fighting. You should spar, but you have to have safety factors in your training or you will be so injured that you will not be able to train. This is counterproductive, and will lead to a dismal showing in your upcoming fight. I use a padded stick, headgear, some hand protection and groin protection for most of my stick sparring. This way I can spar at full speed and power while minimizing the chance of injury. It should be clear, though, that as good as sparring with a soft stick is, there is no substitute for sparring with naked rattan and minimal body armor. Just know that you will get banged up. I do that on occasion, which helps my preparation for my Dog Brother fights.

Here is an easy and effective formula to greatly enhance your stick sparring. Follow it, and I assure you that you will improve tremendously in one month. First thing to do is to get a partner, gear up, and start sparring. After a few rounds, you should be very aware of some weaknesses in your game. This is what you want, because you can now apply the formula for martial success. Write down your weak spots, do drills to work on the necessary techniques and attributes to enhance those areas, do isolated sparring that help you work those techniques, then go back to full sparring.

This is the formula used to achieve greatness in all fields of endeavor. You apply your trade, note your shortcomings, train to improve those areas, then apply your trade with more skill. Then repeat the process. The key is to actually try stick fighting, rather than spending all of your time drilling techniques that you will never be able to do when you have to face a strong, fast opponent who is trying to remove your head from your shoulders! There are countless possible techniques in weaponry based fighting, but the truth is that when you go against a resisting opponent who is swinging hard, only a handful of techniques come into play. You will never understand this unless you try your art out at full speed and power. If you do, you will discover weaknesses in your approach. Discovering your weaknesses is very beneficial because your training will now have focus and meaning. Here are some remedies for common stick fighting ailments.

Are you getting hit in the head? This is usually due to improper distancing, poor blocking skills, or telegraphing your attacks. Time to do some drills. Put on the helmet, give your partner a padded stick, and have him or her slowly swing at your head. Not in front of your head, but at your protected head. Practice slipping back out of the path of the stick. As you get better, have your partner pick up the speed and add faking. This will enhance your sense of distance, and your ability to read the attack.

Next, blocking practice. Have your partner feed a forehand shot at your head and work your block. I almost always do this with rattan sticks to better feel the impact. Helmets are mandatory because one mistake can mean a trip to the ER. Pick up the intensity as you get better at keeping that stick off of your helmet.

If telegraphing your strikes is a problem, work on hitting the heavy bag with as little preparatory motion as possible. Now that you have worked on these elements, do some isolated sparring where you and your partner will only strike towards the head. Get rounds and rounds of this in so that you get very comfortable with defending your head. Now it is time to go back and work on the full sparring again to find more weaknesses. Make sure to isolate head only and hand only sparring. Also isolate combinations like hand and head only, or head and leg only. These will force you to use tactics that you are not familiar with, and you will again grow. If you are being taken down easily, start in the clinch and just work on throws. If your ground game is bad, pick one position and drill from there. Spar to find your worst positions, then work to make it a strength. Train diligently, and that fight next month will be much easier.

I think it is important for martial artists to learn how to actually stick fight, rather than just learning to be a baton twirler. In actually learning how to apply your knowledge you will understand the blueprint for success in all areas of life. This is the greatest benefit to martial arts training, but is only gained if you take your training to the limits!

13. FIGHTING THE BIG GUY

How do you deal with an aggressive attacker who is much bigger and stronger than you are? This is a question that plagues all martial artists who are in pursuit of a functional self-defense methodology. Some people may tell you that size and strength don't matter, but the truth is that they matter a great deal when the aggressor is determined to use those attributes to his advantage. How many combat sports do you know of that do not have weight classes? Boxing, kickboxing, wrestling, and no holds barred fighting all implement weight classes so that smaller contestants can get in and use their techniques and training against an opponent of a similar weight. The reason that this has evolved is that when two fighters of comparable weight compete, the contest will be determined by superior technique, tactics, and conditioning. If two fighters have similar skill levels, but one is considerably heavier and/or stronger, the larger opponent will usually win. A much larger fighter will almost always be more powerful, and power counts in a fight. A street situation has no weight classes or rules, so we must be able to use our tactics and skill at implementing those tactics to make up for the size advantage of a much larger attacker.

To better understand the tactics we must employ, let's look at the different ranges of empty hand combat, broken down into the three most basic components. These would be kickboxing range, the clinch range, and the ground fighting range. Most martial artists have been trained primarily in the kickboxing range. This is where you punch, kick, elbow, and knee an opponent without actually grabbing him. The second range is the clinch, where you are grabbing the opponent, he is grabbing you, or both. The ground fighting occurs when one or both fighters are on the ground. I hope we all agree, now that we have reached the year 2000, that any serious martial artist should train to be functional in all three ranges. We may not have a choice of ranges in a real street fight, so we had better be prepared for anything. Each of you probably has a range that you feel most comfortable in. If you got into an altercation that you couldn't walk away from, which distance would you prefer to fight in? Do you like to duke it out and win the fight standing, are you a clinch fighter who grabs the neck and throws knees and uppercuts, or do you like to grapple on the ground, looking for superior position? Now imagine that your opponent is 6 inches taller than you, outweighs you by 100 pounds, and is very strong. Which range would you prefer now?

Most of us would prefer to stay away from a big man, opting for long range techniques. I was asked by Sumo grand champion (yokozuna) Akebono what I would try if I had to fight him. I am 6' 1" tall and weigh about 190 pounds. Akebono is 6'7" tall, weighs about 450 pounds, and is a fantastic athlete. I said that if I couldn't run, I would try some low line kicks, hoping that he would bend over so that I could score an eye jab. He paused, smiled, and then agreed that it was a good strategy. But let me tell you, I would not want to have to try it for real! Good footwork along with low line kicks and eye strikes may work if the aggressor is not determined to enter, but if you are close enough to hit the eyes or groin, a much taller attacker will probably be close enough to land a big punch that will rattle your brain. The simple haymaker can spoil many long-range techniques from a larger foe due to its tremendous power. Even more problems come up if the big attacker is very aggressive with striking, and you don't have the space to maneuver. Or, he might just try to run you over. You always have to be ready to go to plan B!

What is plan B? Working for the clinch may be a logical next step from long range, but it is difficult when there is a considerable size disparity. If you can grab a big man's hair, you may be able to pull him down to take away posture, thus minimizing his strength. This is a possibility, assuming that the opponent has hair, and that you can reach up to grab it without being crushed. Grabbing the neck is another way of off balancing an opponent, but you have to be so close that you are in real danger of being lifted off the ground and slammed. In most instances, the clinch is the last range that you want to be stuck in with someone who is bigger and stronger.

Where is it that a big man has the least power, and is less of a threat? When he is on his back. A sound tactic for dealing with the big guy is to shoot in low and hit him with everything you have. If you can achieve a good angle and hit a clean double leg takedown at the knees of a large man, you have a good chance of bringing that big tree down. Most large people are extremely uncomfortable on their backs. Putting someone there will give you a chance to escape from the situation, or if necessary, put you in position to strike down at the felled opponent. If your grappling is very good, you may be able to control the big man while looking for submissions. Of course, you first have to score the takedown. Pulling off such a takedown takes work, but so does anything that is worth doing. The knees are the weakest link in that giant's stance, and if you can shoot in hard and fast from a good angle, you can take down someone who is double your weight. You just have to ensure that you don't get stuck underneath him if he sprawls at the right time.

A large attacker has the advantage of raw power, so you have to be able to develop the skills to deal with that power. The two safest ways to accomplish this both involve manipulating the range at which the fight occurs; either stay away and strike from the outside, or get in deep and put him on his back. Easier said than done, but with proper training you can do it! If you are a stand up fighter, find excellent wrestlers to work with on your takedowns. If you are a grappler, get with a mobile striker to help with your evasive footwork and striking power. Don't neglect the clinch either, because you may end up there, and your skill at close range will allow you to transition to long range or the ground. Work it all so you don't have to let a big guy get you down!

14. THE ART OF FIGHTING WITHOUT FIGHTING

Anyone who has watched Bruce Lee's "Enter the Dragon" knows this line well. What a great set-up, complete with a hilarious follow-through. Years later, this line can provoke important questions for those interested in developing the functional fighting skills that Bruce Lee advocated.

What does this line have to do with our training? Here is the first point. In a real situation, the best option is to be able to find a way out of the confrontation without coming to blows. This could be referred to as the art of fighting without fighting. In JKD Unlimited, we stress that the main goal in a street confrontation is to "Go home safely". The goal is not to beat the other person up, or pull off a nice sweep, or get to an armbar. The main idea is to use the most efficient (and legal) way to get yourself out of there. The best way to do this is to avoid those places and circumstances where belligerence usually occurs. You know the spots. Local taverns after midnight, dark alleys in the bad part of town, etc. Avoidance will help you to go home safely. If an aggressive person confronts you, your next best option is to have the skills necessary to talk yourself out of the fight. This is something that must be practiced, just like all of the physical portions of the art, so that you can develop useful tactics in this realm. If someone decides to take out their frustrations on you, but you find a way to talk them out of it so that you can go home safely, then you have succeeded in using the art of fighting without fighting. You should congratulate yourself for dealing with an ugly situation in such a beautiful manner. There can be times, though, when there is no amount of clever conversation that will get you out of a fight.

People that pick on others for the sport of it are not gentlemen, and may not be easily dissuaded from picturing you as a punching bag. If you can't get away, you will have to apply your fighting skills until you can make an exit. Just like the verbal skills mentioned earlier, you have to practice fighting skills to be able to apply them. This is about as obvious as fighting concepts come, so why do I bring it up? What does this have to do with the art of fighting without fighting? I am glad that you asked.

The emphasis that I want to make, as I have done before and will continue to do, is that we must be able to apply our skills in a realistic setting. People spend years in martial arts schools "perfecting" fighting motions without learning how to apply the motions against an attacker. Which arts do that? Nearly every art. Okay, now I've got you riled. I can't be talking about your art, can I? Well it really isn't the art, but the way people practice applying the techniques of that art. A real attacker is going to attack you ferociously, suddenly, and will probably not stop to touch gloves with you before he begins the assault. The attack will be delivered with 100% of the attacker's power, and with full resistance. Most arts, for safety's sake, never allow their practitioners to engage in full-out sparring. Safety in training is very important, but at least allow the students to practice unlimited sparring go at around 70% intensity while wearing protective equipment. Without the sparring, there will be no timing. No drill will develop the timing like sparring, because a drill has too many restrictions and patterns built in. Drills are great for perfecting a single move, or isolating a portion of a fight. A real fight has no pattern, but is chaotic and must be adapted to. Those who have spent lots of time sparring, especially in all ranges combined, are much better prepared to apply their technique against a resisting opponent because they have done so many, many times.

Earlier I mentioned that nearly every art could be practiced without learning proper application. But how about muay Thai? Thai boxers do go 100%, which makes the art very good. Unfortunately, you can find people all across the U.S. and the world who are training muay Thai techniques and conditioning without any sparring. You can find tons of instructors in JKD, the Filipino martial arts, Indonesian Silat, aikido, kung fu, and other arts who have never sparred at all, let alone at 100%. Instructors who haven't tested their skills against resistance in turn create legions of students who will not test their skills in sparring, and will therefore be ill-prepared to handle a street situation. How about Brazilian jiu-jitsu? Unfortunately, BJJ technique is now being taught in many places without the sparring that develops the student into a competent fighter.

What would you call it when martial arts techniques are taught without any sparring time? I would call it the art of fighting without fighting! Don't delude yourself. If you want to learn how to fight, you must practice fighting against someone who is fighting back!

15. STREET GRAPPLING: THE JEET KUNE DO PERSPECTIVE

As more and more martial artists take up grappling to round out their repertoire, many of them seem to forsake their standing game in favor of the ground work. They get hooked on grappling, and they seem to think that their standing fighting is useless. It is easy to fall into this, as the reality fights show again and again the value of ground fighting in a one on one situation. I too enjoy my grappling training immensely, and I certainly plan to continue this vital portion of my training for the rest of my life. But since the primary objective of the JKD practitioner's fight training should be to prepare him or her for an all out street confrontation, focusing solely on the ground fighting aspects of the martial arts could be a fatal mistake.

Street fighting has no rules. It is illegal, and therefore has no parameters, no referee, no favorable flooring, and no guarantee that the fight will be one on one. Some cultures have unwritten codes of ethics, but even then there is no guarantee. We have to understand this to train correctly. If I or any of my students enter a fighting competition, the first question I ask is "What are the rules?" The next thing I want to know is who the opponent will be. Once we know what the rules are, and who the opponent will be, we can devise a training strategy to prepare the fighter. We adjust the training to prepare specifically for the event and the opponent. If we don't know who we will fight against, we must assume that he will be strong in all aspects of that particular sporting match. We want to make sure that we do everything we can in our training to ensure victory.

When preparing for the street, the training must be much broader in scope. We know that there are no rules, so the fight can take on many different characteristics. It may be a stand-up affair, or a ground fight, a knife attack, or all of these. We don't know who the opponent or opponents will be, so we must assume that they will be big, strong, aggressive athletes who are highly trained in all aspects of fighting. This assumption is crucial. If we decide to prepare for an unskilled, unathletic foe, what is going to happen if we have to face Godzilla? We simply won't be prepared, and if you fail to prepare, you should prepare to fail. The quality and quantity of our preparation will determine our performance in an altercation. Therefore, we must train very well for the toughest situations that we can imagine.

Is it important for the well rounded fighter to spend time practicing fighting on the ground? Of course it is. Street fights often go to the ground, so it is vitally important that you are comfortable there. As Matt Thornton, head of the Straight Blast Gyms in and around Portland, Oregon says, "If you can't fight on the ground, you can't fight." What we must understand is that it is important to modify the sport aspect of ground fighting to fit into the true "no rules" parameters of the street. Punching, eye gouges, and biting will change the game.

Grappling does have it's limitations, just as standing fighting does. You don't want to go to the ground against more than one attacker. Recently, an acquaintance of mine who is a Black belt in Brazilian Jiu-Jitsu got into an altercation with a few opponents. He was trying to break up a fight when he got hit from behind, so he wasn't thinking clearly as he took his opponent down. He mounted the guy instinctively, and was still trying to shake off the first hit when someone booted him in the head. He was knocked out cold, and was indeed lucky that he wasn't seriously injured or killed after he was unconscious. Luckily, the group ran away and are now in jail. It is possible to defend against more than one on the ground, but you will have to pay a price. Enson Inoue got into it against three attackers on the street, and he took one to the ground got to his back, and slid back against a wall for protection. He tried to use the first attacker for protection, but the other two got in a lot of hits and kicks before Enson choked the first one out. The others then ran away. Enson related that the experience was "No fun."

This brings up one of the reasons that you should train ground fighting. It is very important to understand grappling so that you can get out of the range. If you have to go against an opponent who knows ground fighting, you had better be able to fight better than him on the ground, or know enough so that you can stand back up. Especially against multiple opponents, you have to be able to make your way back up to your feet efficiently in order to ensure a desirable outcome.

The other reason to know the ground is that you may find yourself in a situation where you want to take the opponent to the ground. If you know that it is going to be one on one, or if you are outclassed standing, the ground is going to be your friend. It is a great option to have, provided that you have trained properly.

In order to train the ground fighting correctly, you should primarily concentrate on getting to and holding favorable positions. If you can get to dominant positions, you can control the fight. After you obtain a dominant position, you can strike, choke, or lock. Remember, "Position before submission". After you are comfortable training positions, add the arm bars, leg locks, chokes, and striking into the game. Striking will change the way you make transitions from one position to another, as you will have to protect your face, neck, and limbs while making the moves. Drill safely, but realistically and you will progress quickly.

Grappling is an essential part of the JKD fighter's game plan. It must be adjusted for multiple opponents and for weaponry, but the time spent on the mat will make you better than you have ever been before. Your standing game will change and improve as well when you take the ground game into account. Find a good instructor, and train well!

16. CHOKE 'EM OUT!

A very interesting thing happened recently that is very pertinent to all those who are interested in developing functional self-defense skills. We must keep in mind that when borrowing techniques and training methods from the combat sport environment, we may also bring along some tactics or habits that are designed specifically for the sport. And those can be detrimental in a life and death self-defense situation.

Imagine that you decided to choose Olympic style tae kwon do for your street self-defense system. You spar in the sport TKD style where no clinching is allowed. One day you get into a real fight, you throw a kick, but end up chest to chest, so you put your hands to the side and wait for the referee to separate you from the opponent. But wait! There is no referee! The attacker grabs your body, lifts you into the air, and slams you to the concrete. This is an extreme example, but the same logic applies to many other sport combat systems.

As we know, ground fighting is a must if you want to be fully prepared for a street altercation. The normal method of learning effective ground fighting is to learn Brazilian jiu-jitsu, wrestling, sambo, or some other form of effective grappling. The sparring is usually geared towards the competitive aspect of the art, so certain moves are prioritized over others. For example, a person who is comfortable fighting from his or her back may purposely put the opponent into the guard, and begin attacking armbars, triangles, and sweeps from there. This is a great way of training, as it make the person a formidable fighter even when in a bad position. The problem comes when the techniques that the person tries for are prioritized in the sporting manner.

This was illustrated recently in a real street fight. Three young men, all highly skilled in Brazilian jiu-jitsu, were out on a Saturday night. It was after two in the morning when they found themselves on a street near a few popular nightclubs. While standing and talking, a man approached them from across the street. It was another accomplished Brazilian jiu-jitsu practitioner, but he was from a rival school and was know for his belligerence. The rival picked out one of the three and started arguing with him. It became heated, and the one being abused said, "Let's go. Let's do it". The belligerent one said no, because he was too "wasted". After a few more words, the aggressor turned and walked back across the street. The three friends were upset, but stayed there talking about the brazen attitude of the other jiu-jitsu guy. A few minutes later, the aggressor appears again, but this time he comes across the street with two very large, muscled cohorts. They all charge, the BJJ bully attacking the one he had verbally abused, while the large guys go after the other two friends. They two big guys are quickly convinced to stop fighting, but the BJJ bully and the BJJ good guy are going at it. The good guy gets in position for an armbar from the guard, laying on his back and keeping his opponent away. There is no tapping out on the street, so he extends the arm until he feels the elbow popping in a few places. He lets go of the arm, knowing that the fight is over. In any tournament it would be over, but this was not a sanctioned competition. The bully, favoring his arm, jumps on top of the good guy and bites him several times on the face. As the good guy moves, the bully stabs a finger into the eye of the downed fighter, looking to seriously maim him. The good guy retaliates by putting fingers in the bully's eyes, and the two are finally separated. They go off in different directions before the authorities arrive. The next day our good guy has a severely bloodied eye, bites all over his face, and serious swelling in his elbow and shoulder from rolling around on the street. He had to miss a few days of work, which isn't good for the well being of his wife and baby. I am not sure what became of the aggressor.

What is the moral of this true story? I hope that the first thing you pick up is that hanging around on a street near the night clubs when the Saturday night crowd is drunken and/or drugged out is not a good choice if you value your safety. The second lesson is that once the belligerent one left the first time, the three friends should have left too. By not being there, no fight would have taken place.

Once the fight did happen, what could the good guy have been done differently? A fight is fluid and unpredictable, and it is impossible to say that it should have gone this way or that way. But, since our good guy did get to an armbar, he would have been better off immediately transitioning from that armbar to a position where he would be on top, or to a position where he might be able to apply a choke. Easier said than done, but it clearly would have been a better choice.

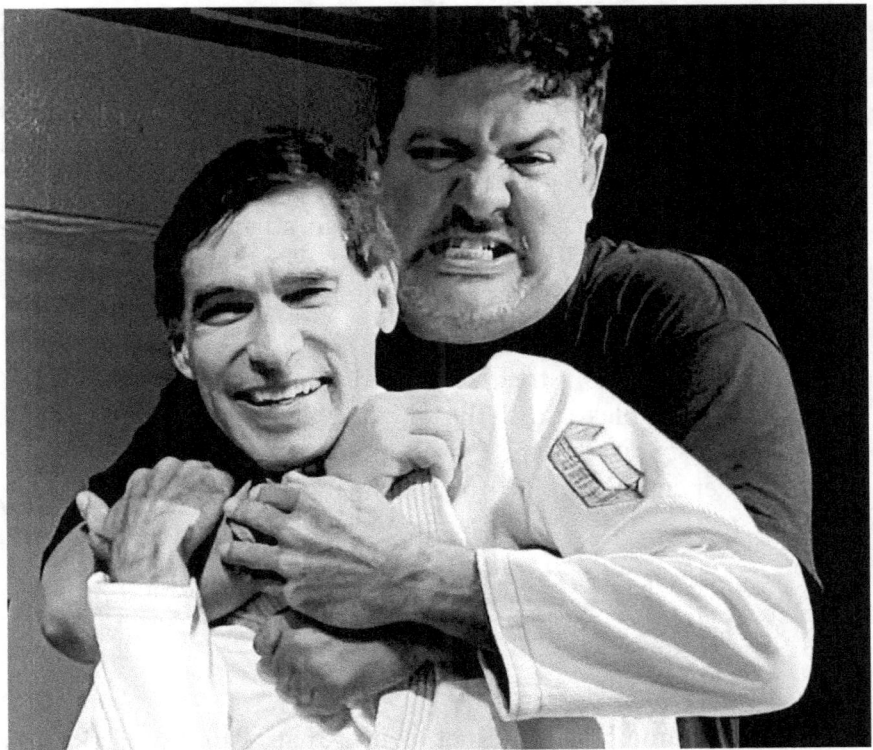

This fight illustrates the point that popping an attacker's elbow may restrict the movement of the arm, but it doesn't necessarily end the fight. If you are going to prioritize your techniques in training, and you are training for self-defense, you should be working on getting to a position where you can choke the opponent out. An unconscious opponent is no threat to you. Techniques like arm bars, arm locks, ankle locks, knee bars, etc., are very useful and essential to train, but the choke is the ultimate problem solver when it comes to street self-defense. If you can get a choke on an opponent, whether it is a rear naked, collar choke, triangle, or other similar technique, the adversary is going to stop fighting. He has no choice. It takes the durability factor out of the equation. An attacker on drugs can continue regardless of punches to the head, knee shots to the groin, and broken arms.

Another point is that the bites and eye gouges, while painful, did not stop either man from continuing to fight effectively. Those who choose to rely on such techniques instead of learning grappling should swallow their pride and get on the mat. Eye gouges and bites are rarely fight stoppers.

From a humane point of view, choking an attacker to sleep is the most desirable method of subduing him. You don't have to cause serious head trauma and you can avoid exchanging blood with the attacker, which is always a preferable.

If you are training for street self-defense, prioritize getting to the choke and being able to finish that choke when the opponent is really fighting against you. It is the most humane move that you can apply to an attacker, and is certainly one of the most effective.

17. BLOODY MESS

From time to time I visit internet forums that relate to martial arts training. If I feel I have something to add from my experience that may be helpful to others, I do so. A very interesting turn of events occurred recently on a forum. I believe it is vital to understand if we are going to make progress in realistic combat training.

There was a thread on a forum where the author asked very sincerely about the difference between functional training and drills that were "dead patterns" in the Filipino martial arts. I chose to respond, as I

have two decades of experience in this field, and have been fortunate to train with many of the great masters. (Inosanto, Ilustrisimo, Sulite, Giron, Gaje, Ricketts, Diego, etc.) I have also had the benefit of being one of the original Dog Brothers, learning first hand what works and what doesn't in real contact stick fighting. I mentioned that there are drills that developed and had been passed down that just aren't very helpful in producing a formidable fighter. The truth is that many styles of Filipino martial arts were expanded and embellished by people who had never actually fought. A practitioner may create a drill that is fun to do, but has little to do with the actual realm of full power, full contact stick fighting. Currently, there are relatively few drills that do. I pointed the differences out, based on the experience of myself and others that have actually fought full contact many times, striving to help a sincere student who was looking for answers. There was also discussion of dead patterns related to empty hand fighting. What happened next was telling.

A fellow JKD/FMA instructor chose to counter my assertions by writing a scathing rebuttal. I am all for this, as we should be looking for truth and listen to other's opinions. He is very fond of the drills that were described as dead patterns, and therefore chose to justify their effectiveness. His method of doing so was questionable.

He said that a student of his had visited my school many years ago, and that the student had "trashed" me in a sparring session. (On a subsequent post, the instructor said that the word "trashed" was maybe too harsh a word.) A private e-mail by someone close to this instructor asserted that even if the student did not trash me, it was a fact that the student had bloodied my nose.

The curious thing is that this never happened. Both the instructor and the e-mail author admitted that they were not present at the alleged trashing. I think we would all agree that if someone came into your school, sparred with you, and bloodied your nose, you would remember it quite well! This imaginary event simply didn't occur. BUT, here is the important thing to remember about this. Whether I got my nose bloodied by someone or not isn't important.

It is entirely possible that a student could visit my school and bloody my nose. A student could possibly come in and choke me out or submit me. Why? Because mistakes happen in sparring! I don't know any boxer who has not had his/her eyes blackened or nose bloodied. I don't know of any grappler who has not been taken down or submitted numerous times. This is the goal of the game, and it happens. Champion boxers get knocked out. Brazilian jiu-jitsu black belts are forced to tap. That is part of the game, IF YOU PLAY THE GAME! It isn't a disgrace; it is an extremely valuable part of the functional learning process. We learn from our mistakes.

As Bruce Lee admonished, "If you want to learn how to swim you have to get in the water." I'll add that if you get in the water, you are going to get wet. The only way to avoid getting punched, kicked, taken down, or submitted is to avoid sparring, and that is the greatest danger. If we set up a culture where it is unacceptable for an instructor to get punched, kicked, bloodied, etc., then we are setting up the circumstances that encourage instructors to avoid all types of "alive" training. When that happens, stagnation occurs and the fanciful reigns.

Alive training is simply where your partner is fighting back. He or she does not just let you do the technique over and over in a contrived manner. You partner tries to stifle your attempts so that you develop timing, distancing, and strategy in real time. A dead pattern is where no resistance is present. Dead training simply does not prepare a person for an "alive" situation. You can work on memorization and coordination, but timing, distancing, and the vital ability to read an opponent is developed best in "alive", even very light sparring. If an instructor wants to always look good (and we all do) he or she may be tempted to avoid the "alive" stuff and stick with the dead patterns and techniques that can be so impressive. I know this intimately because I did this for a long time!

I am sure that many, many instructors feel what I felt. I had progressed from the ranks of student to the level of instructor. Along with that, I attached the silly notion that a martial arts instructor should be infallible. When standing before a group of students, especially when you first start teaching, you want to impress them, to make them (and yourself) feel that you deserve to be leading the class. Fear of looking bad and disappointing the students creeps in. The ego takes over and you create an image that nobody can honestly live up to. Without thinking, you then do your best to keep that image alive by training dishonestly. You don't spar, you don't take chances, and you cover up mistakes with explanations. You get to where your image becomes more important than the truth.

Yes, I admit that I went through this whole thing. It is an easy hole to fall into, and a very difficult one to get out of. I assure you, however, that there is nothing more satisfying than dropping that false, imaginary image and getting back to the person you were when you first started your training. Get in there and play again, training with aliveness and enjoying the process of personal development. A great side benefit is that your students will respect you more for your efforts. If you present yourself up as a coach rather than a deity, your students will develop with the same healthy mindset. Isn't it interesting that a professional coach in basketball, soccer, or any other sport isn't expected to perform better than the players? But that expectation remains in the martial arts. The coaches should be best at developing the skills of their students while continuing to develop their own skills.

The big question for all instructors is this: What do you value more, upholding an image of infallibility or constantly improving yourself? The only people that don't get punched and kicked, thrown, or submitted are those who never play with a worthy opponent. If you are worried that your actual fighting skills are not up to par, go find some top fighters and start training with them. Those willing to put their glorified self-image aside and spar with the best are the ones who will be extremely formidable in a few short years.

Do your students a favor, and do yourself a favor. Just be you. Your students will admire you, and you will have freed yourself from the bloody mess of projecting a false self-image.

18. FIGHT LIKE A GIRL!

Fight like a girl? What is that all about? In a real street situation, it is called being intelligent. When most men train for self-defense, there is this vision of going at it hand to hand, until the assailant is lying in a heap, defeated. Let's get real.

A real attacker is not going to attack unless he feels that he has an advantage. He is not in it for the glory of overcoming the odds. He wants to beat you, humiliate you, and take something from you. He may want your money, he may want your life. One thing he doesn't want is to pick on someone who may give him a fight. This means that the person who will attack you will either have a weapon, a couple buddies, or will be significantly larger than you. If we are going to be REAL, we will REALize that dealing with a weapon or multiple opponents is very, very difficult. We must train to deal with these situations to improve our odds of survival, but the weapon or multiple opponents give a huge advantage to the attacker(s).

A larger, stronger attacker is difficult to deal with, but this type of assailant makes an assumption. He assumes that his size and strength give him an advantage over his victim. Fortunately for us, skill and proper tactics can overcome this sort of disadvantage. But what kind of skill should we develop? I believe that we should begin with those techniques, trained with progressive resistance, which are most effective in nullifying the size advantage of the attacker.

I am fortunate to have a group of women who train in my classes in Honolulu. These women train very hard, and have a great time doing it. They partner amongst themselves, and with the men. We practice in all the ranges (kickboxing, clinch, and ground), much of the time spent in light sparring. The women in class have helped me tremendously in changing the women's curriculum, prioritizing those techniques that work when the opponent is much larger. They don't just learn techniques, they try to apply the techniques against someone who is trying foil every attempt. The skill level of each woman has continually improved, and they consistently surprise guest students with their skills. Well, as obvious as it is, a big breakthrough in our training was staring at me in the face, but it was only recently that I actually saw it.

For years I would train men one way while guiding the women in a different manner. The basics were pretty much the same, but strength techniques that were taught to men were modified or skipped altogether for the women. I had it backwards. Instead of modifying techniques to work for women, I now prioritize those "women's" techniques that work best against a larger stronger opponent for everyone. Therefore, men and women learn the same curriculum, with a few modifications on positioning.

I am sure that many will say that most systems prioritize techniques that work against bigger opponents, but the truth is that many of those techniques are hard to actually apply against a large opponent who is really fighting back. The JKDU women test the techniques against larger opponents every single class. If a woman faces an attacker, we always emphasize escape. The woman must do whatever it takes to go home safely. The same goes for the men. If we face a much larger opponent, we should do what we must to escape. This changes the prioritization of techniques. Instead of looking for the finish, we look for a way out. If there is no escape or we can't escape because we are protecting others, we work hard to finish the fight. Still, we must realize that a strong, aggressive opponent who significantly outweighs you requires different techniques and tactics than when dealing with a sparring partner of similar weight.

When a large opponent is coming at you hard, kickboxing range doesn't last very long. There is so much forward momentum and so little time that standard kickboxing doesn't apply well against a rushing attacker. Kickboxing matches start out at a certain range and tend to maintain that range. An angry attacker tends to move forward very quickly, getting into punching and clinch range immediately. Not to mention that that many attacks start in close range. The primary emphasis is on evasion and dealing with that aggressive onslaught.

Clinch range must be tested against larger opponents. Wrist locks, standing arm locks, and many takedowns in the clinch are nearly impossible against a large, aggressive opponent. We first work on techniques to avoid being taken to the ground, along with maneuvers to offset the opponent's mass. Techniques that may be prioritized in a wrestling match may not work well against the big guy. Moves like the arm drag work well against larger opponents. Pulling the arm and passing by the elbow not only gets you to the back, but also provides an escape route.

Ground techniques have to be prioritized to deal with the opponent's weight and ability to lift us off the ground. If a woman tries to arm bar a large man from the guard, he may stand and slam her. We must be very aware of these dangers, and so we first emphasize positions and techniques that keep distance and provide the opportunity to escape. This is why we now teach the butterfly guard first. Instead of wrapping the legs around a larger opponent, we put the feet inside their thighs to keep the weight off. It is also much easier to get back to your feet from the butterfly guard. We work the closed guard a little later for more attacks, but this works best against someone who is close to your own weight or smaller.

Once the students understand utilizing leverage and are able to maneuver well, I add in simulated eye and groin strikes to the sparring. These help close the size and strength gap, but we can't rely on these to end an altercation. Attackers in drugs or with mental issues may not feel anything. Leverage is prioritized.

Want to be effective in a self-defense situation? Then I say to train like a girl, and if need be, fight like a girl. Watch our women train and spar and you will see what I mean.

19. REJECT WHAT IS USEFUL

I know what you are thinking. "Either the title for this column is wrong, or Richardson has really lost it. He has been out there on the edge for quite awhile, but this time he has fallen over it." Come with me to the edge and see what you think.

The JKD world adopted this wonderful phrase (emblazoned on an iconic plaque by Sifu Dan Inosanto) "Absorb what is useful, reject what is useless, add what is specifically your own." These few words sum up the scientific approach to any endeavor. We want to make the "useful" part of our expression, be it in martial arts or in baseball. We want to dismiss those things that are not useful to us, those things that would dilute our ability to perform well. We also want to add what is specifically our own, as we are all creative individuals with different bodies and inclinations. This is an excellent, truthful, profound phrase. Let's take it one step further.

What kind of telephone do you have at home? Do you have a cordless phone, or possibly a hands-free device? You probably also have a cell phone. Why don't you have a rotary dial phone in your living room? Because at some point, you rejected the useful for something even more efficient. Even with something as impersonal as a telephone, getting rid of that old rotary model may have been hard. I remember my parents using the rotary dial to call my grandparents. I made my first phone calls on that old black, heavy rotary phone, talking to friends and family from a distance. Let me tell you that the rotary phone worked very well. I could call anywhere in the world with that phone, and I remember a sense of sadness when it was replaced. The truth is, however, that you don't use a rotary phone because the current technology is so much better and more efficient. This illustrates what happens all the time in our martial arts training.

If we can become emotionally attached to something as inanimate as a telephone, how attached can we become to martial arts techniques that become a part of our minds and body? Now think of certain techniques that you have actually used effectively. We are talking heavy emotional attachment. Now what happens when a new technology comes our way? Are we eager to drop the old and get on to the new? Of course not. We are happy with the old techniques or methods because they have served us well. We can't just let some new technique come in and bump the old ones out. Where is our loyalty? If we want to be our very best, we must come back to being loyal to the truth.

How do we go about finding the truth in the fighting arts? Simple.

We must fight or we must observe others fighting. If we are dedicated to finding our own truth, we must put ourselves into the realm where truth is expressed. A fight is where two persons (or more) try to subdue each other through striking, locking, choking, etc. If we want to know the truth about a particular fighting technique, we must put it into that environment to test it. Let's take a technique that was deemed useful. Bruce Lee learned the centerline blast from wing chun kung fu. He was able to use this technique with excellent results, as have many other people. After Lee move to America, he found that many fighters used a boxing or kickboxing structure, which was very mobile. He found that the shuffling footwork of wing chun did not work well against these fast moving opponents. It may work well in tight quarters, but if there is room to move, it is just not quick enough. The footwork was changed to make the platform for the straight blast quicker and more mobile. It became a fast run while the hands blasted away. The blast was again working well in a more mobile environment. Should we stop there? Of course not.

A few years ago, we made another adjustment. I had the good fortune of training with Vitor Belfort before he ever entered the Ultimate Fighting Championship. I had trained with him for over a year before I even knew that he did any boxing. Vitor used a technique where he runs towards his opponent while throwing straight boxing style punches. He takes a step with the left foot while throwing a right punch, then a step with the right foot while throwing a strong left punch. In essence, he is throwing a series of crosses, thereby developing great power. The punches come with a turn of the body and the chin is protected by the shoulder. Vitor used this very effectively against the top NHB fighters in the world. I found it to be much better than the running centerline blast for a few reasons. One, there is much more power in a boxing style punch where the punch comes from your shoulder than when it comes from the middle of your chest. Two, since the shoulders are up you are more protected from a wild swing. So, I dubbed it the boxing blast and many JKD and MMA people are using it effectively today. Note that the wing chun centerline blast still works, but as technology advances, we should be ready to pick up something even better should it come along.

Another example is with takedowns. Wrestling takedowns work very well, and have been used effectively for thousands of years. This is a fact. One wrestling maneuver that I use consistently is the single leg takedown. It worked in the days of the Greeks, and it still works today. The great wrestling champion and coach Dan Gable says "The single most important skill in determining a champion wrestler is his ability to finish the single leg takedown." The single leg is about as useful as you can get, and I have had very good success with it. Enter Baret Yoshida. Baret is one of the world's greatest athletes in the world of submission wrestling. Submission wrestling is a combination of Brazilian jiu-jitsu, wrestling, sambo, and anything else you can throw in there to be effective. Baret is a BJJ black belt champion, and an NHB champion. About a year ago I was told that Baret was to start teaching private lessons, so I jumped at the chance to train with him.

We started with sparring. Each time I tried my single leg takedown Baret would counterbalance so I couldn't get him to the ground, push my head off to his side, lock in a head and arm guillotine, and finish it with incredible pressure. I weigh just under 190, and Baret weighs about 145. He was killing me each time I tried that move. I was definitely ready to reject the useful. Because Baret is a great guy who doesn't hide technique, he showed me how to modify the single leg takedown so that the guillotine was no longer available. A new version of the single leg is now in use, and working with great results while protecting from the relatively new head and arm guillotine. Baret has had to modify many, many moves and positions that no longer work in today's game, and he continues to push forward staying ahead of the curve. He is a great example of someone who rejects the useful to absorb or create the even more useful.

The original centerline blast from wing chun and the single leg from wrestling still work. This has been proven over and over again. But there has been progress, and you would be wise to seek out modifications that make you sparring even more efficient. Apply the same methods of advancement to your life, and you will have a better and better existence. If you use a microwave oven or drive a modern vehicle, you have already accepted this idea. Apply it to your martial arts and you will garner the same superior results.

20. MEMORIZATION VERSUS PERFORMANCE

Did you know that there are really only two types of drills that we do in our martial arts training? Take time to think about all the different ways you practice and you will find that when it comes to practicing technique, you will either be working on memorization of the move or on the ability to apply that move. It is important to understand this because if you only work on memorization, you will not develop the essential skills necessary to be able to use the technique against a real attacker.

Memorization drills vary from doing solo forms to partner forms to repetition of a technique on a cooperative partner. This is how we actually get the precision of the move into our bodies so that we don't have to think of every single step in the technique. For example, let's say you are learning how to do the basic outward block against a big right swing, grab the opponent's neck and throw a knee. Most martial arts systems have this move as part of their arsenal because it has proven effective over the ages. How is the instructor going to teach this to you? First, she shows you how to do the block correctly. She shows proper hand placement, and where to contact the opponent's arm. Next you learn how to grab the neck properly, then how to deliver that knee. It may seem like there are only three components to the move, but you try it for the first time and it is not as easy as it seems. Your arm is in the wrong place, you are off balance when you grab the neck, and your knee strikes are not comfortable. The problem is that you have not actually memorized the move. You have the basic idea, but your body isn't sure where it should be. What do you do to memorize this move? One option is to shadow box the move in the air without a partner to help ingrain the movements and make them natural. A better option is to have a partner throw wide punches at you so that you can work on more precise movement against a human body. A third option is to go over the move in your mind, seeing and feeling yourself doing the move correctly over and over again. All three of these methods are great for memorizing the sequence and details of a technique, but memorization is not enough if you want to be able to use your techniques against someone who is fighting you.

You can think of each technique as a tool. Over time, you can develop a great number of techniques to have in your toolbox. You may have worked hard at polishing those tools so that they are like gleaming gems, a beautiful sight to behold. The problem is that having the tools does not mean that you know how to fix a car. I could go down to the hardware store and purchase the finest set of auto repair tools available, but I wouldn't be able to change out the air conditioning unit on my car. Having the tools is only useful once we have developed the skill necessary to use those tools to solve problems.

The second type of drill is what we in JKDU call Performance Games. Performance Games are when we add that all-important ingredient of resistance. I use the word "game" because it should be fun and a challenge. There is variability instead of rote memorization. Knowing the technique is not enough. Being able to apply your technique against someone who is trying to nullify your efforts is what counts. The only way to achieve this skill in application is to practice fighting against someone who is fighting back. It is that simple. By having my partner try to foil my attempts to apply my technique, my body adjusts and develops the timing, sense of distance, and sensitivity needed to make the move work. At the same time, the fine details of the move are honed; details that are not apparent when practicing without resistance. Going back to our basic technique, when under pressure you will learn quickly why the block must be applied at 120-degree angle. (It will collapse if done vertically.) You will understand why the hands must be clasped behind the opponent's neck, and not just lying on the shoulders. (He will escape quickly.) You will learn the balance needed to throw the knee when the opponent is trying to escape. As many a wise philosopher has pointed out through the centuries, you learn by doing.

Now for a vitally important question: How long should a student do the Memorization Drills before moving on to the Performance Games? Six months? A year? For me, usually about five minutes. Yes, that's right. Five minutes. It does not take long to get the basic idea of a technique down, especially those techniques that beginners will use. How long does it take to learn an outward block? Probably less than five minutes. Once the move is memorized to a reasonable degree, it is time to go into a Performance Drill to begin skill development. Many people are afraid of Performance Games because it sounds too intense. Actually, we vary the intensity to match the skill and goals of the student. When a new student comes in we start with very light resistance. If the student just learned that outside block, we have another student, with good control, move around and try to "land" the blow. Not full power and not full-speed at first. Not even with a closed fist, but usually open hand to begin with. Nice and easy, but trying to put the hand on the target. Over time the speed is brought up and power is added. It will eventually be integrated into the overall sparring.

One word of caution on the Performance Games. If you always isolate techniques it will be difficult to have a complete flow in a real fight. It is imperative that the student is allowed the ability to play with few restrictions, but still monitoring intensity according to each person's goals and abilities. The most complete drill is where we start in either the kickboxing range, in the clinch, or on the ground and just go wherever the flow takes you. It will depend on your skill and the skill of the opponent, but it is great fun!

How about those Memorization Drills? Once you have learned a technique should you only try to apply it in sparring and forego the repetition? Most combat athletes spend very little time in each training session working on particular techniques without resistance. The vast majority of the time is spent conditioning the body and doing Performance Drills. Shadow boxing and mental training is done when there is no partner available to train with. Wrestling legend Dan Gable would train like a madman on the mat, then would go home and shadow fight alone in his basement for hours. He visualized the opponents and practiced defeating them. This is only effective if you have spent the time with the Performance Drills so that you know what it feels like to have an opponent come after you.

Memorize the technique through Memorization Drills then put it into action with Performance Games. This is how you will develop into a skillful martial artist, and have a great time doing it. If you need help with these drills, feel free to write to me through my website: jkdunlimited.com.

21. ERIC'S STORY

As we go through this journey of life, those who choose to face their weaknesses then work to strengthen them are the ones who get to enjoy the proudest moments. Many of my students have taken, and continue to take this more difficult, yet fulfilling path. This month I want to relate a particular story that shows the profound benefits realistic martial arts training can yield.

One of my students approached me after class with this story. Eric had trained for many years in different styles of martial arts where sparring was not emphasized. These classes went over techniques, drills, and such, but did not engage in actual fighting practice. That's fine, as many people prefer to work on their physical fitness while learning an art form. As time went on, Eric found himself in a few confrontations. Taking the path of the martial artist, he was able to walk away from each confrontation without fighting. He displayed excellent self-control, but something was wrong.

Eric was lamenting his predicament to a friend. "Some guy gets in my face, I do the right thing by walking away from the fight, but I don't feel good about it. I feel all twisted up inside for days." His friend saw through his problem. "You didn't walk way because you didn't want to hurt the guy, you walked away because you were afraid." His friend was right. Eric told himself that he was being the bigger man, but actually he was shrinking away because he was fearful of getting hurt.

Some time goes by and Eric finds our school. I remember when he first came to class that he was a bit tentative about the whole atmosphere. We don't wear uniforms, music is played during class, and we don't salute each other. Respect is shown by your actions during the training and discipline is displayed through your ability to choose the right techniques during the pressure of sparring. Eric eventually dedicated himself to the training, and improved rapidly. During sparring, each pair is allowed to go at whatever intensity that they choose. Whoever wants to go lighter dictates the pace of that round. Some students go very light all of the time. Others often go hard of the partner is fine with it. Eric usually chooses to spar at pretty high intensity. He as improved steadily and continues to make excellent progress. Like all of our students, Eric finishes the training session with a big grin on his face.

A few weeks ago Eric took his two sons down to the beach to teach them how to surf. After awhile the older son wanted to try some of the bigger waves. Eric let him go, staying inside to help the younger boy. A while later the older boy came in upset. He told his father that he caught a wave, another surfer dropped in on him and dinged his board without any apology. (This is very bad surfing etiquette!) Eric was not happy, especially since the other surfer was a full-grown adult. Eric waited for the bully to come in to shore.

When he came in, Eric confronted him. Eric gave the guy a talking to, and the bully started yelling and posturing like he wanted to give Eric a beating. This is all happening in front of the two boys. Eric kept his calm, and was able to finally walk away without a fight. But, something was still bothering him.

"Should I have hit him?" Eric asked. I asked him if he was scared during the argument. "Not at all" he replied. I told him that I thought he did the right thing. He confronted a guy who was bullying a young boy, he felt no fear during the yelling and posturing, and then let the guy go without stooping to the level of physical violence. I told him he should feel great about the whole incident, especially since he stood up for his sons like that. I am sure that they will never forget that. Eric said that he was wondering if it was okay to let the guy get away with it. I asked, "Do you remember how bad you used to feel when you walked away from a possible fight because you were scared?" Eric said, "Yes." "Well that's exactly what that surfer is feeling right now." Eric smiled, realizing that the bully didn't get off so easy.

Realistic training gives us the confidence to face physical situations without the self-doubt that plagues most good people. If you want to be able to walk away from a fight with your head held high, I suggest that you work hard to develop the skills that work in a real situation, in case the other guy doesn't walk away. The training is tough, but the benefits are priceless.

22. FEEDBACK!

As we continue our journey of the martial artist, certain principles appear that are useful not only for the benefit of fighting, but which can also be applied to any aspect of life. One such principle is that the true goal of those wishing to be able to defend themselves in a real situation is to develop fighting skill. Not just skill at forms or skill at memorized sequences, but the ability to apply your fighting techniques against someone who is fighting back. That is what skill is, right? The ability to apply a technique. Just because a person can swing a golf club with perfect form does not qualify him or her as a skillful golfer. The skillful golfer is one who can get the ball into the hole in few strokes. Knowing the song does not make a good singer. What we want to develop is skill, and there is a simple formula for doing that.

The secret to developing skill is to PRACTICE, CORRECTLY, and CONSISTENTLY, over TIME. I have gone over this formula many times, explaining how I came to it and why it works. I have also explained in the past the many components of each category. Of course, all things can be improved. I am thankful to have understood this formula even better in recent months, especially the category of training CORRECTLY. Interestingly enough, it came to me from an endeavor outside of the martial arts.

I have been working on the craft of writing screenplays for about eight years now. Well, actually, I have been working on the craft for about two years. I started work on my first effort eight years ago, finished it three years later, then put the hobby aside. When I decided to get back at it, I realized that I had not followed my formula for developing skill in the craft. I did not really practice it, I had no real way of knowing if I was doing it correctly, I certainly was not consistent, and I just did one and stopped. Guess what happened? I developed no skill. What many people don't understand is that writing a screenplay is an acquired skill. There may be a certain amount of talent to begin with, but just as a new martial artist may be blessed with athleticism, talent alone will not produce great results. Our talents must be coupled with a great deal of learning and hard work to yield the results we desire. Once I realized the errors of my ways, I resolved to start taking classes and get on a daily routine of working on the screenplay stories that I had floating around in my head. I also resolved to be patient with myself as I keep working on this craft.

Sure enough, I found out that I didn't know much about writing a screenplay at all. It's like an athlete who goes into a grappling gym thinking that he can take anyone in the room. Once he spars with someone who is skillful, he realizes that he does not understand the game. The classes and books helped me tremendously, but I was soon to find another aspect that is as important in writing as it is in martial arts training. I hired a script consultant (one with a lengthy career as a producer in Hollywood) to read my third screenplay. She came back with a ton of notes, pointing out many subtleties that would have taken years of classroom study to discover. What did she give me? Feedback! Solid, skillful feedback. Instead of me looking at the work and thinking that it was pretty good, my coach showed me where it was good and where I was missing key elements. This experience made me understand that having high quality feedback is an absolutely essential part of training correctly.

Imagine training as a boxer, but without ever having anyone throw a punch at you. You may have a coach telling you to keep your hands up, move your head, etc., but you will never know if your defense is good until you have someone give you a little fistic feedback. Here's an example using grappling.

I knew a guy who was an instructor in a stand-up art. He had trained with me a bit, and had brought a few grapplers into his school for seminars. That was the extent of his grappling coaching. I hadn't seen him for over two years when we got together for a private lesson. I asked him how his training was going, and he said "Great, especially the ground." I asked him whom he was training with. He told me that he just rolled with his students. Now this is a great thing, and it is impressive when an instructor will put the ego aside and spar with his students. I figured that he must have improved tremendously from the hours and hours of sparring. When it was time for us to roll I was surprised indeed. Basically, everything was wrong. Every aspect of his ground game had huge flaws. Why? He had sparred for two years, but he had never gotten QUALITY feedback. He was grappling with students who knew less than he did, which meant that none of his partners could capitalize on his mistakes. This led to him believing that his grappling was very advanced when in reality it needed a complete overhaul. We all need good feedback.

Someone e-mailed me recently asking how he could advance his Brazilian jiu-jitsu ground skills to the purple belt level. I told him that he needs to train with people who are better than he is. Why? Because that way he will get the feedback he needs to advance his game. This is why sparring is so important to the martial artist. You get feedback. In my classes we have a particular mindset that helps us in welcoming feedback. I always say that if you want to do your partner a big favor, be sure to hit him or her as many times as you can. We do this safely with proper equipment and intensity, but it makes it fun for everyone. It becomes a game to see who can do the most favors for his or her partner. We also make sure that if our partner hits, kicks, throws, or submits us we thank them for making us better. Good feedback means good improvement.

Do you want to advance your martial arts skill? Is there another area of life where you want to develop skill? Do you want to write a screenplay, a novel, or a song? If so, do yourself a favor and find a great coach who will give you high quality feedback. Your rate of development will be much faster and more enjoyable.

23. DETAILS, DETAILS

There is a saying that goes "The devil is in the details." I have come to understand that great success is in the details. That's why I prefer to say, "Divinity is in the details." As we train in martial arts, we become aware of how important small details can be. Your instructor may tell you to keep your hand up a little higher than you normally do, but it may not seem very important to you. It is just a minor detail. Let me tell you a personal story about that small detail that hit close to home: literally!

Many years ago (in the mid-80's) I trained at the Main Street Boxing Gym in downtown Los Angeles, California. This was an old, but very famous location that drew the very best professionals to its old rings and worn out heavy bags. I was able to see many high level fighters there, including the one and only Muhammad Ali. One day my boxing coach put me in the ring to spar with a very large opponent. I weighed about 200 pounds at the time, but this man I was to face weighed 280! He was the body guard of another famous boxer, later turned actor, Tex Cobb. Imagine how formidable this man must be to bodyguard Tex Cobb!

As I got into the ring my coach gave me one last bit of advice: "Keep your hands up." I said nonchalantly said okay, knowing that I always had my hands up, just under my chin. The bell rang and we started to circle each other. This large man stepped in with a very fast, efficient, extremely powerful jab. I saw it coming, but by the time my hand went from under my chin upward into position to protect my face, it was too late. Maybe a millisecond too late, but late is late! My head snapped back as the full force of his weight and explosiveness transferred into my head. I bounced off the ropes, and fortunately was able to avoid the huge right cross that followed. Enlightenment! At last I understood. Having my hands at my chin did not mean that my hands were up. When a skillful fighter steps in with a very fast punch, I would have to first have to recognize the strike, then raise my hand up to the level of the punch, and then block it. That is one step too many. If my hands were already around eye-level I could skip the time consuming process of raising my hands. I immediately held my hands higher and have kept them there ever since! I learned a lot from that arduous sparring session, but the detail of having my hands up higher was the most important.

I recently released a new set of MMA For The Street DVDs that cover the entire range of street combat. I make it a point to go over the fine details of each technique so the students can actually use the moves with great efficiency. I don't want people to just be able to mimic a move against a cooperative partner; I want them to be able to use the technique against someone who is fighting back. An experienced jiu-jitsu fighter who purchased the tapes wrote to me with the greatest compliment. He stated that the details that I presented on the triangle choke are the best he had ever seen. Better yet, he was able to use those details a few days later at the largest submission wrestling tournament ever held in the United States. He was able to finish two opponents with triangles on his way to his first ever, 1st place finish. He said that it was the details on the DVDs that made the difference. This is a good illustration of how important the small points can be. This student had entered many tournaments and was an accomplished fighter. Learning and applying a few fine points allowed him to leave as a champion.

The smallest details often make the difference between success and failure. If you are in school the small detail of doing your homework before having fun will make a huge impact on your scholastic achievement. If you are in business, the small detail of returning phone calls and e-mails promptly can be the deciding factor between great success and bankruptcy. The small things that we do every day become the habits that consistently push us ahead in life. The little details that we neglect each day will consistently hold us back. Remember the little things that are easy to do are also easy to not do! Whether it is in the martial arts or your everyday life, become a master of those details so that you can enjoy the benefits that come with being your best.

24. LESSONS FROM THE RING

If you are interested in self-defense you would be wise to look at some of the lessons revealed through the evolution of martial sports, especially no holds barred fighting. Let's start with jiu-jitsu.

This art was developed in Japan for self-defense purposes. Jiu-jitsu utilizes all types of striking, throws, and ground fighting to defeat an attacker. In fact most of the techniques are so dangerous that they could only be practiced in a slow, controlled environment. Nobody wants to get injured training, so great care had to be taken during practice. Along came a man named Jigoro Kano who decided to take a portion of jiu-jitsu and turn it into a sport. He created judo where the participants cannot strike, but are allowed to do many throws along with some grappling. The participants of judo did not practice in that slow, controlled environment, but instead practiced applying their techniques against someone who was fighting their every move. Guess what happened? The judo practitioners developed a very high level of skill. Through sparring they developed proper timing, improved the techniques, and developed themselves into combat athletes. When a good judo player sparred with a good traditional jiu-jitsu man, the judo player dominated. It became apparent that whoever practiced athletically, even if he had fewer techniques to choose from, would become the better fighter. Being able to demonstrate techniques against a cooperative opponent just did not translate well to applying those techniques against someone who was fighting back.

About this time a very good jiu-jitsu teacher moved from Japan to Brazil. He ended up teaching the Gracie family the art of Japanese jiu-jitsu. Things are different in Brazil, and the Brazilians had no problem competing with jiu-jitsu with very few rules. Instead of slowly practicing the more dangerous techniques of jiu-jitsu with a partner, they got in the ring and went all out against anyone who would step up to the challenge. This environment changed the direction of jiu-jitsu. The Gracies had to be innovative to adapt the art to the "no rules" arena. Of course, the result was Gracie jiu-jitsu, which is quite different from the original jiu-jitsu. There are many techniques drawn from the original art, but the key is that they practiced athletically, like judo, but without so many rules. Guess what happened? When a judo player went against a Gracie jiu-jitsu player, even without striking, the jiu-jitsu player invariably won. The circle was completed. The lesson is that if you train athletically with fewer restrictions you have more options that you can actually apply.

Fast forward to the nineties. Gracie jiu-jitsu comes to America in the Ultimate Fighting Championship. Royce Gracie enters and beats strong, athletic fighters with his jiu-jitsu skills. He proves time and again that he can enter and take a striker down to the ground where he dominates the fight. The world learned the value of grappling. But again, this was taking place in a new environment. It isn't long before wrestlers learned to deal with the jiu-jitsu submissions and positioning. Wrestlers started to win. Then kickboxers began to learn how to avoid the takedown of the wrestlers and jiu-jitsu stylists. World champion kickboxer Maurice Smith would get a few shots in against a grappler then be taken to the ground, but Smith had learned enough ground work to survive on the ground until he could get back to his feet. He would continue this tactic until his opponent was weary, resulting in a kickboxing match between a tired grappler who could not explode in for a takedown and a world champion striker. Smith knocked out many opponents this way.

The art of the ring has now advanced to the point where the majority of the fighters are very complete. They can strike on their feet, avoid takedowns, apply takedowns, and fight well on the ground. Everyone knows that the next opponent may be a better kickboxer or a better grappler. The only solution is to be able to handle all the distances so that they can try to survive the tough spots and work into a range where they can dominate. Like Bruce Lee admonished, we should strive to be a complete fighter. This is good advice for anyone training in the martial arts, even if you never plan to step into the competitive arena.

A professional fighter knows who his next opponent is going to be. He has an idea of his strengths and weaknesses and trains to deal with that opponent. If you train for self-defense, you don't know who may attack you. It may be a large thug who used to be a boxer. It might be a drunk in a bar who was a college wrestler. It may be a thief with a knife. We need to remember that street self-defense has no rules at all, and we must train in that environment if we want to be effective, but we must train our techniques athletically against a resisting opponent if we want to develop usable skills. We must train to be complete fighters because we don't want to find ourselves in unfamiliar territory. We have to be good at striking, grappling, and weaponry if we want to be truly prepared to defend our loved ones. Have fun with your practice, but apply the lessons of the ring. You will become better than ever!

25. STAND UP!

We all hope that we never have to use our martial arts skills in a real situation. If a situation does occur, we want to be well prepared to defend ourselves properly. Proper practice is the only way. With that in mind, let me ask you a question. If you were attacked and fighting for your life, would you rather fight standing up or would you rather be on your back? Not a difficult question, is it? Few people will choose to fight from their backs, not even jiu jitsu fighters. I have a good friend named Baret Yoshida here in Hawaii who is known as having one of the best guards, if not the best, in the entire grappling world. Ask the most famous Brazilian jiu jitsu fighters who they think has the most dangerous guard and Baret's name will always come up. Does Baret want to fight from his back in a real fight? Not at all. As great as Baret's guard is, he spends a lot of time practicing standing up from the ground to get back to his feet. Think of the advantage you would have if you knew that even if a grappler did take you to the ground, you could stand back up and start striking again. The key is to actually practice this essential skill properly.

It is easy to say "If someone takes me to the ground, I will just stand back up." It is much harder to do against someone who is skilled at keeping you down. One of the JKD Unlimited Performance Games (isolated sparring drills) that we practice is the "Stand Up from the Ground" game. One person starts on their back, the other person starts on top in any number of positions. The top person can be standing, throwing kicks at the downed fighter. The top person can also be on the ground in the guard, half guard, side control, etc. The person on the bottom must try to get back to his feet while the person on top tries to keep that from happening. We vary the level of resistance so that the bottom person gets to work on their escapes without being overwhelmed. What everyone learns is that there are specific techniques and tactics to escape from your back and get to your feet. The person on top learns how to use their own technique to counter all of the escape attempts. The result of playing this Performance Game is that the person on the bottom becomes very skillful at escaping while the fighter on top becomes skillful at keeping an opponent on their back.

Another good friend of mine is Robert Follis, a Head Trainer for the Team Quest Fight Club near Portland, Oregon. This is UFC legend Randy Couture's team, one of the very best in the Mixed Martial Arts world. Follis visited Hawaii recently and trained my class. We worked on standing up from the ground, and he emphasized a few very important points. When people try to stand up, they usually try to push the other person away to make space. This is not the best idea, especially against a strong opponent. They will lean forward and strike down at you. Instead, we always need to push ourselves away. It is as if you are too close to a giant rock. Instead of pushing the rock away, push yourself back from the rock. As you push away from your opponent, try to do so at an angle by getting to the side and pushing on his ear. If you push straight back, you may still get hit hard. Pushing to the side not only gets you out at an angle away from the striking, it may also set you up for arm locks and chokes if you can't get all the way to your feet. Just like when you are sparring on your feet, you want to try to get to the side and attack from various angles instead of coming straightforward.

Another important point is to make sure the opponent does not sit up while you stay flat on your back. If he gets elevation, he will drop those punches and elbows down hard! If he sits up, you must sit up with him. If he starts to push you back down, try to use his movement to push and angle to the side to start your escape. These few concepts can be translated into many different techniques, but as long as you are not getting hit and you can get back to your feet you are doing a good job.

Of course, knowing the technique is just the beginning. Take the techniques and play with them in the Performance Games. Playing the "Stand Up" game is especially important for all of you who specialize in striking arts such as kickboxing, Tae Kwon Do, and Karate. You can set and throw your punches and kicks with all your power, knowing that if you end up on the ground, you will be back on your feet in no time. Spend time doing this drill in each practice session and your confidence will soar. The same goes for your life. Develop the mindset that no matter how hard life throws you to the ground, you will always get back to your feet and hold your head high!

26. ENVIRONMENTAL IMPACT

What is the ideal environment for your martial arts training? Most of us try to have a wide-open space with a smooth, flat training surface. It is also nice to have that surface padded for takedowns and ground work. Is this the type of place that the typical street attack occurs in? Not at all. There are a number of environmental factors that can affect the way a fight takes place. Your physical surroundings, your clothing, and the clothing of your opponent must be taken into account.

Most real fights occur in locations that are not spacious. You will probably have barriers, such as walls, poles, cars, or furniture to deal with. These barriers can be used to your advantage if you have included barrier training in your practice sessions. If not, they may be used against you. The most common barrier is the wall. The best use of this barrier is to clinch and pin your opponent's back to the wall so that he cannot move well. You can get to a position where he cannot maneuver or strike well, but you can. Typically this means tying up both of his arms and pinning him with your shoulder, while remaining in position to fire strong punches and knee strikes at him. Since he is pinned, he cannot generate much power with his knees. There is an art to getting someone against a wall and keeping him there, so you must train this to become proficient. Here are three very simple drills that are essential for familiarizing yourself with fighting at a barrier.

First, start in the clinch with a partner, both of you standing a few yards away from the wall. Work in the clinch while trying to guide your partner's back to the wall. He will try to do the same to you. You will learn how to push and pull with proper leverage and set-ups to get your partner's back against the barrier while keeping from being pinned yourself. If you don't have a suitable wall, draw a line on the ground and try to push your partner across that line, back first.

The second drill is to start with your partner's back against the wall. He does his best to get away from the wall, while you do your best to keep him there. You can do this without strikes to focus on leverage or add strikes to make the drill more real. If the fighters are proficient in dealing with strikes while avoiding being pinned, add takedowns into the mix.

The third drill is the same as the second, but you start with your back to the wall. Your partner attempts to keep you pinned while you try to escape. Again, you can do this without strikes or while including strikes, eventually adding takedowns as well. Doing these two simple drills will give you the awareness and skills necessary to use the barrier to your advantage in a real altercation.

A note on the takedowns. It is often easier to take an opponent down after pinning him to the wall because you take away his ability to sprawl. If you go for a double leg takedown when his back is against the wall, he simply cannot move his hips and legs away from you. Defensively, you will need to learn how to turn your body and use a whizzer to avoid takedowns.

Another environmental factor is the surface you must fight on. If you are lucky, you might be on a flat, soft surface as in a carpeted room. You may just as well find yourself on a sloping asphalt parking lot that is covered with pebbles and broken glass. If your main techniques rely on dropping to your knees for a takedown, you may want to add a few more options into your repertoire. I know of a very good Brazilian Jiu-Jitsu fighter who recently broke his knee after dropping down onto concrete to shoot on his opponent in a street fight. You might get away with pounding your knee on the cement a few times, but it would be wise to avoid the risk altogether if you can.

The sloping surface is important to take into account, especially for sweeps. If you end up on your back with the opponent in your guard, you might immediately go to your favorite sweep. Most people will tend to sweep to one side, rather than having both sides equally trained. But if you try to sweep an opponent to your right, and the surface is sloping upward to the right, it just isn't going to work. You want to sweep downhill. The same with standing sweeps. You need to be able to maneuver your opponent so that you can sweep downhill instead of fighting gravity.

Another major concern is clothing. You can use the opponent's clothes against him. You can use the collar to choke and you can grab his pant legs to make takedowns and guard passes easier. He can also use your clothing against you, so you need to know how to defend against those same techniques along with the simple grab and punch scenario. An untrained streetfighter will instinctively grab your jacket to pull you into his punches. You need to know how to deal with that situation. You can also use your own clothing to stop an attacker. There are several chokes that can be done with the aid of your own collar or sleeves.

Shoes are another factor. Are your shoes slippery? Do they have a good toe and heel to make your kicks more potent? Are they going to fall off in the middle of a tussle? These should all be considered and practiced before you get into a bad situation.

The environment in a real fight is far different than most martial arts studio environments. I suggest you take some extra time to practice against the wall, in your street clothes, and outside on uneven terrain. You will be better prepared for a real attack should you ever have to defend yourself or loved ones.

27. OVERCOMING ADVERSITY

The essence of the martial arts is to develop skills that will help you to overcome adversity. An attacker who is trying to take your life is the ultimate in adversity. We train in the martial arts to learn ways of defending and triumphing over each adverse situation. We learn how to block punches, kicks, and other strikes. We practice the art of turning an opponent's force back against himself. We train ourselves to be able to take charge of a bad situation and turn it to our favor. This is exactly why the practice of the martial arts is so important for our everyday lives.

Most people reading this will never be attacked on the street. That is a fortunate fact, but I can guarantee that each of you will have to deal with adversity in your life. This is just the way it works. Situations arise that we have no control over, but thankfully, we can control how we respond to those situations. It is just like in a fight situation. Proper training will pay off.

If an untrained person is attacked, he or she must rely solely upon instinct to get them through the situation. A well-trained fighter responds differently. Through discipline and technique, the martial artist can efficiently counter the attack and prevail by making good choices at the right time. The difference is that the trained fighter has an effective approach to handling the adverse situation. The same applies in your day-to-day life. Bad situations will arise. The question is, are you going to react out of instinct or respond well due to proper training?

Imagine that you are running late for an important meeting that could mean a lot for your career. You rush around the house looking for your keys, run up to your car, and drive away in a hurry. Then you hit traffic. You get frantic. As the traffic starts to move, you weave in and out of lanes to make up time. The light turns yellow as you approach the last intersection, so you speed through. Unfortunately, you are a little late. Even worse, a policeman was watching you. You hear the siren and see the lights. Now you are late for sure, plus you are getting a ticket and your insurance rates are going to go up. Absolute frustration sets in.

You finally get to your meeting and guess what? The other person is even later than you are. All that stress for nothing. You could have taken your time, enjoyed listening to an educational lecture in the car, and arrived without a care in the world. Instead, you put pressure on yourself and made life miserable. You actually created the adverse situation.

The whole incident could have been avoided by simply planning well and leaving on time. Once you were late, you could have thought the situation out calmly and reasonably by realizing that rushing will only make matters worse. It isn't good to go into a meeting in a flustered state. Instead of letting natural instinct take over, you could have applied the calm mind of the martial artist to get you to the meeting. Being calm upon arrival, you could have confidently approached the meeting as a strong warrior approaches battle. It is all a matter of controlling your mind instead of letting your impulses take over.

You can also use the positive mindset of the warrior to overcome adversity. When things are going bad in fight, we don't give up. Never! We instead look for a positive solution. This is how you should approach those unfortunate circumstances in life. I can use myself as a good example of this.

A few years ago I took a blood test to renew my life insurance. I eat very healthy, (high protein vegetarian since 1990) and take care of myself. Imagine my surprise when the tests came back with a problem. A bad problem. I was diagnosed with a serious autoimmune disease. My body's immune system had decided to attack my liver. It is rare, but that was the circumstance I found myself in. Without treatment I would have only lasted another couple years. Luckily, I take a medicine that reverses the disease and keeps it in check. There are severe side effects of the medicine, but it keeps me alive. Now, I have to say that my first reaction was despair and a feeling of "why me?" Thanks to my training, I quickly changed that into a "What is good about this?" mentality. As tough as the medicine is on me I found some good side effects. It is a powerful anti-inflammatory, which means that I can work out very hard without being so sore. It is also a muscle relaxant, which has allowed me to improve my flexibility. So, I focus on the positive and am very happy that, hopefully, I will be around teaching and training for decades to come. My life is lived in the positive because of my martial arts training.

Train hard and take the lessons out of the gym and into your everyday life. As Abraham Lincoln said, "A man is just about as happy as he decides to be."

28. BE PREPARED!

Here are two extremely important questions that all martial artists should consider: What happens when a martial artists gets into a real self-defense situation? What determines whether the martial artist will win or lose?

Of course, there are many variables. How skillful is the opponent? How big is he? How strong? Does he have a weapon? If you look at all of these factors you can see that they have one thing in common: they are all out of the control of the person being attacked. You, as a martial artist, can control one thing: your preparation.

One of my favorite quotes is from college basketball coach Bobby Knight. He said, "Everyone wants to win, but few people are willing to do the preparation it takes to win." Preparation is the key. How well you train, how well you plan your training, and how hard you work are all up to you. These are the aspects that you have control over. You prepare well so that you can apply your training in a fight. After a fight, adjustments can be made to your preparation so that you can perform even better. You might ask, "what fight am I getting into so regularly that I can use it as part of my training?" It doesn't have to be your fight. If you train only for self-defense, you may never have a fight in your whole life, and that is our preference. But fight experience is crucial to know what happens against an opponent who is giving his all to beat you down. This is why combat sports competitions are so valuable to our understanding of fighting and for our training methods.

The great thing about competitions is that we get lots of feedback about our training and preparation. If you choose to compete, your performance in the fight will tell you how well you prepared. You can then adjust your training to better prepare for the next bout. Without this kind of feedback people can train for years and years in methods that don't work well against a strong, aggressive opponent. You may be saying, "I don't want to compete." That is fine, as you can learn from people competing in extreme martial arts events. You can take the lessons from these events and apply them to your own training. If you know what a successful fighter did to prepare for a bout, you can follow a similar procedure and produce similar results.

If your main goal is street self-defense, I suggest you try what we do at JKD Unlimited. Our training methods are very similar to those of MMA fighters, but we keep street aspects in the training. We safely include groin strikes, eye gouges, and throat attacks in sparring. We work with multiple opponents and weaponry also, but the way we practice looks very much like competition training. We just follow different rules. We know that since we are training for the street environment, our preparation must be for the street environment. There is that word again: preparation.

Being effective is not by chance, but by design. It is easy to watch a great fighter and just see incredible athleticism or talent. While it is true that many of the very best were blessed with talent, it is their training that put them at the top. A fighter will invest hundreds of hours of preparation for a fifteen-minute fight. Why? Because talent alone is not enough. I had a friend in high school who was an incredibly talented athlete. He never practiced, but was one of the best baseball players in the league. He went straight from high school into professional baseball at the 1A level. This is three levels away from being in the Major Leagues where the top professionals play. It wasn't long before he was moved up to the 2A level. His talent had taken him very far, very quickly. But as great as he was, he never got beyond 2A. Why? Because he never applied himself in practice to maximize his abilities. He relied solely on his talent. Once he got to 2A he was surpassed by other athletes who had similar talents, but who also practiced diligently. He was eventually cut from the team because the coaches knew he would never go farther due to his lack of commitment to preparation. While you have no control over how much talent you have, you do get to determine how well and how often you practice. This is why almost anyone can become an effective martial artist. You just have to put in the time, practicing effectively.

Guro Dan Inosanto tells a pertinent story about Bruce Lee. I think we can all agree that Lee was gifted with incredible speed and athleticism, along with a brilliant mind. After a training session in the Los Angeles Chinatown school, Inosanto and some of the other students decided to walk to a nearby restaurant for lunch. Lee was on the wooden dummy practicing a simple block, grab, and hit technique. He had been doing the same move over and over again for five minutes when Inosanto asked his instructor if he wanted to go to lunch. Without stopping his practice, Lee said, "No, you go ahead". The group went off to lunch. An hour and a half later the group returned to the school. Guess what they found. Bruce Lee was still practicing the same move over and over again with speed, power, and precision. It wasn't luck that made Bruce Lee so great. It was his dedication to preparation.

Whatever your goal in martial arts or life, find someone else who has succeeded with the same goal. Find out what they did to prepare themselves for success and do the same with relentless pursuit. If you follow a similar path, you will arrive at a similar destination.

29. BRUCE LEE'S FIVE WAYS OF ATTACK

Bruce Lee, the founder of Jeet Kune Do, was an amazing innovator. His philosophy of searching for the truth in combat without being bound to tradition allowed him to explore new areas of the martial arts. One of his great contributions to the arts is his categorization of the different ways of attack.

Through his training, sparring, and research, Lee came upon the concept that there are five ways of attack. These are: Single Direct Attack (SDA), Attack By Combination (ABC), Attack By Drawing (ABD), Immobilization Attack (IA), and Progressive Indirect Attack (PIA). I will address each briefly, and will then explain why it is important to understand the five ways.

Single Direct Attack is just that: a single attack delivered all by itself without any immediate follow-up. This could be a quick finger jab to the eyes, or a strong kick to the groin. It can be an attempt at a foot sweep or a hip throw. The idea is you make one attack and stop to reassess.

Attack By Combination is simple as well. This is where you launch a series of attacks strung together. This can be a jab, cross, uppercut combination or a few kicks thrown in succession. It can be a front kick, overhand punch, to a double leg takedown. Any two or more attacks put together are an attack by combination.

Attack By Drawing is a tactical ploy. This is where you purposely leave part of your body vulnerable to invite an attack. In normal circumstances, you don't know if the opponent is going to throw a jab, a swinging punch, deliver a leg kick, or try to tackle you. ABD is great because, if the opponent falls for trick, you will know exactly what he is going to throw. This greatly enhances your ability to counter effectively. The key is to leave an enticing opening without letting the opponent know that you are doing it on purpose. If he perceives that it is a trick, he can use your tactics against you by countering your counter (counter time).

Immobilization Attack is where you immobilize the opponent in some way in order to control him or facilitate an attack of your own. In JKD, people usually think of hand trapping, but it actually applies to all methods of physically controlling the opponent. It can be as simple as a hair grab, or as sophisticated as a crucifix position on the ground. Pinning an opponent on the ground or against a wall also fall under the IA category.

Progressive Indirect Attacks work well against an opponent with very good defensive skills. It is half way between a Single Direct Attack and an Attack By Combination. Visualize this: you deliver a right punch toward the opponent's head. He raises his hands to block. You pull your punch back, and then throw a right backhand to the groin. He drops his hand down and blocks it. That was ABC. You threw the first punch, retracted your fist, and then threw the second punch. The PIA method would be to start the right punch to the head, but as he raises his hand to block, you alter the course of the strike, changing it directly into the backhand to the groin before the opponent can adjust to block the groin strike. You did not retract the arm back, but allowed your hand to "progress" toward the opponent while changing its course. Your fist moved "progressively", but not "directly" to the target, thus Progressive Indirect Attack. There are many PIA attacks which are very effective against skillful opponents.

It is important to know the Five Ways Of Attack so that you can analyze your sparring or that of a student. Do you just use Single Direct Attacks? If so, you can improve your performance greatly by adding other methods. It is much more difficult to deal with a series of attacks than with only one, so you should start putting combinations together. If you are doing combinations, are you using PIA? How about drawing an attack from your opponent? Do you use immobilizations? You will have a much better chance at success if you are employing all five ways of attack.

You can also use the five ways to analyze an opponent. By knowing your opponent's habits, you can better set him up. Just realize that some of the attacks work best in a sparring situation where you have time to get a feeling for your opponent. In the street, things happen so quickly that you may just rely on attacking with combinations and immobilizations to subdue an attacker.

Bruce Lee truly was a genius. Understanding his five ways of attack can help you to better understand your strengths while improving upon your weaknesses. Used correctly, you can use these methods to out-think an opponent who is stronger and faster than you are. Being able to overcome a formidable opponent is one of the great advantages of being a complete martial artist.

30. GETTING YOUR TAPS OUT OF THE WAY

In the world of Brazilian jiu jitsu (BJJ) and submission wrestling, the greatest feat is to get your opponent into a submission hold, such as a choke, arm bar, arm lock, or leg lock, and force him to tap out. (Tapping out is when one person concedes defeat by tapping on the mat or his opponent.) Conversely, the last thing you want to do is to have to tap to an opponent. So what is the best way to avoid having to tap? Well, there are two different schools of thought on this: that of the coward and that of the champion.

The coward is the guy who wants to act like he knows a lot, but inside is very insecure. He doesn't want to look bad. The worst thing that can happen to him is to have to tap, because that will be proof that he can be beaten. This is a truly silly notion that is prevalent in the martial arts world, especially amongst instructors. Somehow many instructors get the idea in their head that they are supposed to be invincible. Now, we know that there is no such thing as an invincible human being, but they start to think that tapping out in grappling or being kicked in sparring shows that they are not worthy of being instructors. They also worry about what their students might think of them. Maybe the students will become disgusted and leave the school if they found out that the "master" was actually a human being with faults and vulnerabilities. It is surprising how common this frame of mind is in the martial arts.

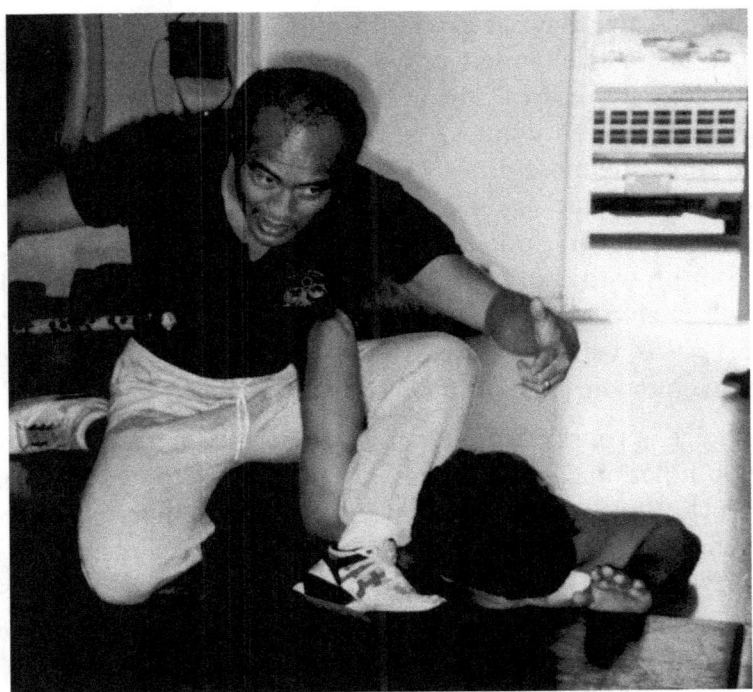

So how does this type of person avoid tapping? By never engaging in sparring. They never take the risk of "looking bad". This is sad, because the only way a person can actually become proficient at fighting is to fight. It doesn't have to be all-out, full power combat, but sparring is the only way to really test your skills and improve. As my friend and BJJ black belt John Machado says, "No sparring, no miracles." It is only through sparring that one can develop the timing and sensitivity necessary to apply technique against a resisting opponent. But still, many people will sacrifice skill development in order to keep the false image of invincibility alive. They avoid the taps by not playing the game.

How does a champion avoid having to tap? By getting the taps out of the way. What do I mean by that? It is a simple fact that if you want to learn how to avoid getting caught in an arm bar, you need to get caught in it many times. Experience is your best teacher. Although you may be aware of how an opponent will get into the arm bar, you have to have the time on the mat playing the game to be able to actually perceive that the attack is coming. Knowing how to counter the arm bar, choke, punch, or any other attack is one thing. Being able to do it at the right time in the correct manner is another issue altogether. The more times you get choked, the harder it will be to choke you. The more times you get kicked in the leg, the harder it will be to land a kick against you. Through real-time training your defense will adapt. You will begin to sense when an opponent is about to throw that kick, or shoot in for a takedown. Little by little, you will be able to recognize the attack and respond with the proper defense. It is a simple process, but you must put your ego aside in order to enjoy the benefits of effective combat training.

The choice is yours. Either you can avoid the taps now, and never develop functional fighting skill, or you can get the taps out of the way and become a formidable martial artist. Whether in kickboxing, clinch fighting, or ground grappling, if you put the ego aside and have fun playing the games, you will see great improvement in a short period of time. You will then earn the right to be truly confident without being arrogant.

31. MMA FOR THE STREET

There is no doubt about it. The well-trained modern No Holds Barred (NHB) or Mixed Martial Arts (MMA) athlete is a fighting machine. He or she can fight very well in the kickboxing, clinch, and ground ranges. Athletes in the sport of MMA train to fight skilled opponents through the use of striking, throwing, and submission holds. Rules prohibiting head butts, eye strikes, groin attacks, biting, and other tactics are in place for the safety of the participants, but other than these constraints the fights are as real as they get. Competitors prepare for the sporting event through rigorous training. Sparring against uncooperative opponents is the main method of preparation, along with massive conditioning. Without sparring in all of the ranges, the fighters would be lost when matched against a skillful opponent. Bottom line: the training methods work. It is from my extensive training in MMA and full contact stick fighting that I was able to distill the JKDU philosophy of training into one phrase. That phrase is: "If you want to learn how to fight you have to practice fighting against someone who is fighting back!" This is what the MMA athlete does daily.

Now, what happens if such an athlete, who trains within the rules of the sport, has to take on an aggressive street attacker outside of the ring or cage where there are no referees? In the great majority of incidents the trained fighter is going to dominate the situation. (An ambush from behind is another story, but no type of training will help you there.) Why? Because all fights take place in the kickboxing, clinch, or ground ranges, and often within all of the aforementioned distances. Someone trained in all of these ranges will generally prevail over an adversary who can only bring aggression to the fight, even without the use of "street" tactics.

On the other side of the equation, you have probably heard of many instances where traditional martial artists who spend most of their time practicing forms and static technique sequences, along with limited sparring, have been overwhelmed in a self-defense situation. Even though the traditional martial artist had eye strikes and groin attacks in his arsenal, he wasn't actually able to apply his training when real resistance came crashing down on him. So if the MMA fighter fares much better than the traditional martial artist in a real fight, we can come to a logical conclusion. If a main goal of your training is to develop usable self-defense skills, you should then train in the sport of MMA. This is where we at JKD Unlimited have a different point of view.

The reason MMA fighters can fight well is because of the training methodology of practicing against a resisting partner in all of the ranges. This is the key to skill development. Knowing the techniques is not enough. You must develop the skills necessary to be able to apply your techniques against someone who does not want you to succeed. Is a real attacker going to resist you? Of course he will. The true art of self-defense lies in your ability to overcome that resistance, not just in memorizing a litany of deadly techniques. You can learn the punches and defenses of boxing rather quickly, but just because you can demonstrate them doesn't mean that you are ready to fight the champ. You have to learn the techniques, and then practice them in the proper environment to prepare yourself to skillfully apply them in combat.

Once you know how to train correctly you must direct that training to address the "rules" of the event you are training for. In MMA, different fighting organizations have different rules. Some fights allow head butts, kicking a downed fighter in the head, and elbow strikes while these same tactics are illegal in other organizations. Fighters adjust their training to allow for the rules. As the rules change, the training and tactics change. If you are primarily interested in the self-defense aspects of the martial arts, then I believe that you should train for the "rules" of the street. As we all know, there is only one rule, which is "There are no rules."

Some will say that this is all nonsense, and that your best bet is to just train as an MMA fighter would train. You are probably never going to get attacked on the street anyway. If you do get attacked, the theory is that you can spontaneously adjust to that environment and add in the foul tactics. I say that theory needs to be scrutinized.

The entire principle of training is to create habits within our bodies so that we will not have to think about what we are doing in a stressful situation. We want our bodies to be able to automatically react in a positive and safe manner when under the stress of combat. Let's go back to that theory that if you are in a street fight you can spontaneously adjust to the lack of rules. My question is this: If you don't train to protect your groin, what would prompt you to think about doing that in a real fight? Answer: Receiving a solid strike to the groin! Do you want to wait until you are kicked in the groin to adjust your clinch stance? Do you want to wait to start protecting your eyes until after you have been gouged? No. If we are talking self-defense, this attitude of training for the sport then making an instantaneous adjustment in the midst of a street attack is dangerously backwards. In JKD Unlimited we do the following:

We train primarily for the street environment, and then make adjustments to the training for those who want to enter competitions – Not the other way around.

We play in all the ranges against a resisting partner, just as we do in MMA sport training, but we always have the street tactics included as we do our training. The idea of training one way, then making a spontaneous adjustment to a mode that you don't train is not practical. It would be like training solely in submission grappling when you are preparing to enter an MMA competition. With this philosophy, you would say "I am going to work on my takedowns, guard passes, and submissions without any strikes allowed. Then when I get in the match, I will just adjust to the striking." We all know that does not work. You have to train for the parameters of the event. You don't only train collegiate wrestling techniques if you are going into a submission wrestling match. You wouldn't just train boxing if you are fighting in a Muay Thai kickboxing match, just as you wouldn't only train kickboxing if you are going into MMA. When you change the rules of the event, the techniques, tactics, training methods, and structure must change to accommodate the particular rules. As effective as sport-oriented MMA is, you should go beyond MMA if you are training to be prepared for the arena of street self-defense.

One drawback of including the street tactics is that you can't actually gouge your partner's eyes or hit him hard in the groin. But you usually don't actually try to knock out your partner in training either. A great thing about grappling is that you can apply your technique at full tilt with minimal risk of injury. MMA athletes don't go all-out with their punching and kicking in training, as there would be too many injuries. Does this mean that they don't add striking to the face at all because it isn't at full intensity? No. in MMA we strike, but with proper protection and at a safe level of intensity. In JKDU, we also add eye strikes, groin hits, and simulated bites to the training in a safe, fun manner to play the game at the street self-defense level. We also include the most dangerous street element: weaponry.

BJJ, kickboxing, and MMA can be very effective in a street fight, but the best MMA fighters don't just train BJJ or Muay Thai or Greco Roman. They cross train specifically for the event. We cross train with MMA style training methods, but with the street environment as our first priority. This can be done by anyone of any level of physicality. We adjust the intensity of the training to suit the individual's current physical condition and goals. It is extremely fun, healthy, and mind expanding. If you aren't planning to compete in the sporting event, but want street self-defense, I suggest that you train primarily for the street environment.

32. WHAT WOULD BRUCE LEE BE DOING TODAY?

I believe that if Bruce Lee was alive today, he would probably be following the same philosophy that he advocated while he was alive. I think that results-oriented philosophy was the key to Bruce Lee's success.

He had a very clear directive on how the martial arts should be approached. He did not believe that an art should be "static" and unchanging, but rather, a living, evolving entity. For some martial artists embracing evolution, that change can be very random for some, adding whichever techniques were most pleasing to the eye. But for Bruce Lee, there was one guiding principle: Only use what works in a real fight!

Because of this, I believe that Bruce Lee would be doing just what he was doing at the time of his death, which is what we are pursuing in JKD Unlimited. We are simply looking for ways to improve our fighting abilities in the street self-defense environment. This is what

Bruce Lee preached and applied. It was a scientific approach and I follow his lead.

I am sure that Bruce Lee would have used his considerable wealth to hire the greatest fighters in the world to train him. He would have thoroughly studied and would now be using portions of Brazilian jiu-jitsu, not for the sport, but to enhance the chances of prevailing if the fight went to the ground. He would have practiced ground fighting in order to more easily stand up from the ground, or finish an opponent there if the opportunity presented itself. He would have added techniques and training methods in the clinch from Greco Roman wrestling and used other aspects seen in MMA competitions, but with the important modification of using, eye, throat, and groin strikes in the training to make it street-functional. He would have included weapons in training to prepare for the worst case scenario.

He would have continued to explored the emotional aspects of fighting. And of course, he would have continued you test everything through lots of sparring. I think that he probably would have trained more with firearms too, especially if he had continued to live in Los Angeles!

All in all, I believe that Bruce Lee would have continued his incredible evolution of the martial arts through research and development, and would have continued to be very far ahead of his time in the world of realistic self-defense techniques and training methods.

33. BLITZ JKD INTERVIEW

Do you have a favourite quote or lesson from Bruce Lee perhaps one that you think summed up his approach and would best guide people who choose to follow his example today?

- My favorite quote from Bruce Lee is on the last page of the Tao of Jeet Kune Do. It is: "Self-knowledge is the basis of Jeet Kune Do because it is effective, not only for the individual's martial art, but also for his life as a human being."

For me, this is the whole purpose of training so diligently in the martial arts. Most will never have to use their art in a real street encounter, but if we train true, we can use the principles that we use in sparring and fighting to better handle the resistance that life throws at us. If I can overcome a skilled opponent who is doing his best to counter everything that I do, I can then use the principles that developed this level of skill to become more skillful in other areas of life. This includes personal relationships, business, and achieving goals in other endeavors.

What are the main differences between the path that you have taken with JKDU and that of other JKD groups, including the Bruce Lee Foundation/ Jun Fan Jeet Kune Do group represented by Taky Kimura, Ted Wong, Shannon Lee Keasler and Linda Lee Cadwell?

- First of all, let me express my profound respect for all of those you have mentioned. I respect Taky Kimura for obvious reasons, but also because of his humility and kindness. Look at his son Andy Kimura. He is a wonderful person and martial artist, and is proof that Taky Kimura is a great leader. Ted Wong has worked very hard to preserve the original teachings of Bruce Lee, and actually can express the art physically as few others (if any) can. I have never met Shannon Lee Keasler, but her willingness to take on this task of preserving the original art is admirable. Linda Lee Cadwell is a phenomenal person. I have such respect for her. Brandon Lee introduced me to her, and she was so gracious and powerful. The next time I saw her was at Brandon's memorial service, and I will never forget her poise. Despite all the tragedy she has endured, the last time we met she remained strong and kind. She is truly a person to emulate.

To your question, my background is science. I won the science award at Carson high school in Los Angeles, was a biology major at U.S.C, and did research on multiple sclerosis at UCLA medical center. There is the "scientific method" that we follow. Basically, you have an idea, then you test that idea under realistic conditions and you get a result. If the result is not what you want, you change a few things then test again. Once you get a favorable result, you test again and again to be sure that the result can be reproduced consistently. This is what I do in the martial arts, which is the same approach that Bruce Lee took. Research different arts, then put on the gear and spar hard to see what works and what doesn't. He took this so far, that it was easy for me and others to carry on the work. He laid the foundation of so many principles which would have taken a very, very long time to find. So my approach is to only use what works, and to know what works we must engage in rigorous sparring with great fighters in a wide variety of disciplines. Again, this is exactly what Bruce Lee did to create Jun Fan Jeet Kune Do.

Does the very nature of JKD's purpose and philosophy "using no way as way, having no limitation as limitation" make it difficult to set down a syllabus for a JKD organization?

- Great question. My answer is: It depends on the goal of the organization. I believe that the Bruce Lee Foundation will have an easier time of it, because they want to show exactly what Bruce Lee did during his lifetime. Now that is a vast undertaking, because it is clear that Bruce Lee was constantly evolving as he met different top martial artists from various disciplines. But, if your goal is to stay on the cutting edge of combative effectiveness, then the curriculum will undergo changes as the evolution occurs. This is natural, but can make creating a curriculum difficult. What I have done with JKDU is to break it down conceptually, so that the student progresses in all the ranges in a logical, functional manner. It has taken twenty five years of training to be able to create an efficient curriculum, but I always tell my students that changes will occur in the future.

The Bruce Lee Foundation's website says that "You do not make up your own JKD - Bruce Lee's art has a definite set of techniques that are deeply entrenched in philosophical principles. It is through the continued practise of these techniques and principles that one continues to improve, discover and deepen their understanding of JKD". Would you agree with this, and if so, how is a balance found between teaching the JKD structure and developing the art as evolution deems necessary?

- I see their point, that Bruce Lee's art has a definite set of techniques. These are what Bruce Lee himself did, and that is Jun Fan (Bruce Lee's) JKD. But if we aren't limited to what Lee did in his lifetime, then there is much more. This is why I call my organization JKD Unlimited. I don't want people to think that I am just sticking to what Bruce Lee did over forty years ago. As great as his personal art is, I don't want to represent myself as teaching exactly what Bruce Lee did, although there are many aspects of his art that are clearly visible when we train and spar. Evolution is another matter altogether. I am sure that Bruce Lee had never heard of Brazilian Jiu-Jitsu. Now, if one is not very well-versed on the ground, he or she is at a huge disadvantage. I don't think that he was

able to train in Greco-Roman wrestling. That clinch work is vital to today's training. Without a good clinch, one will have a very hard time handling a good MMA fighter. Bruce Lee got together with the best fighters of his time and sparred. He learned from them, while passing valuable lessons on to them. In 2006, if one wants to emulate Bruce Lee, I believe that you must simply do what he did. Not just his techniques, but his methods of researching. That is why I spar with BJJ, MMA, and kickboxing champions. There is no theorizing when you spar at that level. There is just "what is". If I spar with Randy Couture, and he crushes me with a takedown over and over again, I know that I need to work on countering that, and making sure I have that move in my arsenal. Each time a training partner is successful, it makes your defense that much better. Same with the other champs I work with. If you want to "Absorb what is useful", you need to spar with great fighters to see what really is useful at the highest level.

Shannon Lee Keasler said in an interview that "There's confusion about what JKD is" and revealed the Bruce Lee Foundation's intention to clarify it and implement an instructor syllabus based on JKD as it was when Bruce died - essentially making it a fixed entity. What's your opinion/feeling on this move?

- I admire her for working on this. I think it is great that there is a dedicated group of people who want to preserve what Bruce Lee did himself. It would be such a shame if that was somehow lost. So I say "good for them", and I hope that they are successful in creating a place where people can go if they want to see what Bruce Lee did himself. I do hope that they will encourage their students and (especially) their instructors to train outside the curriculum so that they can spar and experience a wide variety of martial arts, just like Bruce Lee did. Sticking to one art creates a false sense of security.

In JKD, who do you personally look to for guidance and inspiration?

- I guess it is clear that I still look to the writings of Bruce Lee for inspiration and greater understanding. Amongst the living, I just love spending time with

Sifu Dan Inosanto. He is just a wonderful person to be around. I again hosted him here in Hawaii recently, and we had so much fun hanging out and talking martial arts. He knows the original JKD inside and out, but he has decided to continue to research every art imaginable. He is truly the most knowledgeable martial artist on the planet. I also enjoy spending time with Sifu Larry Hartsell and Sifu Richard Bustillo. They both have vast knowledge to impart.

My best guidance would come from my sparring partners. They are the ones who show me my strengths and weaknesses. This gives me confidence in the moves that I can pull off consistently, and inspires me to work on those techniques which I need to improve. It is a wonderful, humbling, and enjoyable process.

In your opinion, what does the future hold for JKD as a whole?

- As a whole, I believe that there will be a lot of bickering and politics! (Laughs). That is inevitable, because many people have different points of view on what JKD is and what JKD isn't. But, I truly believe that those who spend a large amount of time sparring with high quality partners will have their heads in a very different place. We become obsessed with the art of fighting, with improving, with having a better performance in sparring. I spend a lot of time sparring kickboxing, clinch, ground, and with weapons. This is what develops my skills as a fighter, my insight as a teacher, and my character as a human being. It is through this that I understand what Bruce Lee meant when he wrote that quote that I love so much.

34. PRINCIPLES OF JKD UNLIMITED

My main emphasis for JKD Unlimited is to provide practical martial arts training for as many people as possible. It is very important to me that the techniques, tactics, and training methods that I teach actually work. Practicality is first and foremost. There are plenty of places to learn martial arts that are theoretical, so I choose to focus passing on what works against an opponent who is fighting back. But the road to functionality is narrow, and it is easy to stray off the path. In order to keep myself and my instructors under me moving in the right direction, I needed some guiding principles to keep us in line. These are the four principles that keep us training in a realistic manner, instead of drifting off into the world of martial fantasy. They are:

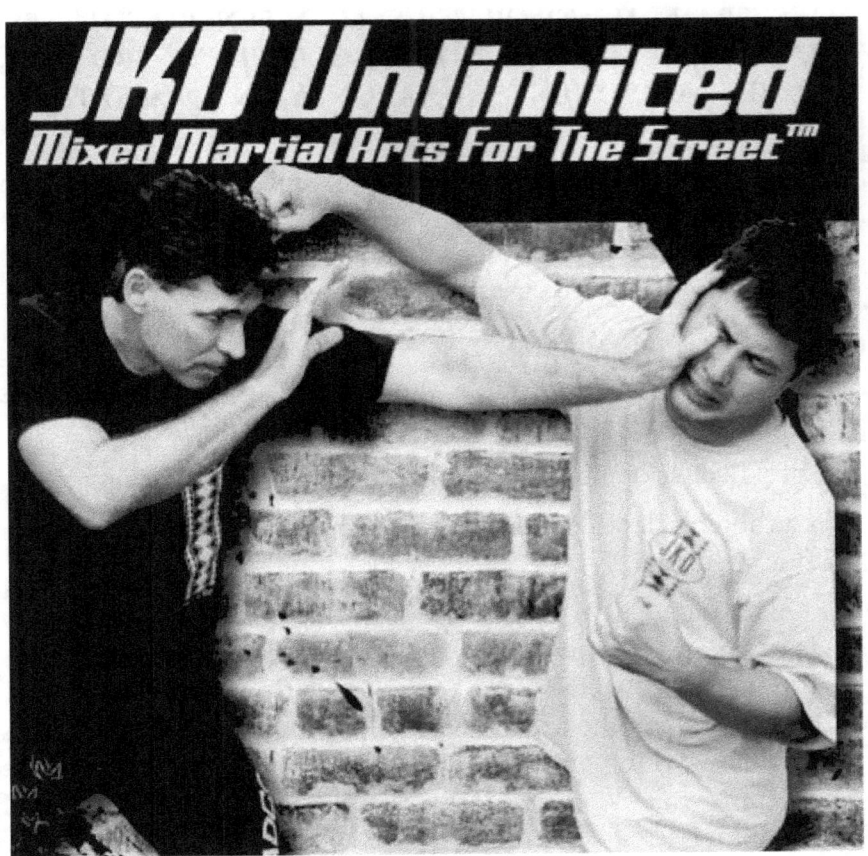

1. WE TRAIN FIRST AND FOREMOST FOR STREET SELF-DEFENSE.

We train to be effective in the street environment, then make adjustments to the training for students who wish to enter sporting competitions. Not the other way around.

2. WE TRAIN WITH PROGRESSIVE RESISTANCE.

A real attacker is going to resist your effort 100%. If you want to learn how to fight, you have to practice fighting against someone who is fighting back. Progressive resistance allows everyone, regardless of experience, to do this in a safe, fun training environment.

3. WE TRAIN AS COMPLETE SELF-DEFENSE ATHLETES: ALL THE RANGES (STANDING, CLINCH, & GROUND), MULTIPLE OPPONENTS, WEAPONRY, IN A VARIETY OF ENVIRONMENTS).

We train to be prepared for almost any situation. We want each student to actually train in as many self-defense scenarios as possible so that if a student gets into a bad situation, then they already have experience in that particular situation.

4. WE HAVE FUN DURING THE TRAINING SESSIONS.

The more fun you have training, the more often you will train. This will lead to a greater

rate of skill development while enhancing your overall quality of life.

(For a more in depth explanation of each of these guidelines, go to jkdunlimited.com)

I am planning to train for the rest of my life, and I assume that my students will do the same. That means that we are going to spend a great portion of our lives practicing the art, thinking about the art, and passing along the art to others. If we are going to spend this much time working on developing functional skills, we should be having fun while doing it. This is also very practical. You see, if each training session is enjoyable, we will tend to practice longer and more often. We won't get bored, or just plain tired of going to that class. Each meeting will result in a very good time for everyone, while training hard to improve practical fighting skills. The more you practice the faster you will improve, so by maintaining a great environment, students will train more often and therefore improve at a faster rate.

Those who are training for a competition will have to take a different approach. They can still have fun, but they will also have to push their bodies very hard and do a lot of very uncomfortable and painful training. Competitions often go for a very long time, so the level of conditioning must be significantly higher for a combat athlete. You simply can't get tired. Therefore, extremely difficult cardiovascular work is a necessary part of the training. It is never easy, and rarely would it be considered fun. But if you are going to fight in the ring, you must be very well conditioned.

If you are training for self-defense, you will still work very hard at times, but you won't be grinding out the majority of your training and dreading the next class. Our classes are held in a very relaxed, but disciplined atmosphere. Lots of laughing and joking while training hard. As Bruce Lee said, "You should train seriously, but don't seriously train." That is exactly what we are after. We work hard, and pay attention to constant self-improvement, but we do so with a smile on our faces. The result is that we develop extremely skillful martial artists who are fun to be around. If you plan a trip to Hawaii, drop into one of our classes so you can experience this great group of people yourself.

35. THE FIGHTER'S PERSPECTIVE

I received a very interesting email from my Performance Group Leader in Portugal. Luis Barneto has been affiliated with JKD Unlimited for some time now, and has attended my seminars in Italy hosted by JKDU Full Instructor Augusto Baracco. Luis was able to practice the empty hand portion of our curriculum well, but the weaponry training was a bit more difficult, as I only have a small amount of time to cover weapons on my seminars. I have an outline for my upcoming Battlefield Kali program which emphasizes only those things that work in hard stick and knife sparring, and Luis asked if he could read the outline to help him progress faster with the weapons. I agreed.

Luis received the outline and read it thoroughly. It seems that he understood much of what was written, even if there were no photos to go with the text. The only problem was that the primary training method in Battlefield Kali is isolated and full sparring using padded weapons and body protection. Luis had ordered padded weapons, but they had not yet arrived in the mail, so he could not yet engage in the sparring exercises. But, he did have that written outline.

Since he had studied other forms of weaponry, the outline was understandable. Various elements of posture, footwork, positioning of the weapon, basic strikes, combinations, how to set up your opponent, etc., was all very logical. The sparring progression made sense too, as it starts with isolating certain targets or strikes and progresses to unlimited sparring. So, Luis had a good grasp of the material. Or so he thought! Something happened which would change Luis's perspective on weaponry training. His padded sticks and knives arrived.

Eager as always, Luis took the weapons to class, got a partner, and started sparring. In all his years of doing martial arts with weapons, he, like many martial artists, never actually sparred with weapons. The normal practice session for weaponry is to do forms or to do two person sets. Some systems also do flow drills or practice techniques to counter various attacks. But, just as in empty hand martial arts, doing drills or techniques with a cooperative partner is nothing at all like sparring full speed against a partner who is not cooperating at all. So, Luis got a big surprise during his first sparring session. I wasn't there to see it, but I am sure that the stick came much faster than he had anticipated, and the aggression of his opponent was different than he had ever experienced doing drills and techniques. I'm sure his partner took a lot of hits from Luis, but I imagine that Luis got his fair share as well.

After the session, Luis read through the Battlefield Kali outline again. He said "It was like reading an entirely new document." Strategies and techniques and the progression of training now had a whole new meaning to him. Why? Because Luis was now reading the outline from a fighter's perspective. He was not comparing the ideas in the outline to slow drilling, but instead he could relate the material to actual fighting. Battlefield Kali was developed through countless hours of sparring, not theoretical drilling. Due to his stick fighting experience, Luis was able to comprehend the outline at a much deeper level of understanding. This brings up a very important point.

Luis was able to change his perspective because he had the courage to spar with his students. Many instructors are afraid to do this due to the fear of looking bad. They want to maintain the illusion that they are invincible. To me, that is very sad. It means that the leader of the class is so fearful that he won't actually practice his art in front of his students. One of the ultimate goals (for me) in martial arts is to learn to live without fear. What does it say when the head of a class is afraid of sparring. By participating in sparring at various levels, the instructor can help the students and help himself at the same time. And this will also ensure that the instructor and students will maintain the fighter's perspective when exploring new areas of the martial arts.

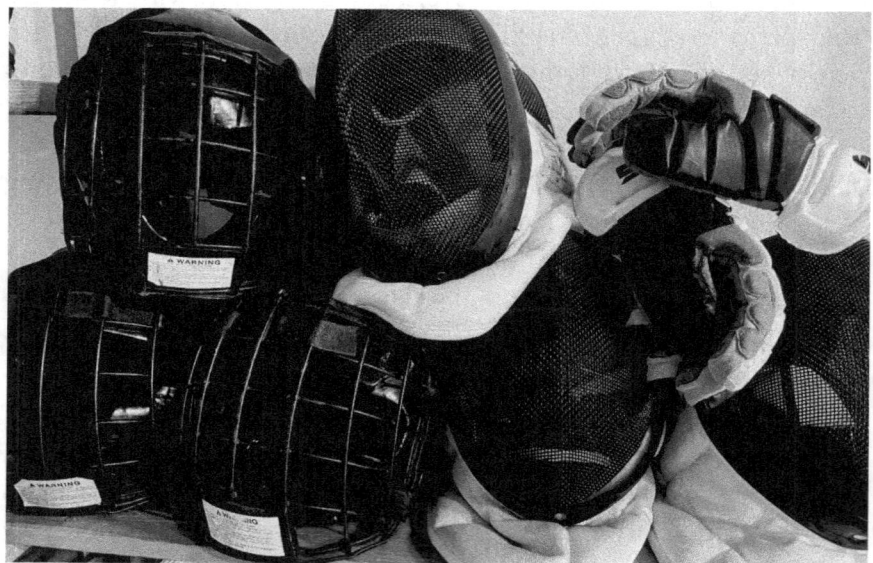

There is only one way to achieve the fighter's perspective, and that is to earn it through actual fighting. You can do this safely through the use of protective equipment and you can vary the intensity depending upon the goals of the student. But you have to spar if you want to understand actual fighting. There is no other way. I am sure that many martial artists will dispute this claim, and I know why. It is because they haven't fought enough to earn the fighter's perspective. How about you? If this seems wrong to you, please do yourself a favor and go to a boxing, kickboxing, or MMA gym for two months. Make sure it is a fighter's gym where there is lots of sparring. After two months, see how your perspective has changed. If you haven't spent time sparring with combat athletes, the experience will definitely make you a better martial artist and person. I went through that same process myself, and I am so glad that I did. The martial arts are more beautiful than ever when we can see them with the fighter's perspective.

36. FIGHT FOR SUCCESS!

Just as a fighter needs to look at past performances in order to spot strengths and weaknesses, we are wise to look back at the last year and determine which areas of our lives need work. The best time to do that is RIGHT NOW!, so if you are tough enough, grab a pen and a paper and use the next few minutes of your life for a little "post battle" analysis.

If I am reviewing one of my fighter's bouts, the most natural approach is to look for all of the mistakes. But watching the fight as a whole can be a little too much to digest. A method that I have found useful is to write down fight categories on a paper, then as I view the fight, I can put down my assessment in an organized fashion. For an MMA fight, I will make columns with the following headings: boxing, kicking, takedown attempts, takedown defense, clinch, work against the cage/ropes, ground & pound, ground positioning, and standing up. That might seem like a lot of extra work, but it actually makes it easier. I watch the bout and jot down each error in the proper column. When I review the match with the fighter, we can concentrate on one category at a time instead of jumping back and forth between ranges.

Let's do that same thing with your everyday life. Take out that pen and paper and make the following columns: family life, health &

fitness, diet, business life, personal relationships, personal goals. Now think about how you fared in each of these categories last year. Quickly write down the mistakes you made in your family life. Just write a few things that come to mind that you could improve upon. Maybe you didn't spend enough fun time with your family. Maybe you need to call your Auntie on the mainland more often. Just write these down quickly. Now do the same with health/fitness. How did you do there? Did you watch your diet? Did you cut down on the alcohol? (I hope I don't even have to mention cigarettes!) How about business? Did you do a good job serving others and bringing home the cash? Where did you fall short? And how about those personal relationships. Did you keep in touch like you should? This whole exercise should take about ten minutes, looking for and writing out your weaknesses.

After I review a fight a few times to look for errors, I watch again and write down all the good things that occurred. We don't only want to work on strengthening the weaknesses; we want to further strengthen the strengths too! That makes for a tough competitor. Now do the same with your life review. Note all the things you did well in each column and vow to further improve those in 2009.

Now that you know what you want to work on, set a goal for each column. Make sure that the goal is specific, and be sure to actually write it down. That makes it more real than just being a thought in your head.

The next absolutely crucial step is to figure out how you are going to practice so that you can reach your goals. That's right, just like training for MMA. In the fight game, after we discover the weaknesses and strengths, we make a training schedule to address those issues. Do the same for everyday life. If you have a hard time passing up candy in the store, figure out a way to practice passing up on the sugar. Go to the store after you have eaten and practice saying no to the junk. It sounds silly, but it works. Just like in the cage, the way you practice determines the way you are going to perform!

Take the time to check your past performance, note the good along with the bad, develop drills, set a practice schedule, and then get to work.

37. ON BRUCE LEE'S TEACHING

Black Belt magazine's editor asked me to answer the question, "If you had to teach a student only one element of Bruce Lee's teaching, what element would that be and why would you choose that? Here is my answer:

If I had to teach a student only one element of Bruce Lee's teaching, I would ingrain the principle of training against a resisting opponent in all the ranges rather than merely doing isolated drills with a cooperative partner. Without complete sparring, you will not be able to apply any of the techniques and tactics that will help to defeat an attacker. Sigung Lee called this principle of constantly testing your skills against an uncooperative opponent "alive" training. Particular moves and strategies are very important, but the most difficult and immediate obstacle to overcome in a real fight is the immense amount of pressure and resistance given by the attacker. And if you don't practice dealing with real, unpredictable resistance, you will not develop the ability to automatically adjust to the myriad of obstacles that a real opponent will present. Through intelligent sparring with many different types of people from a variety of backgrounds, a student will learn how to deal with various structures, tactics, and pressure. Of course, I would teach the students how to keep the sparring as safe as possible. I start with light intensity sparring in all the ranges from the very first day of training so that the student immediately begins to learn how to deal with resistance, but it is a very low intensity. It is a game, not warfare. As the student progresses, instructor candidates must progress to the highest level of training by doing what Bruce Lee admonished- that students "should wear suitable protective equipment and go all out." Suitable means that the equipment will provide a good level of safety to the practitioner during vigorous sparring. Is that a bit extreme? Yes, but this essential experience of high intensity sparring is why Sigung Lee also stated, that "JKD is not for everyone." One must be extremely dedicated to engage in high intensity sparring. But that is the best preparation. As I like to say, "No sparring, no JKD".

Another very important reason for the emphasis on sparring is that it will give actual, empirical feedback that will help the student "Absorb what is useful, reject what is useless, and add what is specifically your own." In order to know what is useful and what isn't, a student must test each technique him or herself. JKD is a personal experience, which means that each individual must experience combat (hard sparring) for himself or herself in order to find out what works and what doesn't for him or her. Just memorizing techniques from an instructor and doing light drills will not create a great fighter. If we merely look at a technique from afar, or test ideas against cooperative partners, then we are not applying a scientifically valid test. Testing a new sunscreen at night does not give you a good idea of how the product will perform at noon! We must test our techniques and tactics under conditions that are very similar to the actual combat environment if we want to know what works for us, what doesn't, and to also discover nuances that are specifically our own. Since it is both unethical and unadvisable to purposely get into street fights, sparring in all the ranges becomes our best means to develop complete, functional fighting skill. If you don't believe me, then consider Bruce Lee's own words:

"There is nothing better than free-style sparring in the practice of any combative art."

38. A LITTLE BIT EVERY DAY

◯

Way back in 1986, I took a trip to Tokyo, Japan, staying with my friend Sensei Yori Nakamura and his wife Hiromi. The reason for my trip was to shoot my very first instructional video. Yori was kind enough to set everything up, and he even assisted me in the video.

Yori was one of the first Shooto champions, and is now one of the top administrators in the Shooto organization. For those who don't know the history, Shooto was the first MMA type organization in Japan, created years before the UFC was started. Shooto was founded by professional wrestler turned combat fighter Sensei Satoru Sayama when he got tired of professional wrestling matches being billed as real. He decided to make an "almost anything goes" sport, and Shooto was born.

Being in Japan was a great experience for me in many ways. I was able to really get a feel, if only for two weeks, of the lifestyle that most people live in Tokyo. The apartment was extremely small by American standards, but it was just fine and very functional for the Nakamuras. That was an eye-opener. We walked down the small side streets to go to the "furo" (bath house) each evening. There was no need to waste space having a shower in the apartment when the bathhouse was affordable and provided great service.

Yori also took me to training sessions with his instructor, Sensei Sayama. What an experience that was! I taught him some tricks with the butterfly knife, and he gave me an insight into hard core fight training. Sayama was and is the real deal, and his methods of training primed me for my later venture into MMA training and coaching.

I really learned a lot on that trip, but one of the most important lessons was given to me in a brief moment by Yori.

Each night before bed, he would take time to do some stretching.

Not a long session, but as I recall, maybe ten minutes or so. Yori had great flexibility, and mine was very poor. I asked him about it, and his basic philosophy on improvement has influenced me in many aspects of my life to this very day. Yori explained, "A little bit every day is better than a lot every so often." Great wisdom.

I use this idea in all of my endeavors. Time goes by regardless of what we do, but we often put things off because we "don't have the time". Isn't that true for you? I know that I had been guilty of using this excuse throughout my life. It is very convenient, and is readily accepted by most people. When giving this excuse, most will chime in with, "Yeah, me too. I don't have time to do anything." But, this just isn't true.

Do you want to become a solid martial artist but you feel that you just don't have enough time? I know a lot of people who feel this way, but the truth is, you can make constant improvement towards your goal with just a little training each day. You don't have to go into the gym and train for six hours a day unless you plan to be a professional fighter. If that is your goal, then other aspects of life will have to be put on hold. But if you have a long term goal of becoming a very good fighter or coach, then a little bit each day will lead you to the destination of your desire.

If you do a one hour workout twice a week in class or with a partner, and then spend just fifteen minutes shadowboxing the movements on your off days, I am sure that you will reach your goal of being a proficient mixed martial artist. I have no doubt at all. It will take longer than someone who can train for hours every day, but I know that you will get there. And isn't that what counts? It's that fifteen minutes per day of focused training that will make the difference. Be patient and work progressively towards your goal. The reward will be worth the discipline to do your training a little each day.

Imagine that you have a lofty goal, and that I told you that it will take ten years for you to reach that goal. Would you quit? I'm here to tell you that the year 2019 is coming and it will be here before you know it. (At the time of the printing of this book, 2019 is far in the rear view mirror! I'm so glad that I applied this principle well since 2009.) You might as well do a little everyday so that you can reach your goal when the magic year rolls around. What were you doing back in 1999? If you had started doing a little bit each day in '99, you would already be at goal today! Time goes by, so just plug away until you feel that thrill of achievement.

How about other goals in your life? Let's take something very difficult. Let's say that you want to write a novel, but you don't have the four to ten hours per day that professional writers spend on their work. No problem. Just do a little bit every day. Let's say you can sit down for twenty minutes per day. I am sure that you can find twenty minutes. Use the first few weeks to write a good outline. If you aren't sure of how to write an outline, spend a few weeks using your twenty minutes a day to read up on the art of writing a novel. Then do your outline over the next few weeks, or whatever it takes. Then start writing. Twenty minutes a day, every day. Can you write a full page in twenty minutes? Maybe not. How about half a page? I'll bet you can. Sit down and write half a page per day, and guess what happens after two years? You have 365 pages. Does two years seem like an awful long time? If you started this in 2005, you would have two novels finished by now (in 2009). I started writing my first novel at the end of last year, a little bit each day, and I finished my second revision in July of this year. Whatever you want to do, just chip away at it and it will be done.

The one thing that you will have to supply in order to make this method work is the discipline to do your task each day. The best way to do this is to form a good habit. Pick a time of the day, preferably early in the day, and discipline yourself to work towards your goal for twenty minutes each day. (The later in the day you start, the more chances of distractions derailing your efforts.) It might be hard for awhile, but after a month of using discipline you will create a habit that runs by itself. Once it is a habit, you won't need willpower to keep it going.

What if you are an MMA fighter who has the luxury of training for several hours per day? I'll bet that there is still some technique you have been wanting to work on that you just don't have time for in practice. Simply add an extra five minutes a day to work on that move. It will become sharp over time, and you may find yourself in a position where that extra practice makes the difference between a loss and a win!

Whatever you want to accomplish, be it in the martial arts, in your career, or with your family, work at it a little bit every day. The years will go by, and you will be able to look back and be proud of the progress that you have made in all areas of your life.

39. THE GRAPPLING DUMMY: THE 7 BENEFITS THAT YOU CAN'T GET WITH A LIVE PARTNER

Let's get this straight- training with a grappling dummy is not a substitute for rolling with live partners. Grappling is about feeling an opponent and timing your attacks and defenses, and the only way to do that is to roll. I earned my black belt in BJJ (2006) by sparring for countless hours with a huge variety of people. But, I can unequivocally attest that my hours spent working on a grappling dummy helped me to get to the black belt level much faster.

A grappling dummy is not a substitute for rolling with a partner, but it is an amazing supplement. Just as the heavy bag is supplemental equipment for a striker, a grappling dummy should be used by a grappler to supplement his or her rolling time. When you are practicing your striking, you can't just pound away full power on a partner for rounds on end. No partner would take that kind of a beating, so you use the heavy bag to get in thousands of reps of full power striking while working your form and conditioning. The same principle applies to grappling. No partner is going to let you arm bar him as hard as you can for reps, so you should use a grappling dummy to get in all full power training. You get better and nobody gets hurt. Pretty simple.

Here are the seven major benefits of training with a grappling dummy that you can't get training with a live partner:

1. Unlimited Repetitions- It is said that "repetition is the mother of skill". The problem is that a live partner will not sit there all day long while you choke him hundreds of times. A grappling dummy does not complain, and will endure any number of chokes, locks, and strikes that you can throw at him. You can work on precision and accuracy at your own pace, as many times as you like.

Anytime you are learning a new technique, you must first memorize the steps and develop the coordination necessary to apply the move. That comes before finding the timing to apply it. When I am working on a new move, I use the dummy to get that move into my "muscle memory". When I go back to sparring, the basic memorization and coordination phase has already been taken care of, and I can concentrate on the timing and set-ups needed to pull off the move in real time.

2. Unlimited Access- We have a limited amount of time that we can train with partners, but a grappling dummy is available 24 hours per day. Whenever you have extra time, you can improve your technique, movement, and endurance. If I have ten minutes free, and I can use that time to work on some of my basics. Those short sessions add up over time! While your next opponent is resting, you make your competitive edge a little greater.

3. High Intensity - Your training partners don't want you to slap on submissions at full power, strength, and intensity. This gets old in a hurry, and there is too much risk of injury. But, you can go all-out with a grappling dummy, especially if you are training for BJJ For The Street (self-defense) or MMA fighting. Choke as roughly and as powerfully as you can. Crank those heel hooks past the point where an actual partner would be injured, and do so with full force. Rip into arm locks without trepidation. Stack him on his head as hard as you can as you work your guard pass. This kind of training feels more like a real fight, so it trains your killer instinct as well as your physical technique.

4. Full Power Striking- Simply put, you can hit the dummy as hard as you like and as many times as you like. You can sharpen all of your striking tools while you train from different positions; fists, elbows, knees, kicks, head butts, etc. This helps to ingrain powerful, accurate striking into your grappling. Often, people don't strike in the grappling range because they don't do it in training. You can solve that problem by working your hitting on a grappling dummy. The fact that you can hit as hard as you like also helps you to fine tune your balance while you apply your strikes on the ground.

5. Practice BJJ For The Street Techniques- For self-defense purpose, a grappling dummy is fine with letting you perform all of your street tactics. You can throw head butts, strike to the groin, tear at the throat, and gouge at the eyes. No partner will let you do that! You can be at the back working a choke while you heel kick him in the groin. You can have the dummy in your guard and grab his throat hard to make space and stand up. Work all the street tactics that you may need in a life and death situation. Because of a grappling dummy, you can work on all those severe methods that MMA or grappling schools don't allow during training.

6. Choke Endurance Practice- With a grappling dummy, you can constrict any choke for as long as you can to enhance your endurance. Squeeze that rear naked choke with everything you have and see how long it takes for your muscles to give out. Constrict that triangle until your legs give out. Doing this will increase your muscular endurance and allow you to know just how long you can hold a choke without gassing. You will also improve your ability to constrict those chokes while accurately targeting the carotids for quicker finishes. This can be done with all chokes, including collar chokes for BJJ and self-defense practitioners.

You can also cycle your endurance training. Do a certain number of rounds holding various chokes. For example, do the rear naked choke for twenty seconds, then rest twenty seconds before doing it again. Then switch to the triangle to work your legs for a number of rounds. Then switch to the darce, arm triangle, or any other choke you want to strengthen. Believe me, your arms, hands, and legs will get a great workout, and you will find that partners will tap much sooner when you land the position during your rolling sessions.

By squeezing full power for an extended period, you will also discover where you have any space in your choke. Take away those spaces and your choke will become technically superior.

7. Full Power Throwing- You can stand a grappling dummy up and practice throwing as hard as you can. Instead of the allowing the gentle landing that you need to provide to a live partner for safety, you can practice driving the dummy through the mat over and over again. You can land with your full weight on it, and he won't be injured. Or angry! Work all the high amplitude throws, and land him on any part of his body that you like. Just like in a real life and death fight.

It is clear that this supplemental training with a grappling dummy offers tremendous benefits that you can't get when training with a live partner. You must train with a live partner to get the timing and body feel for offense and defense, but you should also train with the dummy to help you improve the quality of your techniques even faster. Anyone who scoffs at training with a high quality dummy has never done it well. As MMA and self-defense continues to evolve, we should see as many grappling dummies in the gyms as we now have heavy bags and Thai pads. It is an invaluable piece of training equipment.

40. LUCKY DOG SPEAKS

Manila Times - You are one of the most well rounded teachers in the martial arts drawing from varied sources among them Chinese, Filipino, African, Thai and Brazilian. Can you tell us a brief account of your martial arts career?

Burton Richardson - I was very fortunate to grow up in Carson, California, about a mile away from the original Filipino Kali/Jun Fan Gung Fu Academy headed by Dan Inosanto and Richard Bustillo. Sifu/Guro Inosanto was Bruce Lee's right hand man and Sifu/Guro Bustillo was a student of Bruce Lee and Dan Inosanto. I started there in 1980, and the philosophy of constant improvement and refinement resonated with me and my science background. I continued to train with Inosanto, and through his guidance was able to train with the luminaries of many different arts. After I became an instructor, I continued to train with Guro Inosanto (as I do to this day) but also set out to travel the world and learn from the very best in as many disciplines as I could. That led me to at least 12 training trips to the Philippines along with journeys to China, Japan, Brazil, South Africa, Europe, and all across the United States. Today, I continue to research and put everything to the test through hard sparring.

MT - You visited and trained in the Philippines a number of times; can you tell us how much the FMA influenced you as a martial artist and a man?

BR - The FMA has been a great, positive influence. Martial arts-wise, I have had so many different points for view on functional combat from Grandmasters of the FMA, including Tatang Antonio Ilustrisimo, Bert Labaniego, Tony Diego, Topher Ricketts, and Jose Mena. That was just in the Philippines. I trained with many more GMs in America. I so appreciate the incredible tactics and techniques learned from men who used the art to survive and thrive.

As a man, I learned from the incredible generosity and good humor of the Pilipino masters. Each man merely wanted to share, and showed great joy when I was able to understand a concept or move. Probably the most impactful character lesson that I learned is from GM Bert Labaniego. After a lesson, he told me, "Always avoid a fight. But if you must engage, don't just fight for yourself. Fight for your family and loved ones, because they will be badly affected if you are killed." The concept of doing my very best out of love of my family and friends has shaped my life. I am very thankful.

MT - You are an original member of the Dog Brothers, notorious for their "Higher Consciousness Through Harder Contact" philosophy of live-stick sparring; can you tell us what you've learned from that experience and how did you earn the moniker "Lucky Dog"?

BR - I learned that theories need to be tested at full speed, power, and intensity in an environment of fear. It is one thing to practice moves against a cooperative partner, or in light sparring. It is something else altogether when failure means severe pain and injury. Being one of the original Dog Brothers helped me to streamline my approach and use only what is proven functional under heavy pressure. This way, I know that my students are equipped for a serious incident. I was dubbed Lucky Dog because, when asked how I pulled off some move, I would often reply, "Luckily, he stepped in the right spot" or "I was lucky that I was able to block that strike."

MT - You got involveE in the training of some professional MMA fighters every now and then; can you tell us more about it plus your thoughts on traditional martial arts and MMA?

BR - As you can tell from my other answers, I believe in pressure-testing before teaching. MMA is the ultimate sport for pressure-testing many techniques, tactics, and training methods. When I train UFC fighters, the moves MUST work. Traditional martial arts often go down the road of theory without real pressure-testing. That said, MMA is a sport and most traditional arts are designed to deal with an initial surprise attack where weapons, multiple opponents, and other aspects take it outside the realm of sport. My answer is to train traditional arts, like FMA, JKD, Silat, etc. in the same manner I train MMA fighters. Lots of sparring is essential. Proper preparation is key.

MT - How would you describe the martial arts curriculum you're teaching today and what are your current projects?

BR - My main guiding force is Bruce Lee's JKD philosophy of "having no way as way and having no limitation as limitation." Since people tend to impose limits on themselves, I call my overall method JKD Unlimited. Using only what works, but not limiting ourselves to a particular method. All of my programs only use the most functional aspects of the martial arts. JKDU is also known as MMA For The Street. My weaponry program is Battlefield Kali- an FMA-based method that safely blends a Dog Brother mentality to functional training. I also include some Zulu stickfighting. I also have a Silat For The Street program which is the empty hand portion using Silat and Kali principles and techniques. Next year my BJJ For The Street program will be out. So, I am all about using what works to protect those we love.

I have been hired to do the fight choreography for a major motion picture on the exploits of David and his Might Men from the bible. Lots of sword fights where I will draw heavily from FMA!

I would just like to conclude by giving my sincere thanks to the people of the Philippines. Your culture continues to have a very positive influence on me and my students worldwide. Maraming Salamat Sa Inyong Lahat!

41. FINISH THE CHOKE!

In a real self-defense situation, our main priority is to go home safely. That's the goal. Any means of reaching that goal, so long as it is within the law, is acceptable. (Some say do whatever you must, regardless of the law, but I don't want my students to end up in prison.) How do you go home safely? Run. This is always a good option if available. If you don't have the space or means to run, or if you have someone you must protect, try to talk your way out to the situation. If there is no time or opportunity to quell the situation before hand, you must fight your way to escape. While punching, kicking, arm bars, and arm locks are great techniques that really work, our primary goal is to get in position for a choke. If the attacker is on drugs or mentally deranged, cutting off his air supply is the one sure means to safety.

There are many methods and positions for the choke. There is the sleeper choke, collar chokes, guillotine, triangle, arm triangle, reverse sleeper, and many variations of each. There are many ways to set up and get to each move also. With sparring comes the skill to get into the proper position for these techniques. Once there, you must know how to finish the move against someone who is struggling to get out. Close doesn't count in fighting; you have to finish to make it count. Here are a few pointers that may help you out.

Regardless of the particular type of choke you are trying to apply, the main concept is to constrict the vessels that allow blood to flow to and from the brain. If the blood cannot flow, oxygen cannot get to the brain. No oxygen, no consciousness. If possible, we avoid putting severe pressure on the windpipe, as this can cause trauma and swelling which can lead to the death of your attacker. We want to go home safely. That means to your house, not the big house (prison). Merely putting lots of pressure behind the neck usually doesn't do it. Pulling on the neck, while painful, doesn't work well either. You have to constrict those blood vessels that run next to the throat to shut off the oxygen supply. Be sure that your technique is focused on constricting that area rather than just squeezing whatever you have as hard as you can.

If you have gotten to the back of your opponent and secured the position by controlling the opponent with your legs, be sure that your sleeper choke is applied with constriction and not just by pulling. If you have your right arm around the neck properly (inside of your elbow lined up with his/her trachea, no space between your arm and the trachea), the main choking motion is to get your right forearm to squeeze toward your right biceps. Doing this constricts the neck. If you just pull back, you only apply a lengthening pressure. Bear down and get that constriction. The idea is to close the blood vessels. To help bring your forearm to your biceps, use your left forearm/elbow to push. Since your right hand is locked over your left biceps, use your left arm to squeeze inward to aid the constriction. To add more pressure, put your chest into it, again aiding with the over-all squeeze.

The triangle choke is about constricting those arteries and veins as well. If your right calf is behind the opponent's neck, the main choking motion is to pull down with that calf while pulling up with your right hamstring. The hamstring in the side of the neck is what will create the actual choke. Of course, this alone is rarely enough to finish an opponent. Pulling the head/neck into the hamstring while doing a spiral squeeze with your thighs will help tremendously in finishing the choke. It is helpful to have the opponent's arm across in front of him, but not necessary.

Just as the sleeper, you don't want any extra space around his neck if you can avoid it. Try to get the back of your right knee as close to the neck as possible, and the inside of your left knee as close to the head as possible. Also, the more your right calf is behind your opponent's neck the better the choke will be. You want to choke the neck, not the back.

The collar choke follows the same principle of constricting the side of the neck. There are many hand positions and variations on the collar choke, but you use the material of the lapel to constrict the blood vessels, or you use the collar as a leverage point so that you can hold the person close and use the forearm to finish. Even if the opponent only has a t-shirt, bunch that material up to make it stronger and use it against him. The collar chokes should be practiced because they come up so often. It is a valuable tool to have in your arsenal.

One last note. If you feel that you have a choke on pretty well, but the opponent is not tapping out, don't re-adjust the choke. It happens often that someone gets to a choke, squeezes for a few seconds, doesn't get the tap, and so figures that it is in the wrong spot. The person then adjusts the choke and starts the squeeze again. But each time you adjust, you allow that precious oxygen to start flowing to the brain again, and must essentially start from scratch. If you have done this in sparring you have probably heard your partner say; "I was about to tap, then you let go for a second." If the choke is on, keep up the pressure the fight is finished. Getting to the position is only half the game. The other half is finishing the choke. Then you can go home safely and enjoy your life.

42. HIGH PERFORMANCE!

High performance. Isn't this what we are all after in our martial arts training? Isn't this what we strive to achieve in all aspects of our lives? We want to be able to perform at a high level of proficiency. Put another way, we want to become extremely skillful at our endeavors in life. What is it going to take to become a high performance martial artist?

I started using the term "High Performance Martial Arts" in the early nineties. The idea was to be able to perform our martial arts at a high level of proficiency, much like the difference between a regular automobile and a racecar. This was a fine goal, but my definition of High Performance was somewhat varied. I had not made a solid distinction between the entertainment part of the martial arts and the combative portion. As I entered more tournaments, and fought in different arenas, I realized that my path would primarily be one of teaching functional fighting and training methods to those who were interested in self-defense techniques that work under extreme pressure. High performance took on a different meaning for me.

What I found was that, regardless of how well I could flow my techniques together with a training partner, almost none of that coordination translated to sparring proficiency when I tried to apply the techniques against someone who was fighting back. I realized that for me, skill in actual fighting was what mattered most. I no longer wanted to be a person who taught thousands of techniques, but had never been able to actually do any of them in sparring. I changed the way I was teaching, and used the concept of High Performance Martial Arts as a guiding principle.

There was one major obstacle standing in my way of going in this new direction. I was making my living teaching JKD Concepts seminars, and the people who came to my seminars expected a certain style of teaching. I had a reputation for teaching in a very detailed manner, while exploring the thousands of variations that are available in the various arts. I had come to a point in my training where I realized that 99% of the intricate variations had a very low chance of working in a real fight. What to do? I knew that I could not continue teaching in the same manner. I had to tell the truth that I was exposed to.

What I did at first was to show a few functional techniques at the seminars, then go into what I referred to as "the art part" of the curriculum. I figured that this way, everyone would be happy. They would get some functional moves, and then also get to play with lots of "fun" techniques and drills. Each individual could then decide whether to pursue the fighting or demonstration art. It sounded like a good idea, but what I found was that most of the seminar students could not distinguish between functional and fantasy techniques. It was the same trap I had fallen into. Due to a lack of consistent sparring, these good people had no frame of reference to judge what worked and what didn't. Regardless of how I presented the material, people still went away with the feeling that they could somehow use these fantasy techniques in a real situation. I feel responsible to train students to be able to defend themselves in a real altercation, so I was in another quandary. Again, what to do? Was I going to just give up teaching the "art"? I really didn't have much choice, because it was clear to me that I wasn't helping people become better fighters; I was just adding to their delusion. I decided to speak with a close friend of mine about this situation.

Matt Thornton had restricted his teaching to the functional for several years. Matt encouraged me to just teach what I believed in. His advice was great. He told me that I would lose a lot of students doing this, but that many others would come who had similar goals to my own. He was right. I changed the seminar curriculum to cover only those things that either I or someone I knew of had been able to actually use in hard sparring or fighting. It is a simple concept. High Performance meant the ability to perform your techniques and tactics against someone who is totally resisting you. We train with progressive resistance so that the students begin sparring in a very safe, controlled environment, and gradually increase the amount of resistance as their skill level improves. I knew that I was risking my living by changing my approach, and my seminar schedule dropped off precipitously. But it has all worked out wonderfully. I really had no choice, because I cannot teach something that I don't believe in.

Over the years the fighting methods have improved almost daily. Training is better, application is better, and we are having more fun than ever. I also teach solo work with weapons and empty hands for the mind-body connection and flow, but these cannot be mistaken for functional fighting. I take the High Performance ideal and use it in every aspect of my life. I train in the fighting arts and other areas using the High Performance way. I take classes and work to become more skillful in other areas, from writing to business to charitable works. The different aspects of my personal life are working great. Keeping High Performance at the forefront of my mind keeps me moving in a positive direction in every endeavor I choose to undertake. You can do the same thing.

High Performance is a creed that you can live your life by every day. Is your life working for you, or do you seem to be stuck in a situation that you don't want to be in? If you are not happy with your life, it is probably due to your way of approaching life. Living well is a skill that can be acquired. If you don't like your results, change your approach. You must learn to believe in yourself, and only do those things that you believe are best for you. If you want to teach martial arts for a living, but are not taking steps to make that a reality, then you are short changing yourself. We get to make the choice to either live our dream, or just settle for what others believe we should do each day. Be bold and do those things that you want to do. Seek out the best teachers and train hard so that you can live the High Performance lifestyle.

43. IN THE CLINCH

Our first philosophy in JKDU is to look for the truth. This may seem simple, but it is a difficult thing to do for us humans, as there are many implications to this endeavor. To look for the truth, we first must admit that we don't know the whole truth. This takes humility. If we find a new truth, this often means that something that we have been doing for a long time is now outdated and we must change. It is easy to get attached to techniques and drills that have brought us pleasure over the years, and putting them aside is difficult. To substitute the new truth for the old takes courage. This means that we must admit that what we were doing before was not as good as it could be. This takes more humility. A good sense of humor helps also.

In our search for truth we must regularly go through a process of self examination. We must hold up that mirror of truth and take a good long look at what we see. It is not always pretty, but it is the truth nonetheless. One thing to look for is hypocrisy. Many JKD students will criticize traditional arts because the feeder of a punch will often extend the punch then stand frozen until the good guy finishes his technique. The comment is usually "Nobody is going to stand there with his arm out! That is ridiculous!" Ten minutes later you may see that same student pick up a stick, and ask his partner to hit an angle one. His buddy will oblige by extending his stick arm and freezing in position so that the technique can be executed "properly". Do you see the problem? We must always be on the lookout for this type of double standard, then correct it immediately.

About 5 years ago it became apparent that JKD practitioner had a glaring weakness: the ground game. We found out, thanks to the Brazilians, that we really didn't know how to fight on the ground. In one sense, this was horrible! It wasn't that we were missing a few techniques, we were missing an entire range of combat! Some instructors recognized this truth, swallowed their pride, and put on white belts. We got crushed and humiliated, but those who could handle this sort of ego bashing got better and better. It is no longer a weakness for us!

It has recently been brought to our attention that we have another great weakness. Weaponry? No, some of us have fought enough to have a good grip on reality there. Kickboxing range? No, plenty of sparring has led to good skills. Trapping range? Of course not! JKD is known for trapping. We have hundreds of combinations in trapping range. But are they functional? Is there a better way? The answer seems to be yes. At this point of our progression, it seems that trapping range is the weakest area of the JKD fighter.

Matt Thornton of the Straight Blast Gyms in and around Portland, Oregon was the first to bring this to my attention. He worked with UFC fighter Randy Couture. (This was well before he became a UFC Hall Of Famer.) Randy is a great guy, and happens to be a Greco Roman wrestling champ, as well as the only undefeated heavyweight champ of the UFC. In Greco Roman wrestling, a combatant can only take his opponent down with an upper body throw. No leg attacks are allowed. Therefore, these wrestlers become very adept at controlling the upper body of their opponent. Matt worked on this upper body wrestling with Randy and was totally dominated. Randy knows how to tie up his opponent and control him while setting him up for a takedown. Those of us who spar know that many of the compound trapping procedures in JKD just don't work well against an uncooperative opponent. (Note- over 2 decades after I wrote this article, I have an entire video program on how to apply functional trapping in MMA or in street self-defense!) Greco Roman tie ups do. It is as simple as that. With this revelation, we must integrate the pertinent techniques and training methods of MMA modified Greco Roman wrestling into our training.

Anyone who is good in this range will be able to tie up an opponent and strike him at will. You will also be able to take down an aggressive assailant. If you take the fight goes to the ground, you will most likely be on top. These benefits are extremely valuable to the JKD fighter, as we will now have the ability to combine the control tie ups of Muay Thai, Boxing, and Greco Roman wrestling to create a new synergy that will be very difficult to beat. Tying up with someone who has no experience with these methods is like wrestling with someone who has never been on the ground. If you have done your homework, the fight is much easier.

Look for more work in the clinch range from JKDU, and search out instructors in your area who know the tie up game. It is one more big step down the path of constant improvement towards being, as Bruce Lee said, a functional fighter.

44. THE FILIPINO BALISONG / BUTTERFLY KNIFE: HISTORY & USAGE

The Filipino balisong, often referred to as a butterfly knife, has been much maligned in recent decades. It has been described as a weapon of violence preferred by gang members that has is only used for offensive purposes. Some states have banned the possession of a butterfly knife despite the fact that much larger, sturdier, faster deploying knives are absolutely legal to carry. The balisong is actually the most humane self-defense knife due to its ability to be used at various levels of force. Before we go into those aspects, let's go over some history.

- History:

The balisong knife was developed on the island of Luzon, Philippines in the province of Taal/Batangas. There is a barangay (neighborhood) in Batangas by the name of Balisong, which is where this unique knife is assumed to have been first created. There are varying accounts as to the time line, with some claiming that the design was created over a thousand years ago. But certainly, its presence is well documented throughout the 20th century and the epicenter of production is in Batangas.

When entering Batangas coming from Manila, you quickly come across little roadside stores similar to country fruit stands. But the merchants in Batangas are selling butterfly knives instead of mangoes and bananas. It is a local industry which the Batangeunos are very proud of.

The design is ingenious. Instead of having a folding knife which needs two hands to open or a fixed blade that needs a sheath, the sheath and handle are one. The handles encase and protect the blade and the user from accidents while allowing the knife to be opened with one hand. This attribute is important in self-defense as drawing with one hand is essential while the other hand will be occupied warding off the attacker. A tool knife rarely requires a one handed opening except for convenience. To open, a latch is unlocked and one of the handles is pinched. With a circular movement of the wrist and arm, the other handle rotates around and into position while exposing the blade. The handles are grasped together and the knife is ready for various levels of defensive action.

- Defensive purposes/three levels of force:

A big advantage to the balisong is that the knife can be used along several levels of force. The first level is the flourish, where no physical contact with the assailant is made. When sufficiently threatened, the balisong user can produce the knife and go through a routine of opening and closing the knife in a very impressive manner. This flourishing is designed to intimidate and dissuade the aggressor from pursuing a physical altercation.

I grew up in the city of Carson, California which had a very large Filipino population. Around 1982, my sister was working at a park a quarter mile from my house. Four Filipinos in their late teens, who had just arrived recently in the states, were playing basketball on the outdoor court. A group of very large Polynesian kids of about the same age started playing on the other end of the court, but then decided that they wanted the whole court to themselves. The larger boys started threatening the small newcomers. "FOB" was a common epithet hurled at newly arrive Filipinos, and the big guys used that and other unpleasant words to intimidate their diminutive prey. My sister saw what was going on and was headed over to put an end to it when one of the bullies shoved the Filipino closest to him. The small guys all jumped back and pulled their balisongs with skillful flourishes. The big guys high-tailed it off before my sister could even get to the court. This is a great example of how the balisong can be used as a deterrent instead of going directly to deadly force.

The next level of force is keeping the balisong closed in order to use it as a small striking stick. This method is described in the book "Balisong- Iron Butterfly" (Dragon Books, 1985) by Filipino balisong master Cacoy Hernandez. In the introduction, he refers to his balisong as a "deterrent".

One incident illustrates the "Less lethal" option integrated into the balisong. In the book, the author recounts the time he saw his instructor attacked with a bolo (very sharp Filipino machete) on the dangerous docks in Manila. The master stepped in and struck the attacker with the butt of the balisong, dropping the aggressor. He countered a sword attack without using the blade of his balisong. This illustrates the defensive possibilities of employing the butterfly knife without any cutting.

Mr. Hernandez also cited times when he had to go to a higher level of force, utilizing the blade itself. But every single situation described was defensive. Never did the knife come out prior to an aggressor's formidable attack.

In Batangas, the birthplace of the butterfly knife, the use of the balisong is commonly taught to women for self-defense. Whenever I am in the Philippines, I strike up conversations with local people hoping to find someone who is trained in the Filipino martial arts. I have gleaned great information and insight from such impromptu interviews from taxi drivers, clerks, and even from a lawyer.

During one visit, I questioned a young lady who was my waitress in an empty restaurant. I learned that she was from Batangas so I asked if she had learned to use the balisong. Sheepishly, she replied "My father taught me, but just a little". After some coaxing, I handed her a butter knife and got her to demonstrate her methods of self-defense on me. I approached from the front, but she said, "No, grab me from behind." I obliged and she suddenly turned, made one lightening quick non-lethal strike, and escaped. On further questioning, she made it clear that her father taught her to use the balisong in a defensive nature, primarily against an abduction attempt. The goal was to use the balisong to create an opening for escape, not to take someone's life.

- Speed of opening:

The beauty of the balisong as a self-defense implement is that it can be used at various levels of the force continuum. The downside is that, because of its design, it has the slowest speed of opening of any modern self-defense knife.

Here are the steps required to draw and open a balisong compared to opening the most popular type of folding knife that has the "wave opening" feature constructed into the knife. (The wave opening feature is a hook or protuberance developed by famed knife maker Earnie Emerson which snags on the pocket as the knife is pulled out. This results in the blade opening just as the handle clears the pocket.)

The balisong does not clip to the top of a pocket or belt, but instead resides at the bottom of the carrier's pocket. To go from a concealed carry to having the blade in a useable state requires to following steps pocket:

1. Thrust hand deep into the pocket

2. Grasp the unit closed balisong

3. Pull the hand completely out of the pocket.

4. Feel the for the latch and rotate the still closed unit until it is in the proper orientation for opening.

5. Use the pinky or thumb (depending upon orientation) to open the latch.

6. Pinch one handle between the thumb and forefinger so the other handle is free to move. (This is a very precarious grip in a chaotic self-defense situation which leaves the defender susceptible to dropping the knife.)

7. Make a circular motion with the hand and wrist to allow the free handle to rotate to the open position. The most common opening involves 3 distinct circular motions to get the knife open. There are lesser known methods that enable the opening in one motion, but

these require more deliberate and precise generation of momentum.

8. With the handles now touching, the finger pinch grip transitions to a full finger grasp around both handles.

9. To ensure that the open balisong is as sturdy as possible, the latch should be closed. This is involves using the thumb to find and manipulate the latch into the locked position when the balisong is held in a reverse (icepick) grip. When held in a standard (hammer) grip, the free hand must be used to close the latch. If not locked, the handles move considerably, making the grip less secure and the knife unstable.

Opening a standard, modern "wave opening" pocket knife has fewer steps and is therefore much faster to deploy. Most pocket knives have a clip so that the knife can be just inside the top of the pocket for easy access. Many pocket knives have the wave opening (the hook or protrusion that snags the lining of the pocket) so that the blade opens as the handle clears the pocket. The steps to opening are:

1. Reach the thumb just inside of the pocket along the handle while the middle and/or index finger rests along the clip outside the pocket.

2. Pinch to grasp the handle.

3. Pull the unit out sharply allowing the hook to snag the pocket lining. By the time the handle has cleared the pocket, the blade is open and locked into place.

4. Adjust the grip to have a firm grasp on the handle.

Pocket knives which do not have a hook or protrusion to facilitate the opening often have a circular opening at the top of the blade. In that case, after step 3 the thumb and index finger pinch together in the hole and a snapping motion is made to send the handle away from the blade and into the locked position. Then the transition to a full grip is performed.

The balisong has a long history as a defensive implement. When I first started learning how to use it in the late 70's, it was always for defensive purposes; never as an offensive weapon. The balisong is taught in a manner of starting at the lowest level of force (flourishing to dissuade an attack) then moves to striking with the closed handle as a less lethal option, then escalates to using the edge or point when morally and legally justified and absolutely necessary. In my opinion, the balisong is the most humane self-defense knife there is because of the ability to use various levels of force are built into the butterfly knife. With proper training, I highly recommend it to anyone interested in self-protection.

45. A LESSON FROM SOCRATES

Through teaching countless seminars around the world to practitioners of almost every style, I have found a simple method that gets everyone on the same page for training. It is easy to become so absorbed into your particular style of martial art that you have a hard time approaching training objectively. I should know because it happened to me. I was so into my particular systems of martial arts that I passed up opportunities to train with Brazilian jiu-jitsu instructors, wrestlers, and judo players for years. I couldn't see the benefit of other methods of training if it wasn't the same as mine. I looked out at other styles through the prejudicial lens of my own styles. But, if we can look inward, within ourselves, we will find that we all tend to agree on the truths that lead us to training correctly. This isn't about stylistic differences, this is about finding the combative principles that we can all agree on. Once we acknowledge these, we are free to adapt our personal styles to a more complete method of training.

So, how do we find out what we really believe? By asking a good series of questions. This is what Socrates did to allow his students to go beyond cultural programming and look for truth. Answer the following questions and see where it leads you. Remember that we are not discussing the benefits of the artistic side of the martial arts, but are focusing on the best way to defend ourselves and loved ones from a violent, life-threatening street attack.

1. For street self-defense, is the primary purpose of our training artistic expression or fighting effectiveness?

2. Should we gear our training mainly toward the rules of competition or toward the absence of rules in street self-defense?

3. Is it better to just stick to the techniques that were passed down in our particular style or should we be open to use any techniques that

give us a fighting advantage?

4. What is the best way to know whether or not a technique works? Should we take the word of our instructor or should we actually test the technique ourselves?

5. If you test a technique for yourself, should the test be done in a highly controlled environment without any resistance from your cooperative partner or should the test more resemble the chaos of a real street situation? (While maintaining appropriate safety measures.)

After these questions, most everyone agrees that if we train for

self-defense, effectiveness should be our primary concern. We should train for a street environment, using whichever techniques work best. We know the techniques work because we put on the protective equipment and test the techniques and tactics under near street fight conditions. Basically, everyone agrees on this. Let's see what else we can agree upon.

Whenever we talk about self-defense we tend to make assumptions. Many of these assumptions are about the attacker. We assume he will stand in a certain pose. We can assume that he will throw a certain punch in the "correct" manner. Let's step away from our preconceived notions and look within for the truth about real attackers in a worst-case scenario.

1. Should we assume that the attacker is passive or aggressive?

2. Is it better to assume that he is skilled or unskilled?

3. Is it better to assume that he is weak or strong?

4. Timid or determined?

5. Will he be compliant or will he resist our efforts 100%?

6. Should we assume that will stop when he feels pain or should we assume that he will feel no pain?

7. Should we assume that we can dictate which range the fight starts in or should we consider that an attacker may start the fight in any range?

Everyone agrees that attackers are aggressive. That's an easy one. Have you ever heard of a passive attacker? "Please sir, if you don't mind, I would like to beat you within an inch of your life and take your money if it isn't any bother to you." Not going to happen. We all agree that it is better to assume that the attacker is skilled, strong, determined, totally resisting, and feeling no pain. We also agree that an attacker can sneak up on you and strike from a distance, grab and strike, or just tackle you to the ground when you aren't ready. When we understand this, we agree that a fight can begin in any range so we must train in all the ranges. Now that we are clear that we are going to train realistically to defend against a tough attacker, let's ask some good questions about how we are going train to prepare ourselves to prevail in such a situation.

1. Is the possible number of techniques available in the entire scope of martial arts limited or unlimited? (This sometimes takes some discussion, but if you put all of the basics in combination you have a

nearly unlimited number of techniques available to you.)

2. When we train, do we have a limited amount of time or is our training time unlimited?

3. If time is limited, and we want to be effective in a self-defense situation, should we prioritize the most effective training methods and techniques?

4. If a real attacker resists 100%, should we primarily practice against a passive opponent or against a partner who resists our techniques?

5. Can you become a good swimmer without actually getting into the water to practice swimming?

6. Can you become a good basketball player without spending a lot of time playing against other players who are trying to block your passes and shots?

7. Can you become a good fighter without spending a lot of time fighting against someone who is fighting back?

Almost everyone gets to the last question and understands the phrase that is plastered all over this book: If you want to learn how to fight, you must practice fighting against someone who is fighting back." We still get a few here and there who have been so brainwashed that they believe that doing forms in the air will make you a great fighter. That is like a person who shoots imaginary baskets with an imaginary ball believing that he could play in the NBA. The concept of adding resistance is so simple that it is easy to miss. I often say that the path to fighting skill is very narrow, and that one can easily be led astray. The truth is that we only have a certain amount of training time, so if you want to become a skillful fighter, you need to make the most of that limited time and train the most useful techniques in a realistic manner. That means against a resisting opponent. Rarely at 100% intensity, usually at around 70% or less for safety. The great thing is that training with resistance in all the ranges is great fun when you do it right. After you become competent in the basics, there are thousands of more advanced techniques and combinations that are available so you can continue to expand and grow and enjoy the process. But when faced with an attacker intent on doing you or your loved ones harm, you will only get to apply one technique at a time, so we must make sure those basics are very strong. The way you practice under pressure is the way you are going to perform under pressure, so practice with resistance in all the ranges. It is great fun and very satisfying.

46. INTERVIEW WITH RICKSON GRACIE

Rickson Gracie, the champion of the famous Gracie family of Brazil, is training very hard for his upcoming rematch in Japan with Takada. Rickson's lifetime of preparation paid off in the first fight as Rickson controlled the match from the beginning, and ended the contest by sliding to an arm bar from the mount position - a trademark of the Brazilian jiu-jitsu stylists. I had the opportunity to talk with Rickson about his training recently. As usual, he was calm, confident, and very candid about his training and his philosophy of fighting and life. Here is what the great champion of Gracie jiu-jitsu had to say.

Burton- How do you feel about your training for this fighting?

Rickson- My training has been very good, right on schedule. I am just very happy that the fight is on.

B- What kind of training have you been doing for jiu-jitsu?

R- I have been working more without the gi for this fight, more free-style combat training. If you are just grappling, you forget about the striking defense and offense. On the ground I have been working on the traumatic aspect of the art, the strikes from different positions and defenses for the strikes.

B- What concepts do you use when striking on the ground?

R- I work my striking in all positions. My striking is not designed to finish the opponent. Instead, I use the strikes to create openings so that I can apply submissions. I want to create an intersection of options by putting the opponent into a position where in order to survive one attack, he must move in a way that opens up another line. Of course, the opponent shouldn't know that this is happening. The characteristic of a great fighter is the ability to create confusion and take advantage of the confusion.

B- What sort of training have you been doing for the standing portion of the fight?

R- I have been sharpening my blocks for the punches, kicks, elbows, and knees, and I have been improving my strikes. The training is specific for the free-fight. I have to fight in all of the distances. Kickboxing is good in certain ranges, but I must also have the trapping options in the closer distance. I start away, cover all of the elements to clinch and throws. I have to be able to adjust to all of the elements.

B- What do you do to train your takedowns?

R- I have a general picture of training. I do positive cross-training. I always want to use what works so that I evolve in a positive way. My throws are based upon wrestling and judo. Without the gi, wrestlers are the most talented at takedowns. With the gi, judo players are the best.

B- What do your cardiovascular workouts consist of?

R- I do sprints, ride the bike, and go swimming.

B- How about strength training?

R- My strength training is done more to create support for my body so I can avoid injuries. I do a little weight training, but I make sure I keep the muscle flexible, strong, and healthy.

B- What can you tell us about your mental preparation?

R- It is within. I do this for life. I am always ready, 24 hours per day. It is important to keep yourself totally out of commitment to the result. Instead, I just concentrate on doing my best. I work to get rid of the invisible enemies in my mind. I surrender to God, and I am ready to die or kill.

B- How is your spiritual life involved?

R- This isn't just sport to me; this is my life, my tradition, my honor. I am willing to die to support my cause. I fight not for money, but to put my beliefs to the test. I look far beyond the sportive aspect, much deeper. The competition is more important than my physical body. I fight to honor my family, my father.

B- What is a typical day like for you when you are training for a competition?

R- I wake up, eat, do cardio, then go home. I eat again, stretch, then rest. I go to the school and train for one, two, or three hours, depending on the intensity. I finish by stretching for one hour.

B- And your diet?

R- I eat six meals per day and I take vitamins.

B- Do you have a game plan for the fight?

R- No. I go in with an empty mind, ready to find a gap.

B- What advice would you give others training in the martial arts?

R- Try to bring the experience on the mat to your real life. The mat is just a laboratory or school to polish physical, mental, and spiritual being. Work to find the important things inside of you; deep strength. Martial arts are not to learn to beat people up, but to learn about building yourself up.

B- Many people get into martial arts to develop confidence. How should they pursue this?

R- Confidence is related to the beliefs you have inside of you. In order to believe that you can do something, you must have hands-on experience. I can't confidently build a house without experience. Confidence is related to experience in life. I have been in so many situations that I know that I can do well. Jiu-jitsu won't let me down. Put in the hours on the mat. It takes lots of time, devotion, passion, and love. I work hard to have no doubts. I will surrender to destiny, but not to the enemies in my mind.

B- Who has helped you in your preparation for this fight?

R- Everybody, all of my students. I can get better training with anyone.

B- Any words for your students?

R- Training in jiu-jitsu is preparation for life. Don't worry about being the best, just take little steps forward. Feel good every time you come to train. Keep training and you will be good.

B- Thank you Rickson for sharing your knowledge with us.

R- *Thank you, my friend.*

47. ISN'T SPARRING DANGEROUS?

More and more martial artists are coming to realize that training with a cooperative partner can lead to bad habits for fighting, and can induce us to walk down the path of training to be impressive rather than effective. If combat effectiveness is what you are really after, then you must also understand one of the pitfalls of training with resistance.

For those who have missed the resistance train, here is a brief itinerary of the journey. In a real fight, do you think that an opponent is going to passively allow you to perform your techniques, or is he going to resist your efforts? This is an easy one. We all know that an attacker will attempt to quell all of our methods of defending ourselves. If this is the case, we must then be sure to train in an environment that simulates that street-fighting environment. In other words, your partner can't just stand there and let you do all of your moves. Furthermore, if your partner is cooperative, you will probably start embellishing the basic techniques with more intricate maneuvers that ONLY work against a static opponent. I summarize it thusly: "If you want to learn how to fight, you have to practice fighting against someone who is fighting back." Simple but true. If you just perform techniques against a willing "attacker", you will be in for a big surprise if you try out your stuff for real. Over and over again this is borne out when people step into a fighting arena for the first time without resistance training.

The complaint that I get about the idea of always training against a resisting opponent is "But everyone is going to get hurt". Not true. We use the principle of progressive resistance, just as you do in the weight room. When you use an amount of resistance that you can handle, but that is slightly uncomfortable, your body will adapt to that resistance. When it has properly adapted, you can add more resistance. This works very well, and injuries are kept to a minimum. In my classes, people get to "play" (a much better word than "spar") the first day they come into class. No experience? No problem. Just like in the weight room, if you aren't used to the resistance, you start with very light resistance, then build it up over time. Each person gets to choose the amount of resistance they ultimately want to encounter in the gym. Not all weight lifters train to become Olympic champions, and very few of my students strive to compete in fighting events. But training with resistance, from the first day, is the most efficient way to train. The best part of all this? It is also the most fun way to train.

When people just drill techniques without resistance, they are merely memorizing the move. This doesn't mean that they can actually do it. I can show anyone the proper technique for swinging a baseball bat in a few minutes. They will be able to take a short stride, keep the head from bobbing, swing smoothly with proper wrist alignment and hip turn, and follow through well. Excellent. Does that mean that they can hit an 85-mph breaking ball that starts at their head and ends up around their waist? I really doubt it. They have to start hitting very slow pitches. Why? So that they can develop the ability to read what kind of pitch is coming (fastball, curveball, slider, change up), and to be able to properly time the swing with the pitch. The same applies in fighting, except every pitch has the intent to knock you down. A fighter must be able to read and time the opponent so that the proper technique can be chosen and applied at the proper time. This can only be accomplished through playing the game against a resisting opponent. We do drills to memorize the techniques and develop the proper coordination, but safe sparring is where the essential elements of reading and timing are most efficiently developed. Students have great fun when they get to actually play the game with light resistance, instead of just memorizing techniques.

So now that more and more people are training with progressive resistance, another problem begins to appear. Just as techniques developed in the absence of resistance may not work when resistance is present, some techniques that work when there is light resistance fail miserably when full resistance is applied. Going back to the question I asked earlier, everyone agrees that an attacker is going to resist. My next question is, "Will an attacker resist 50%, 75%, or 100%?" Again, everyone agrees that the great majority of attackers are going to resist 100%. (Note the word "attacker". Picking a fight with a small inebriated guy in a bar to test out your stuff doesn't qualify him as an attacker.)

Simple techniques, such as holding a person's wrist to keep him from punching you may work at 75% intensity, but not at all when the opponent flails wildly. It is a different ballgame. In ground fighting, taking a few punches from the guy in your guard is not a big deal when you are playing around. Have him fire at full power and it becomes a very big deal! It is very simple. A real attacker will give all the resistance he can. If you want to be sure that your techniques work, you need to know that they work under full power resistance. So am I saying that all martial arts students should fight at full tilt? No. Not at all. The proper level of resistance in their training depends upon their goals. But, I do believe that all instructors should have experience applying their techniques under full resistance conditions. This way, the "tour guide" will understand the territory that he or she is leading the flock through.

An occasional full power bout will keep you based in reality. My experience as a one of the original Dog Brothers changed the way I looked at weaponry fighting, and empty hand fighting. My kickboxing changed me. I still train NHB all-out once in a while to keep everything in proper perspective. I can then pass along the training methods, techniques, and tactics that I KNOW, from my own experience, work well under the worst conditions. I also use methods that I have seen others apply consistently under full pressure. As mentioned, not everyone will want to go hard in sparring and that is absolutely fine. But I want to make sure that while the students are having fun training with light resistance, the techniques and tactics they are applying in light sparring actually work in a furious street encounter.

48. ISNESS AND IFNESS

What in the world is "isness"? It is simply what is. What in the world does this have to do with our martial arts pursuits? Everything.

Every person I have ever met who practices martial arts believes that there is a self-defense benefit to their training. They all believe that the way they train lends to their ability to develop real skill that could translate to success in an all-out street attack. The truth is that this is seldom the case. The reason is that the majority of people training in the martial arts are wrapped up in ifness rather than isness.

If we want to become good at anything we must strive for the truth. We must look at what we are truly trying to accomplish and set our course in that direction. It always helps to find people who have been there before so that we can learn valuable lessons to make our journey easier, more direct, and less perilous. This makes perfect sense. You find someone who has already done what you want to do and you follow the method that they used to achieve success. What happens in martial arts? The majority of people want to learn how to fight; yet they follow someone who has little or no fighting experience. Why does the instructor have no fighting experience? Probably because the instructor's instructor had no fighting experience.

Here we come back to isness. What is fighting experience? Doing forms? No. While you can become stronger and faster doing forms, the truth is that doing forms will make you good at doing forms. There is no fighting experience. How about doing sensitivity drills like chi sao? That should give fighting experience. No. Practicing drills like chi sao will make you good at chi sao. This is not fighting. Thai pads and focus mitts can make you better, right? While hitting pads will develop many attributes of a fighter and can ingrain certain moves, it is not fighting. It is drilling on equipment. Doing forms is what it is. Doing drills is what it is. Hitting pads is what it is. If you want to develop yourself as a fighter, you have to spend time fighting. Why? Because fighting is fighting.

You can't become skillful at anything unless you practice doing that thing. You may add supplemental training to enhance your attributes, such as hitting pads, but this is just an adjunct to the core training, and must not be substituted for the core training. When I played baseball, I spent at least one hour each day hitting a ball off of a tee and into a fence. This is not hitting, but it was a valuable addition to batting practice and game time. Batting practice was the key element. I took lots of batting practice, but the time there was limited, so I supplemented it with hitting off a tee. It worked very well. What would have happened if I just hit balls off a tee, and never hit a ball that was thrown fast? Would I have done well in the games? No. I would have had good technique, but no timing and no ability to adjust to the pitches as they came in.

What if someone came up to you to teach you baseball and told you that they have the greatest method ever for learning to hit. They proceed to pull out a tee, take you to a fence, and have you hit balls off the tee into the fence. Seems reasonable enough, but what if they told you that this is all you need. You don't need batting practice against a live pitcher. You don't need the batting cages. As a matter of fact, you don't even need to play in any games. You will hit the ball so hard after working off the tee that you may accidentally hurt someone if you play in a real game. It would be best if you only spend time hitting off the tee, and safer for everyone. Would you believe this? I hope not. The only way that you could buy into this is if you have never played baseball. Anyone who actually plays knows that hitting a slider is very different than hitting off a tee. The coach is either lying to you, or he has no actual experience either.

Hitting in a game is what is. Hitting off a tee has benefits, but it is not hitting a live pitch. In martial arts people practice techniques against an "attacker" who stands with arm outstretched like a statue. What is this? Practicing against a statue, and statues don't hit back.

Once this notion of practice is challenged, ifness comes into play. "If the attacker does this" or "if I was in this position" this and this and this would be applied. "If I do this drill long enough I will be able to defeat anyone in a fight." This is "if" not "is". Isness is when you have someone actually fighting you. If we are talking about fighting arts, then the game is fighting. You have to practice fighting to become skillful at it. There is no other way. None. People will now say, "but if I hit mitts with proper feeding, it is like fighting." No, that is hitting mitts with a good feeder. What if the feeder never took the time to set the pads so that you could hit them, but instead punched and kicked and grabbed you the whole time? That would be more like fighting. Then come the excuses. "If we actually fought, someone would get hurt." It depends upon the intensity of the fighting and the protective equipment you use. Just as pitches in batting practice are thrown at about 75% of game intensity, fighting can be practiced at a lower intensity to minimize injuries and allow the participants to improve. This said, you must apply isness to this as well. Sparring at 75% is very different than going all-out. If you want to be really good at fighting, you must occasionally step into the danger zone and go 100%. The intensity you take your training to depends upon your goals.

The truth is that if you want to be good at something you have to spend time doing that thing. Doing forms is doing forms. Practicing static techniques is practicing static techniques and doing drills is doing drills. Only fighting is fighting. If you want to learn how to fight, you must practice fighting against someone who is fighting back! It is what it is.

49. CUTTING THROUGH THE ORIGINAL VS. CONCEPTS CONTROVERSY

Original vs. Concepts; Which is the better approach? This question has been looked at over and over again the last few years without much progress. I believe that just as in any other area of art, sports, or technology, we can go beyond the old way of thinking and find a better way. For clarity, let's first take a look at what the "original JKD" people think, at what the "JKD concepts" people think, and what the two camps think of each other.

Original JKD is comprised of those things that Bruce Lee actually did himself; His techniques, his training methods, and so on. A common phrase from this camp is, "If Bruce didn't do it, it's not JKD." They tend to have a healthy reverence for Lee and everything that he accomplished. They have great confidence in the art that Lee founded, and have considerable pride in teaching the methods developed by the founder. They believe in practicing the basics of Jun Fan Jeet Kune Do with diligence to hone the skills of the artist. Many in this camp look at the concepts people as a group of wayward martial artists who think that accumulation is the key to proficiency. They think that concepts people will practice any art regardless of whether or not it is useful, and most concepts people think "The more techniques I know, the better I must be."

Jeet kune do concepts practitioners believe that the art that Sigung Lee passed on is good, but there is much more to learn in the martial arts realm. Concepts people think that by studying different arts, a wider scope of understanding will be gained, and the student will be better off in the long run. Knowing more techniques is like having extra insurance in case you end up in a bad situation. They also have a strong reverence for Bruce Lee, but they realize that he was only able to study a small portion of the arts that are available today. They also believe that a martial artist should be well-rounded in his or her approach, and the only way to accomplish this is to study a wide variety of arts. Many concepts people think that the "original" practitioners are closed minded, and limited in their martial options. Some concepts people also think that since they practice Jun Fan Jeet Kune Do themselves, it only makes sense that the concepts approach better prepares an individual for a combative situation. If a concepts person knows the same things as an original person, plus knows other arts too, then the concepts person has the advantage.

Obviously, I am making wide generalizations here, and every individual practitioner is different, but this is some of the prevalent thinking on both sides of the issue. What we all want to know is, which side is right? Which approach is better? Actually, I don't think that is the question. I think that what most of us really want to know is "What should I do to become the best martial artist that I can become?" Isn't this the pertinent question? We want to know if OJKD is better than JKDC to be sure that we are practicing the best way that we can. From a fighter's point of view, how to become the best of oneself is the only question that pertains to martial arts training. It doesn't matter if it is OJKD or JKDC as long as we become better martial artists.

I have been very, very fortunate to have studied with Sifu Dan Inosanto over the last 18 years. He is the best of all worlds in the martial arts because he is a great teacher, technician, fighter, and a wonderful person. He is a great student as well, constantly researching and training in various arts under many different teachers. His teaching is on a very high level also, because he encourages each student to find their own way. He will supply everything a person could need to go into any aspect of the martial arts. He also encourages his students to study with other instructors so that the student will have different perspectives on the arts. He encouraged me as I went down one martial path, and he now encourages me since I have changed the direction of my training and teaching.

For years I taught all aspects of various arts, from forms to intricate techniques to the basic fighting drills. My Los Angeles students enjoyed the training, as did my seminar students. As time went on and I entered various full-contact competitions, with and without weapons, I began to re-examine my teaching approach. I finally realized what my problem was; I didn't have a goal for my training and teaching! I needed a goal to guide my training in a particular direction, but I had to first decide what that direction would be. I decided that the most important aspect of the martial arts, that thing that makes it martial arts, is to be able to defend yourself in a life-threatening situation. I wrote out a goal for myself and my students, and used it to guide my research, training and teaching. It has shaped my expression of Jeet Kune Do. Here is the goal. I hope you find it useful.

"You must be able to apply your art under extreme pressure, in all ranges, with or without weapons, against one or more, armed or unarmed, highly skilled aggressive opponents, in a variety of environments." This is the goal of the training and it guides me and keeps me on track. I believe that the underlying theme of Jeet Kune Do that makes it unique is that the art must work on the street. Take a look at the components of the goal and see if they make sense to you and your training.

To be able to handle such a situation, you must be able to actually apply your art. There is a big difference between looking good in class and going for it in the street. In class you may like to work with someone who has good energy, but in the street, an attacker is going to have the worst energy that you can possibly imagine. Instead of giving you "good energy", he is going to try his best to foul up anything you try. Our training must prepare us to deal with that sort of frantic, hostile energy. The techniques you use must be simple, effective techniques that have been proven to work under adverse circumstances. Remember, knowledge is not power, the ability to apply your knowledge is power! To become a powerful martial artist you must be able to apply your art. You must be able to handle the pressure of an aggressive attack. If your training doesn't include dealing with heavy attacking pressure, how do you expect yourself to automatically adjust to a high pressure situation in the street? Be sure you include drills in your training where you feel your partner pressuring you, or create a training situation where you have deal with the nervousness that can hinder your performance.

You must be able to fight in all ranges of combat. Nobody can predict which range a street fight will start in, or where it will end up. You must be functional in all of the ranges, or after years of training you may end up in a position that you are unfamiliar with. You should be proficient in kicking range, hand range, trapping range, you should be able to throw an opponent, and you must be able to fight on the ground. You may be a great stand up fighter, but what happens if you get tackled from behind by an opponent you didn't see? How about a grappler who has to face more than one opponent? If you want to have a fighting chance on the street, you must be functional in all of the ranges.

Weaponry is a must as well. One of the most natural things for an irate human being to do is to pick something up and use it as a weapon. If you want to understand how to defend against a weapon, you should learn how to fight with a weapon. You should understand the difference between fighting with an edged weapon and fighting with a blunt impact weapon. If you know the weak points in your attack with the weapon and you are used to the motion of the stick or knife, you will have a much better chance of surviving an armed attack. If the situation is really bad, you may need to improvise a weapon to save your own skin.

Have you practiced against multiple opponents? Have you seen a mass attack occur? Do you have tactics to deal with this sort of attack? If not, you better get to work. Mass attacks are a common occurrence. You could be minding your own business when a group of youngsters with nothing better to do decide that you are to be the outlet for their rage. Multiple opponents are very difficult to deal with, but you should at least practice the tactics that could allow you to run to safety. Even in your one on one training, you should factor in the chance that the guy you are fighting may have friends on the way. This is why staying on your feet is important. If his friends come around the corner, you can run. When you grapple, you should try to choose positions that are easy to run away from. If you are tangled up with an opponent, he can hold you until his friend arrives to introduce his boot to your brain. Not good. Always factor in fighting against more than one opponent into your training.

I always want to assume that any opponent I or a student of mine faces is highly skilled in all of the ranges. If you assume that the person knows nothing, what happens if you grab him and find out that he is a wrestling champ? You could make a careless mistake and be finished. Much better to assume that the person is highly skilled, approach the situation accordingly, and win easily if the opponent isn't skilled. The best way to avoid underestimating an opponent is to assume that he is very good.

There are environmental considerations to take into account also. Can you fight in the dark? Can you function when it is very noisy, like in a night club. How about when the ground is slippery, or on a hill, or in the snow, or in the water, or when you have lots of clothing on, or when you are in a parking lot, or when you are sitting in your car? You should try training in different environments so you can more easily adapt to a situation in the real world when conditions less than optimal.

So we know what the goal is, but what do we need to become functional? We must have sound techniques and employ proper training methods.

There are millions of possible techniques, but far fewer moves that are probable to work against a highly skilled, aggressive opponent. So where should we draw our base techniques from? I choose most of mine from full-contact combat sports. Muay Thai, vale tudo, boxing, and other combat sports put skilled competitors together to go nearly all-out. They don't talk and theorize about fighting, the go out and do it. You will see certain techniques being used over and over again because they work well. I use these techniques, then add all of the foul tactics such as eye and groin strikes that are illegal in the ring but necessary in the street. The techniques must be simple, and practical, and must be practiced repeatedly in order to become functional. Most of the techniques I teach are those that I have pulled off under pressure, or techniques which I know have been performed by someone else under pressure. If I want to teach a move that I believe is practical, but I don't know of anyone actually doing it, I will tell my students just that. This way I am honest with my teaching and I retain my integrity by staying true to my goal.

I take most of the basic training methods from combat sports also. You must have an efficient way of practicing your techniques that simulates the combat conditions while keeping a margin of safety. If you get hurt during training you are defeating the whole purpose of martial arts training. You learn martial arts so that you can stay healthy, so safety in training is a must. Training for combat sports is designed to win the event, and since our "event" is a street fight with no rules, we must alter the drills to fit our needs. The main goal in the training is to build extremely strong basics in each range, because the fighter with the strongest basics usually wins the bout.

This is basically what my expression of Jeet Kune Do is. I call my group Jeet Kune Do Unlimited because I don't want any of my students or myself to become limited in our thought process, and start to think that we have the "best" way or the "only" way. I call what we do High Performance Martial Arts because that is what it should be; martial arts that you can perform at a high level of proficiency. Some people will like it, others will hate it, but that doesn't matter. The most important thing is to be constantly improving. I am happy with where the training is now, but I know it will get better in the future as I and my research team of instructors experience more training methods from different arts, cultures, and fighters. I want to be the best that I can be, and I want to help my students and friends to do the same. Bruce Lee gave us a great example by showing us what happens when a person sets a goal and works on that goal with zeal. Forget about whether "this" art is better than "that" art. Set your goal, make sure it feels right to you, then get to work on being the best that you can be.

50. KALI WISDOM

The Filipino martial arts have made a huge impact since they were brought to public attention, primarily through the efforts of Guro Dan Inosanto. Inosanto began teaching these arts publicly in the late 70's, and although there were grandmasters who taught outside of their own families before this time, it was Inosanto who popularized these arts through his dedicated teaching schedule. The result is that the Filipino martial arts have been able to take their proper place next to other major arts. Because these arts are derived from battlefield and ring experience, we can assume that there is a great amount of functional material in each system. It is interesting and enlightening to draw upon the wisdom of the great kali masters when it comes to understanding how these and other martial arts evolve.

One of the greatest masters of the Filipino martial arts was a man named Floro Villabrille. Villabrille was a fighter. This term is thrown around rather loosely today, often describing someone who practices tenaciously. But to be a fighter you must fight. It is that simple. Villabrille did so in many (legend says 80) so called "death matches". To envision one of these matches, picture a no holds barred event, like the Ultimate Fighting Championship, but with two modifications. Yes, punches, kicks, elbows, and knees are allowed, along with throws, grappling, and joint locks. The modifications? No gloves, and the combatants use heavy sticks to strike each other with. No protection except your skill. This is stick fighting and Villabrille was the best.

The combatants used rattan sticks, and sometimes used hardwood "swords" that were flat and nearly came to an edge on each side. The tip was flattened too, so there was no point to thrust with. How good would you have to be to survive a few of these? How about 10? 40? 80? It becomes obvious that Villabrille was a true fighting master, because he was able to take his skills into the ring, put his life on the line, and control his emotions enough to apply his art in the most difficult of circumstances. Now if you are looking for someone who has gained wisdom from years of martial arts training, would you prefer to go to someone who has 80 fights or someone who has spent years memorizing forms? It is obvious that wisdom gleaned from the fighting arts is held most readily by those who fight.

One of the most enlightening concepts from Floro Villabrille was passed onto me by my longtime instructor Dan Inosanto. Inosanto tells us that Villabrille said that there are two arts in kali: "entablado" and "matador". Matador is the art of fighting, more literally the art of killing. Most people in our time find this to be an unsavory prospect. Practicing the art of killing is not something that most normal people in our society want to spend time perfecting. I would include myself in that group, as I don't prioritize killing techniques in my personal training or in my teaching. I prefer to focus on combative methods that work against aggressive, skilled attackers. Focusing on killing may not be good for the spirit, although there are those in our society who must do this to protect those of us who prefer to pursue other endeavors. But the fact remains that the base art of kali, eskrima, or arnis is the art of doing battle against someone who is trying to kill or disable you.

The flip side of this (Pinoy humor intended) is the art referred to by Villabrille as "entablado". This literally means on the table or on the stage. Entablado is the entertainment art of kali, whose purpose is along the same lines as the many cultural dances from the Philippines. While derived from the battlefield art, the purpose of entablado is to entertain. It is not intended to be a fighting art. Matador is the fighting art. Entablado consists of many elaborate techniques, beautiful two person sets, and the magic of weapons in motion.

As time has passed, which art do you think has become more popular? Of course it is the stage art. It is more beautiful, less stressful, and you get to avoid those painful stick sparring sessions. Not to mention the fights themselves! Few people are going to dedicate themselves to learning the combat portion because it requires engaging in combat. I remember many times when Dan Inosanto would stop a Filipino martial arts class to explain the difference. He would say "If I was just going to prepare you for a stick fight, I would have you hitting the heavy bag for an hour. Just making an "X" on the bag for an hour. Then some sparring and that's about it. But few people want to do that everyday." This is the difference between entablado and matador. Not only is the goal different, the training is very different too.

Think about your own training. Are you spending any time practicing fighting? I don't mean techniques, but actual fighting. If you don't spend time fighting, you will not be a good fighter. You can hit focus mitts, shadow box, do forms, and swing your weapons in the air all you want, but if you don't spend time fighting, you will not be able to fight well. Some people dispute this. They think that if you are good at doing forms and drills then you will be a good fighter. That makes as much sense as saying that because Randy Couture is a great fighter, then he must be one of the best at martial arts forms. It just doesn't work that way.

Listen to the wisdom of the masters. There are two arts. Know which of these you are practicing and why. If you want to learn how to fight, practice fighting methods that prepare you for battle. If you want to enjoy the beauty of your chosen art, then spend your time perfecting the motions of drills and forms. If you want both, be sure to practice both. Above all else, enjoy the process that will take you towards your goal.

51. NHB VERSUS JKD

There has been a great debate over the usefulness of No Holds Barred (NHB) fighting for street self-defense. Those who train in NHB fighting often quote the motto of the Ultimate Fighting Championship, claiming that the sport is "As Real As It Gets". Many other martial artists look at the rules and claim that it is merely a sport. I have trained diligently in many different "self-defense" arts since 1979. I became a full instructor under Dan Inosanto in both the JKD Concepts and Filipino Martial Arts in 1990. I am also certified in Muay Thai under Master Chai Sirisute, in Pentjak Silat under Pendekar Paul DeThouars, and am one of the original Dog Brother stick fighters. I started training in NHB style fighting in 1995, training with the Inoue Brothers, Randy Couture's Team Quest, Baret Yoshida, and Charuto Verissimo. This background allows me a unique perspective from which I can dissect the issue of NHB versus JKD.

Before we go any farther, let me assure you that a person who is well-trained in NHB fighting will usually do very well in a one on one street confrontation. There is just no doubt about it. The training is so complete and efficient that the skills of a person trained in NHB will simply overwhelm your typical street fighter. With that said, you may conclude that the debate is over. If NHB does work well in the street environment, why have any further discussion? Because if the primary goal of your training is street self-defense, and not to compete in an "extreme" sport, you should look into the modern approach to self-defense training. It is much more effective than confining your training to the rules of the sport.

Okay, now the NHB guys are mad. Just hear me out. First off, there are no magic bullets here. The great thing that NHB fighting has taught us is how to train correctly. The training is usually a blend of Brazilian jiu-jitsu, Thai boxing, Western wrestling, and Western boxing. (Other elements are often used as well.) Each of these combat sports developed methods of training that translated into successful performance against an opponent who was fighting back. But the training in each sport has a different look and direction than the others. Why? Because the rules of each contest are different. One principle that I have come upon is:

"The rules of the event will dictate the training, techniques, and tactics that are used to become successful in that event."

If you train for a wrestling tournament you are not going to practice throwing kicks at your opponent's legs. You will not stand upright like a Thai boxer, as you will be taken down easily. You will not throw an overhand right to facilitate your move into the clinch. The training, techniques, and tactics will be specific for the rules of the event.

NHB events have the least restrictive rules, but there are several different sets of regulations used. Some allow elbow strikes, others do not. Some allow kicks or knees to the head of a downed opponent, others do not. This affects the way the fighter approaches the training and the fight. If head butts are not legal, a fighter can be on his back and hold the wrists of the opponent to avoid being punched. If head butts are allowed, he must use different tactics to defend against the punches and the head butt at the same time. Change the rules and you change the game. Clearly, a fighter who does not prepare for all the possible attacks will be at a great disadvantage during the fight.

This brings us back to our debate.

We all know that there are no rules in a street attack. Therefore, you must be trained to deal with all possibilities. I don't mean just knowing the techniques, but actually sparring with all the possible techniques so that you have the timing and sensitivity necessary to actually apply your techniques successfully in a real situation. This must be done in a safe environment with proper protective gear, but the main point is that if you don't practice protecting from the groin strike in practice, you won't do it automatically under the stress of a street attack. If you are training for self-defense, you should practice with those rules in mind. Now, people always say "But you can't really gouge to the eyes or hit the groin in practice. That makes the training unrealistic." I would like to ask how many of you actually spar kickboxing at 100% intensity without gloves? Is that also unrealistic? The truth is that a very small percentage of martial artists ever compete in kickboxing or NHB events where you fight all out against an opponent who is doing the same. Those who do compete know what it is like to fight at full intensity, and that is a great advantage. If you are boxing at less than full intensity, then adding groin strikes and eye gouges at less than full power can easily be added into your sparring to make it more street specific. If you want self-defense, then train for self-defense.

I would like to now take you through an examination of the difference between modern JKD, as developed in JKD Unlimited, and NHB by looking at the road to fight night for a professional NHB fighter. The first thing that happens is that a date and location is set. This means that you know where and when you will be fighting. This does not happen in a street attack. You will often have no idea that you are about to be attacked. You are minding your own business, then BOOM! You are ambushed. You suddenly find yourself in the middle of a life and death struggle. Instinct and training kick in without thought. This is a very different mindset than having lead time to prepare for a fight.

Besides the element of surprise, there is also the mental issue of giving permission. When you sign to do an NHB fight, you give permission to your opponent to try to knock you out, choke you out, or submit you, within the confines of the rules. You do not give a person in the street permission to attack. It is a total invasion of your space. No rules, no ceremony, just violence being thrust upon you. If you are not prepared mentally to deal with this type of attack, you may be overwhelmed. Preparing mentally for the street is different than preparing mentally for the ring.

Another consideration for most NHB fights is your weight category. Will you cut weight to be at the top of a weight class or will you have to bulk up before your fight? This is not a question in the street as there are no weight classes. You have to know how to deal with a much larger attacker. You need to practice the techniques and tactics that will give you the greatest chance at success against a large adversary.

To prepare well you will need to know how many rounds there will be and how long each round is. You will need to practice pacing yourself so that you don't begin too hard or too fast and tire out. This is very important in NHB fighting, but there is no long term pacing in a street fight. A real attack is a sprint. You must train differently and spar differently in order to be ready to handle the onslaught and to deliver your own at a very rapid pace. You need the anaerobic capacity to sprint hard for a short burst, then burst again if necessary. Professional fighters have incredible cardio, but if you aren't a professional fighter you should be sure that you can burst and recover quickly.

Now it is fight night. You walk into the ring. The surface is padded and level, not too slick, not too sticky. It is ideal for fighting. Not so in the street environment. The surface may be bumpy, sloped, wet, icy, sticky. You may have curbs to deal with, or broken glass or mud. You have to adapt to the environment, but if you train on different surfaces you will be better prepared for a street altercation.

In the ring you are wearing a mouth piece, groin protection, and gloves. I doubt that any of you will be wearing groin protection in the street. You have to rely on your skills to keep you safe below the belt! In the street you will have to change your clinch stance to avoid the groin hits. Your guard will have to change to protect the groin. It is best to train this way if you want your street positioning to be automatic. Your hands will not be protected, so you need to understand what it means to hit someone in the head with bare knuckles. Broken hands are common, so you may choose to practice open hand striking if you want street self-defense.

The referee calls you to the middle of the ring. There are no referees in a street fight. It is up to you to fight and win. You can't count on anyone looking out for your safety if you get knocked out. It is all up to you.

You wear fight trunks and no shirt. The referee instructs you to avoid grabbing the trunks of your opponent. In the street, people wear clothing. You must be prepared to deal with an attacker grabbing your clothing and pulling you around. You should also know how to use the attacker's clothing to control him and possibly choke him. It is important to work with clothing grabs in class so that you are prepared for an actual attack.

The referee continues giving the rules of the game. There are no rules in the street. In the ring you have one opponent. In the street there will probably be many. In the sport your opponent will come after you with punches, kicks, takedowns, and submission. In the street there may be knives, clubs, or firearms. If you get in a real bad situation in the ring, you can always tap out. There is no tapping in the street, no doctor on hand to check your cuts. It is just you and the skills you developed through your training. Training for the street is clearly different than training for the ring.

With all that said, I want to emphasize again the importance of proper training methods. A NHB fighter with good training will easily defeat a martial artist who knows lots of street tactics, but does not train correctly. By correctly I mean lots of sparring. You have to spar against an uncooperative partner in the gym if you want to be able to apply your techniques successfully against an uncooperative attacker in the street. That is the only way to learn to deal with the pressure and movement of a resisting attacker. I phrase it like this:

"If you want to learn how to fight, you must practice fighting against someone who is fighting back."

It is really quite simple. In JKD Unlimited, I have many different training methods that deal with multiple attackers, surprise attacks, weaponry, and other street specific elements. We practice in a way that often looks very much like NHB training so that the students are actually progressing in their skills, not just in knowledge. And we have loads of fun doing it! We have many different "Performance Games" that keep the class lively, fun, and productive. We train for the street first, then alter the training for those who want to compete in sporting events. Not the other way around.

I would like to close with a quote from Bruce Lee, the founder of

JKD. He said, "In sparring there are no winners. In competitions, you do your very best to win. In the street you MUST win!"

In order to win, you must prepare well. By using the concepts of NHB fight training combined with the tactics found in street altercations, you will be well-prepared to thrive in the chaotic world of street self-defense.

52. THE ART OF SELF-DISCIPLINE

One of the many benefits that people equate with martial arts practice is the development of self-discipline. Mention anything referring to the fighting arts and one often gets "That's really good for discipline, isn't it?" Those of you who follow this column know that I advocate training the fighting arts in a realistic manner, one that consists mainly of actual fighting at various intensities. Two questions are often poised to me. First, "Can training in traditional martial arts develop self-discipline?"

What is self-discipline anyway? As one who has studied self-discipline very hard over the years (primarily because I noticed an absolute lack of it in myself), I have come up with this definition: "Self-discipline is doing what is best, even though you feel like doing something else." You want to lose weight, you know it is best to skip the trip to Hagen-Daz, but you really feel like going. Which wins out? It is a matter of self-discipline. If you give into your urges toward the pleasure of the dessert, you will not move towards your fitness goal. If you choose to forego the delectable delight, you advance towards your goal. Can traditional training somehow help you with this? Absolutely.

A basic truth of the universe is that through practice we form habits. If we practice well, in a manner that leads us toward our goals, we will develop habits that allow us to receive the fruits of our labor.

To develop the ability to overcome the urge to give in to pleasure, simply practice doing that. The simple but arduous task of standing in a horse stance is a perfect example. You get into the stance, and not much later, you feel pain in your legs. Your knees start to shake as the burn in your leg increases. This is discipline practice. Your body tells you to get out of that stance and shake out your legs. What do you do? Give into the body asking for a more pleasurable experience, or stay in that stance and grind it out so that you can have stronger legs? By staying in that stance, even a few more seconds, you develop your powers of self-discipline. The same goes for body toughening, stretching, and a whole host of other traditional martial arts activities.

This brings us to another point that has been brought up. "I watched your class, and it looked like undisciplined brawling. Where's the discipline in what you do?" We must always understand that there are two points of view on actual combat; what we would like it to look like, and what it actually does look like. Even in sparring, where each person can punch, kick, clinch, throw, and ground fight, what "is" does not jive with what many people think "should be". In other words, in a real fight, both fighters are trying to be unpredictable, and throw the other person off. It rarely looks just the way you like. When it does, it feels great. Slap that triangle on and get the tap, a great finish to a single leg takedown, or a well-placed strike against someone who is trying to avoid it brings great satisfaction. That only happens through skill, and discipline. Discipline? Oh yes, tons of it. As much self-control as it takes to stay in the horse stance, believe me that the level of self-discipline jumps tremendously when you must do it under great pressure. Being punched in the face tests your resolve! You may get close to a takedown, then the opponent counters and starts with the body shots. Are you going to be disciplined enough to go through the pain and finish the task, or are you going to give up and go back to a more "pleasurable" distance? If you back out, you may never get that chance to finish again. You may spend the rest of the night on the wrong end of a jab, instead of taking a couple more shots and getting the opponent down. Work hard on real fighting, and your discipline must improve. Otherwise, you will just quit when you get in a bad position.

How about something that is less painful physically, but still pits the mind versus impulse? Ever watch a kids class? Ever teach one? You see how difficult it is for them to stay still? The simple act of staying in line and not moving requires great discipline for most children. My parents can tell you all about it. They couldn't go to a restaurant for many years during my childhood due to the scene I would inevitably make. (If only there was a martial arts gym nearby!) Having those kids stand in line without moving is an exercise in self-discipline that could carry over to other parts of their lives. If they understand the benefits of putting off temporary, short-term pleasure for more lasting long-term benefits, they will be way ahead of the game.

This idea of putting off the temporary for the lasting is a cornerstone of understanding discipline. You can practice methods of improving discipline, but logically thinking out your reasons for doing so also helps. Having a good reason for doing the right thing, even though you feel like doing something else, helps you to make the best choice. How can that be? What is another word for "reason"? Motive. What is the state of having a motive called? Motivation. That key word for success, motivation, is really nothing more than having a great reason to keep you on course. Know your goal and have a great reason for achieving it and you will more easily stick to your plan. Stick to a good plan (never quit!), and as simply as following a roadmap, detours, flat tires and all, you will eventually reach your destination. Use the discipline you gain from your training and apply it to your everyday life. With a strong goal, proper reasons, and self-discipline, you will prevail.

53. SUCCESS THROUGH FAILURE

No matter what martial art you study or what your goals are in the arts, one thing is certain. In order to succeed you are going to have to go through a lot of failure. As always, this truism in the martial arts is also true for your everyday life. Want to be great? Then you have to have the courage to do poorly. There is actually a science to this and it is a very important aspect of proper practice. Let's call it the 3F approach.

The first F stands for "Fail". This may still seem strange to you, the notion that in order to achieve you must have setbacks, but think about it. How did you learn to walk? By trying and failing hundreds of times. Over and over again you got all the way up to your feet (which was quite an accomplishment in itself) and you tried to take steps. Down you went. With each "failure" your body made adjustments. Your balance got a little better each time. Your legs got a little stronger. Your coordination improved. Time and time again you tried and failed, until all that failure turned you into a success. As difficult as it was then, you are now a grandmaster of the art of walking. You don't have to think about it, you just do it. You can walk uphill and down stairs, through water and over rough terrain. If they gave out belts for walking you would have one of those old beat up black belts with a bunch of red stripes. What would have happened if your parents didn't allow you to learn how to walk? What if they were afraid of seeing you try and fail, so decided to keep you from taking any steps until you were much older. They might have figured that since three year olds walk very well, they will just wait until you turn three and then let you start from there to avoid the mental anguish of failure. What would happen? You would have been stronger, but you would still have to go through that same process of trying and failing until you learned how to walk. You became very skillful because the unsuccessful attempts taught you what you needed to know in order to make the proper adjustments, not because of your maturity level. It should be noted also that as a baby, the thought of giving up never entered your mind, as it was not a concept that you had learned yet.

This goes for any endeavor you have mastered. For example, I have a few friends/students who spend much of their lives in wheel chairs. They cannot walk like most people, but they have gone through the same failure to success process in many areas. They learned to speak through making mistakes. They learned to write as we all do by making mistakes. No matter what you want to become good at, you have to try, learn from your errors, and improve. In martial arts, if you want to become a good fighter you are going to have to have things go wrong for you. Nobody just naturally has perfect technique and timing. It is developed through failure. In my JKD Unlimited classes we do a lot of sparring. It is done at various levels of intensity, depending upon the skill level, experience, and goals of the individual student, but most of the practice involves complete or isolated sparring. I emphasize that each time you get hit, kicked, taken down, or submitted you get better. So the idea is to do your best to help your partner improve! If you want to learn how to avoid takedowns, you need to know what it is like to really be taken down by someone who is skillful. Your body will make those adjustments if you drop the ego and get in there and train. We have to be smart about it, as we want to make sure that the failure we endure is beneficial. This brings us to the second F.

The second F stands for "forward". This means that the setbacks are such that we actually gain something useful from them. Someone might say "Hey, I want to learn how to fly, so I am going to jump off a twenty story building without a parachute. If I keep doing it enough, I'll learn what I need to know so that I can fly." Pretty obvious that there is going to be one big failure, and the thing that this person learns (people can't fly) is probably going to sink in as he is passing the tenth floor. A little late. In the fighting arts, you can also put yourself into a situation where the failure is detrimental. You could decide that you want to learn how to box, so the best way to do that is to find a boxing gym where up and coming pro fighters train. I have seen this many times in pro gyms. A new guy comes in. Many trainers are only interested in someone who is going to make them money in paid fights. The first thing they need to do is test the kid's heart. Is he a quitter or will he take a beating and keep fighting back? They throw him in with a mean, experienced fighter and the kid takes a colossal beating. If he never quits and shows some promise, the trainer may take him in. If not, he is out the door with a bad head ache and a severely bruised sense of self-esteem. This can be a very bad type of failure, as it can psychologically damage the well-meaning student. We want to fail "forward", not backward. If he goes into the boxing gym and gets to spar lightly, he will get hit and his body will start to adjust, instead of going into panic mode. He will get the feel for moving his head correctly and keeping his hands up. Over time he will become harder to hit, and will be able to look for openings to launch counter attacks. Eventually he may control the sparring sessions, setting up the opponent and scoring often. Even when he gets to this level, he will still get hit and will still be learning. All those little lessons he learned on the way up will be with him, but there is always more to learn.

The third F stands for "fast". We want to get those failures out of the way as quickly as possible to make our improvement happen at a rapid pace. This may be a very Western idea, but we tend to view life as being short, and we want to get where we are going in the most efficient manner possible. This doesn't mean sacrificing quality. We just want to enhance our qualities as efficiently as we can. Let's say that you have been grappling for a while and set a goal of winning a particular grappling championship. What should you do? Wait for that tournament to come around? No. You should enter every competition that you can. This is how you are going to get experience (i.e. failures) so that you can improve your game and be in top form for the targeted competition. When tournament day comes, you will be much better prepared. Maybe you don't know how to grapple at all and your goal is to become proficient on the ground. What should you do? Read about it for a few years before joining a school? Take one private lesson per month? No. You need to get in there and spend as many hours grappling as you can. You will make your mistakes and get them over with, instead of prolonging the process. Great grapplers have been arm barred, arm locked, and choked so many times that it is very difficult to fool them. They failed their way to success. Those who rose through the ranks quickly also paid close attention to their mistakes so that they didn't repeat them over and over again. This is another way to speed up the process. Pay attention to the problems and work hard to fix them.

Want to become a success quickly in any area of life? Then you need to Fail Forward Fast. Get good training, and make your mistakes as soon as you can. Have a good coach who can help you avoid making the same mistakes, and will guide you away from others.

There will be some pitfalls that you can avoid altogether by having a good coach. My baseball coach at U.S.C. always said "Don't make the same mistake once. Let someone else make it and learn from him. But there are some things that are only learned from personal experience. Be smart about it and be sure that you can survive any mistakes you set yourself up for. Don't be reckless, but please don't be afraid of making mistakes. You can be sure that anyone who has achieved anything has made tons of mistakes along the way. Use the 3F principle of Fail Forward Fast to improve quickly so that you can live the rest of your life as a success.

54. A BEAUTIFUL MARTIAL ARTS FANTASY

So you want to be able to protect yourself. Where are you going to go to get the best training possible? Let's indulge our wildest dreams, and imagine that we have absolutely unlimited funds for our pursuit of combative excellence. Now what would you do?

Since this is your passion, you are willing to bring in the very best trainers and fighters from around the world to guide you. Your interest is realistic, workable, self-defense. You don't just want to learn a bunch of moves, you want to actually be able to do them against someone who is trying their best to use their moves on you. With this in mind, you decide to train with those people who actually put their arts to the test. You realize that some of these arts are practiced as sports and are therefore limited by the rules, but you are wise enough to see that this is actually a benefit. You know that you want to be proficient in all areas of fighting, so you will bring in experts in various portions of the arts so that you can put together a puzzle that results in a beautiful, broad, brilliant picture brimming with detail. Who do we start with?

There are many choices, but you reason that most fights involve people punching at each other. You hire a top boxing coach. He works you on your punching skills, both offensive and defensive. A large part of your training is sparring. You didn't realize how important the legs are, but you get the point when your masseuse works on your lower body to knead out the kinks. You progress well, and figure it is time to add another element: kicking.

Your kicking specialist is a Tae Kwon Do champ. She is expert at whipping that foot out with power, speed, and accuracy. You spar each workout. You didn't realize how sore your upper body would be from kicking. Thank goodness for that masseuse!

More elements are needed. You opt for a Thai boxer to add in the low kicks, elbows, and knees. More surprises. Every inch of your body is sore. You swear that your hair is sore from those workouts, but you are loving every minute of it. You see that your boxing and kicking skills are very helpful, but things are different when the knees, elbows, and low kicks are included. The cardiovascular demands are greater than you are used to, but your body adapts as you train and spar. You are feeling comfortable now, so you search out another trainer.

You realize that your striking skills aren't going to do you too much good if you end up on the ground, so you find someone who can teach you how to defend takedowns. Who are the best at defending takedowns? Wrestlers. You bring in a top free-style wrestling coach, along with some of his wrestlers. Soreness again! Changing elevation, penetration steps, finishing the takedowns, sprawling, cross-faces, and getting slammed to the mat take their toll. You don't care, because you are improving rapidly, and you have that personal masseuse. Proficiency creeps up. You love the training, but want to work more in the clinch. Your free-style coach gives you a referral.

In comes the Greco Roman wrestling crew. Your neck wrestling in Thai boxing is very useful, but the Greco positioning and throws bring in a whole new series of elements. You get into the different tie-up positions, and you learn transitions and takedowns from each. You learn how to set up your moves in sparring, and you are getting better at defending the attacks. They also show you how to incorporate the freestyle takedowns into your sparring that are illegal in Greco Roman wrestling. You make great progress, but a question burns in the back of your mind.

What if I am proficient in all these areas, but I still get taken to the ground? Time to bring in a Brazilian jiu-jitsu team. A whole new world opens up. Arm bars, triangles, chokes, knee bars, sweeps, positioning, transitioning. This is going to take a while, but this is what you do. You are loving it, even though you get spanked every day in sparring. You still work on your other areas too, as you pay your other coaches to be on call. You now feel complete, but another question pops up.

How would punching change the clinch and ground game? You decide to start with the clinch. You know about the knees, but what about pure punching from a wrestler type? Your research assistant has good news for you: Senegalese wrestling. You fly in a team from

Senegal to learn their sport. You find that traditional Senegalese wrestling is a combination of hand strikes (no gloves) and wrestling. The winner is determined by knockout or solid takedown. They wear wrap around shorts that have a cord "belt". They grab the belt to aid in takedowns and avoiding takedowns. They start standing, with a stylized probing. As the punches fly hard and fast, an entry is made. You find that while you try to avoid the takedown, you partner is punching you hard with uppercuts and hooks to the face. (You don't care. You have the greatest plastic surgeon on the planet.) The coach teaches you well, and you are able to adapt quickly. Another element added into your game.

How about the ground? As a matter of fact, what happens if I can punch, kick, elbow, knee, and head butt standing, in the clinch, and on the ground? Then what? Here come the "vale tudo" fighters. No holds barred fighting (including head butts) puts everything in perspective for you. You must be able to strike, wrestle, submit, and defend against submissions and strikes in every position. All of your previous training is melded into a contiguous whole. Time passes, and you are feeling very good about your game. One day your eight year old nephew visits. He is feisty. You playfully put up your hands and take a fighting stance. He promptly kicks you in the groin, sending you down for the count.

You regain your composure, and realize that you left out a few elements. What to do? You know that without sparring there is no measurable progress. Techniques are just techniques until you can actually put them into use through sparring. You call NASA. If they can put a man on the moon, they can design a comfortable groin protector that absorbs every milligram of impact. You ask for eye and throat protection too. You realize that you have totally ignored weaponry, so you ask them to make the safest training knife on the planet while you start taking knife lessons with top Filipino martial arts fighters and pistol defense with Krav Maga special forces trainers.

A few months later your pocket is a million dollars lighter, but your groin is protected. You are happy. You spar like a vale tudo fighter with all the targets in play. You learned about scenario training, environmental influences, and weapons draws so you add these in. You hired a couple guys who sole job is to sneak up on you and attack you a few times per month. Your family thinks you are crazy, but you are content. Why? Because you have become a functional martial artist whose training has no end in sight!

55. NEW AND IMPROVED JKD BETTER THAN EVER

Jeet Kune Do. What an enigma. A young man named Bruce Lee, who majored in philosophy in college, used his study of philosophy to improve and expand beyond the norm through his physical expression of martial arts. Philosophy is so important to each of us, because our personal philosophies are what guide our lives. Also, our martial arts philosophies guide our training, and our training is what determines our skill levels and preparedness for an actual street encounter. Observe a training session and you observe the prevailing philosophy of that martial arts group. Watch a JKD Unlimited training session and you will know that our philosophy is to have fun while training hard in all the ranges. You will see lots of serious sparring, and hear lots of laughing. This is our philosophy in action, and it defines us. We test everything for ourselves, so that each person knows what he or she does best.

Why all this talk about philosophy? Because this is what made JKD so special. Rather than forms and dead patterns, which were the norm in the martial arts world, Bruce Lee had the ability to see through the "classical mess" and move beyond it. He constantly evolved toward a better understanding of combative training through research, training, and experience. One needs only look at how the training progressed from his days in Seattle, to those in Oakland, and then to his school in Los Angeles to see the trend of adding functional techniques and training methods while deleting those that no longer proved themselves. The L.A. period alone saw many improvements in a very short time. What does all this adding and subtracting mean? It means that Bruce Lee knew that he didn't have it perfect, and that the art could always be improved. Does that make sense to you? I hope so, because the fact that everything can be improved is a constant in life, just as everything can be worsened if we are not vigilant.

Let's talk about how JKD has been improved since Lee's early departure from our earthly realm. Lee constantly improved the art over time, and it would be a shame for us to not continue that trend. I do think it is valuable to preserve the physical techniques that Lee evolved through during his lifetime, as it gives us a perspective of how much evolution there was. We just don't want to stop there. That would be like going to a Colonial America museum, then adopting that lifestyle in 2002! I prefer driving in a car, using my home theater system, and flying in airplanes to get from here to Europe. The same applies for my fight training. I want to use the best vehicles that we have come across to get me where I need to go.

To see where the improvements have been, let's understand that much of martial art consists of the 3 Ts: Techniques, Tactics, and Training methods. There are other aspects, such as culture, tradition, etc., but let's just look at the fighting aspect right now. Bruce Lee broke technique down into the ranges in which they occur. He described kicking, punching, trapping, and grappling ranges.

KICKING RANGE:

This is a range that has not changed much at all since the 70's. Lee had elements of gung fu, TKD, Thai boxing, and French savate in his kicking arsenal. We have just added a few ways to kick from the ground that were not in the original art.

PUNCHING RANGE:

The punching has changed very little also, since it was based primarily off of Western boxing, wing chun, and choy li fut. The most significant addition would be the "boxing blast" which is similar to the wing chun straight blast, but is much more powerful and the structure is more protective than the wing chun method. The boxing blast is where you would "run" at your opponent with short, choppy steps while throwing a series of fast, powerful crosses. As you run, if your right foot is landing forward on the ground, your left cross is making contact, then as you continue forward with your left foot, your right hand makes contact. This has been proven to work very well, even in championship level No Holds Barred fighting events.

The other modification is that many JKDers are now using palm strikes more readily, due to the trauma that a closed fist often suffers after making hard impact with an unfriendly skull.

TRAPPING RANGE:

This is where major changes have been made. JKD is primarily designed for defending oneself against a street attack. The reference point based trapping techniques have been proven to be ineffective in the majority of combative situations. Is it possible to pull off a trap, such as a pak sau, lop sau, jut sau, etc. in sparring? Absolutely. But the idea of seeking a reference point in order to apply a trap is not efficient. That is the reality. Classical hand trapping works against a defensive opponent; one who is either static, or one who is just blocking. Think about it. If you do a pak sao, lop sao combination, the opponent has to stay fairly stationary while he lets his hand be trapped, then blocks your punch, and then gets trapped again. He is not attacking!!! He is waiting for you to do your traps. A real attacker throws a barrage of punches, pushes you, tackles, and grabs. It is easier to get a single trap in sparring, because there is usually a lot of moving around and sizing up your opponent. During the give and take of sparring, there are times when the opponent's hands are up, but he is not attacking. Simple traps are extremely useful in this environment, but look out for that cross in case he throws it while you are coming straight in. We have added solid head movement with our functional trapping.

We have added a great deal of clinch work, starting with the Thai boxing clinch on the neck. Dan Inosanto stressed Thai boxing training in the late 70's, and continues to do so to this day due to its effectiveness and conditioning aspect. We also use boxing methods to get into the clinch, and in recent years we have rounded it all out with the fabulous addition of modified Greco Roman wrestling techniques, mainly through Greco Roman wrestling and UFC champion Randy Couture. The concept of trapping is to control the opponent's hands so that he cannot strike, while putting yourself into a position to attack. We now have many clinch techniques that put us into this favorable position, even though the attacker is actually attacking. This is a huge addition to modern functional JKD.

GRAPPLING RANGE:

There are two parts to this range: standing grappling and ground grappling. While Bruce Lee had incorporated a few throws and a little ground work, grappling was definitely the weakest link in the JKD chain. The addition of great takedowns from wrestling and Brazilian jiu-jitsu has helped us tremendously. We are better at doing the takedown, and at defending from being taken down. Thanks to the Gracies, Machados, and many others, 90% of our ground fighting is from Brazilian jiu-jitsu, with some wrestling and other components rounding it out. This is a whole world in itself, and must be worked on diligently if one wants to become skillful. Being able to control an opponent on the ground and apply chokes, joint locks, or striking puts you at a great advantage. It is a wonderful addition, as it can help us to neutralize someone who is much larger and stronger by putting them onto their backs where their strength and mobility are hampered.

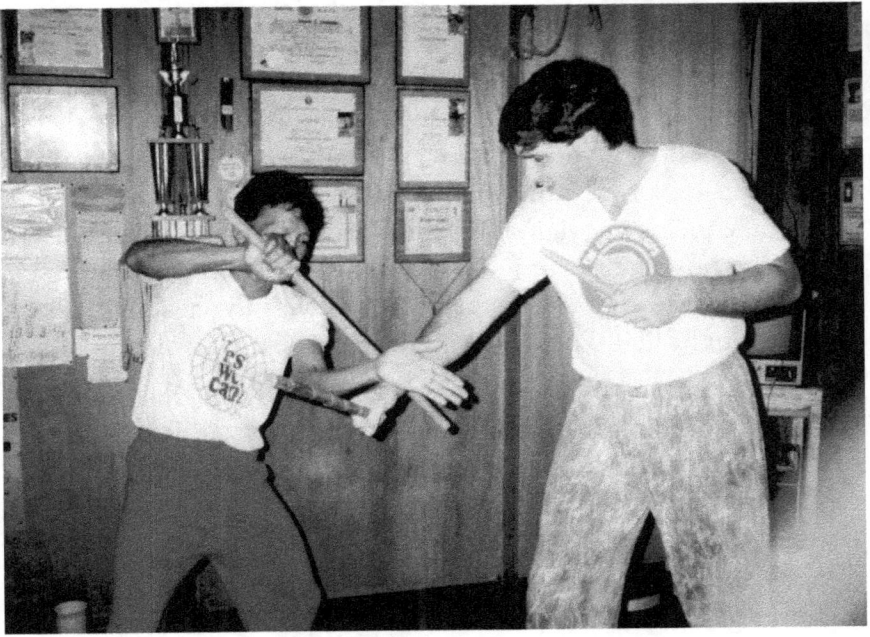

Those are the empty-hand ranges. Today, we usually refer to the ranges as just being kickboxing, clinch, and ground. This is simpler, and deletes the artificial range that must be held for compound trapping to work.

WEAPONRY:

Another area that has been greatly expanded is the use of and defense against weapons. The addition of the Filipino martial arts (thanks to Dan Inosanto) has given us an awareness of how dangerous a knife or stick really is, and has allowed us to hone our skills in dealing with an armed assailant. This is now an important part of our training, as it is likely that someone who is bent on robbing you will be armed. Great influence from my fellow Dog Brothers has guided the current expression of weaponry training amongst those bent on practicing practical weapons defense while simultaneously learning how to utilize a weapon against a dangerous attacker.

We have looked at techniques, but how about tactics? The way you approach a fight depends upon the techniques you have in your arsenal. Having a complete clinch and ground game means that you can now choose to move in and take an opponent to the ground, if you feel it is safe to do so. Since you are aware of how quickly one can be taken down, your kickboxing changes to make sure you are in position to sprawl if an opponent shoots in at your legs. One of the takedowns in original JKD has been modified because it was too dangerous against someone who knew even a little submission grappling. Instead of charging straight in with the head at the side, we place our head in a position where it is more difficult to be choked.

Another tactic we use is to rely on gross motor skill techniques. Under combat stress, we now know that it is very difficult to think, so we must rely on those techniques that are easily ingrained, and require no fine motor skills. This is another reason that compound trapping is not practiced by reality based JKD fighters. If it is difficult to do a technique against a cooperative partner, how are you ever going to do it against someone who is resisting you? The interesting paradox here is that there are complex techniques that can be done on the ground while under stress, because there is less movement there, and it is easier to physically control the movements of an opponent when you have your arms and legs wrapped around them. Even so, we primarily train those techniques that work with the natural movements of our entire body so that we can apply them under pressure.

Another tactic we now utilize is often referred to as "verbal judo". This is the art of talking your way out of a bad situation. There are many ways that you may be able to de-escalate a situation through good verbal skills. Much better than fighting!

Training methods are what really determine how skillful you become. You can have great techniques and superb tactics, but if you don't train them properly you will be lost. Bruce Lee advised us to "get in the water" and do a lot of sparring. Although imperfect, this is still the greatest training method we have. We have improved upon sparring by doing so in all the ranges. This means that we spend many of our rounds where we mix everything together, just as you might do in the street. Kicking, punching, clinch, throws, ground, back to standing, and in whatever order it naturally occurs. We also isolate sparring in different ranges, and may also restrict the attacks so that we can work on one particular area of our total expression.

Another good addition to sparring is the development of drills that simulate the ambush factor. Many real attacks begin as an ambush. The attacker rushes you when you aren't looking, and tries to finish you as quickly as possible. We now have sparring drills that simulate this environment. It is not like regular sparring where a certain pacing always seems to creep in. A real fight is a sprint, not a jog, and we have to practice "sprinting" in order to gain the necessary skill. Being the ambushee always puts you at a disadvantage, but proper practice makes you more prepared for this common assault.

Another training method that we are using is to enter competitions. Many will say that JKD is not for competition, and that is true. We emphasize eye gouges and groin strikes. But JKD sparring usually is kickboxing oriented, so why not do a kickboxing match where you get to go full power against a skillful opponent? You get to deal with nervousness, fear, and lots of other emotions that may come up in a real fight. We encourage people to enter No Holds Barred events if they express an interest and are ready to compete. I competed in kickboxing and stickfighting, and those experiences did wonders for my understanding of the art. It is just another way to bring your training up a notch.

In class, we do spar often with eye and groin protection so that we can kickbox, clinch, and grapple while delivering and protecting from attacks to the eyes and groin. This changes the structure in the clinch and on the ground, and has already made vast improvements in the students.

Thanks to the work of Tony Blauer, we now practice psychological preparedness as well. Tony has also helped us by encouraging the use of scenarios, where students get out of the typical dojo mentality and put themselves in a real-world situation and have to find a solution.

As you can see, JKD has changed dramatically from the time that Bruce Lee first called his art JKD, to the time of his passing, and up until the present. It is constant evolution, and we have Bruce Lee to thank for his inspiration and courage to go outside of tradition and blaze his own trail. He was able to cut that trail deep into the new frontier, and we honor him by continuing that work. Many people inside and outside of JKD have contributed to this effort, and I thank them all. My work with JKD Unlimited has been very gratifying, and my students around the world are very appreciative of the help that we have gotten along the way.

56. PROGRESSIVE RESISTANCE & VARIABLE INTENSITY

Let's talk a little about Resistance. People often get squeamish at the thought of training with resistance, as they envision a hulking opponent smashing them repeatedly in the face. Not a pretty picture. In fact it is one I have been on the receiving end of. I had been boxing for about a year when my coach had me spar with the legendary Tex Cobb's bodyguard at the old Main Street Boxing Gym in downtown Los Angeles. This guy was huge, and weighed in at nearly three hundred pounds! My coach told him to take it easy, as he had boxed professionally. Unfortunately, some people have a hard time turning the intensity down. (This is why we make sure that our students are paired up with others who want to train at the same level of intensity. We also use helmets!)

We got in the ring and I had just started moving with him when he unleashed a tremendous jab that I distinctly remember to this day. Let's just say that I learned the difference between having my hands up under my chin and really having my hands up in front of my face! That thunderous jab drove me back into the ropes, almost off my feet. Up went my hands, and boy did my head start moving! So did my feet. I was all over that ring. Luckily, I was in better shape and he tired out with about thirty seconds in the round. Most people will never go back to training after getting a headache like I had, but my coach was so encouraging that I didn't give up.

This is the normal method in boxing gyms. Many professional coaches first want to see if a prospective fighter has heart, so they toss him in the ring with a pro to see how they handle the beating. If they have heart, they will train them so they can try to make a living off of them. My goal is to get the realistic training to everyone, so instead of "sink or swim", I employ the concept of Progressive Resistance. I got this term from bodybuilding, and I like to use a weight lifting analogy to explain this principle.

Imagine that you decide to sign up at a weightlifting gym. (Martial arts sounded too dangerous!) You have a personal trainer to teach you how to lift correctly and get you going in the right direction. You tell the trainer that you want to work on your leg strength. She says okay, and teaches you how to do a squat. She puts a broomstick across your shoulders, feet shoulder width apart, has you keep your back straight while bending at the knees. She points out that you should sit back, almost like sitting in a chair, to avoid having your knees move out in front of your toes. Better for your knees and better for balance. After a few minutes you can duplicate the squat correctly. Now what did you actually just learn? You learned a technique. That would be like going to our JKDU/HP-MMA class and learning the mechanics to throw a solid punch. It has taken you about three minutes to learn the proper form for the technique called the squat. Now what happens? Do you just practice that technique with the broomstick for the next three years? No.

Your trainer takes you to the squat rack. Why? Because you have to add resistance if you want to get stronger. Doing the technique with resistance is going to trigger the Adaptive Response. If you don't add resistance you are not going to get stronger. If you don't add resistance in your fight training you won't develop fighting skill. Let's now say that your wonderful trainer takes you to the squat rack and proceeds to load the bar with 300 pounds! What is going to happen if you try to squat that much your first day? You are going to break something! Why? TOO MUCH RESISTANCE! You have to start with just enough resistance to make the effort slightly difficult. This causes your body to adapt. You go in the following week and you can add a little more resistance. Over time, depending on your goals, you may be able to squat with 300 pounds.

The exact same theory of Progressive Resistance holds true for our fight training. Too much resistance is counterproductive. You will actually be worse off by adding too much resistance than not training at all. Instead, the trick is to add enough resistance to make it slightly difficult to apply your technique. As you improve, you add more resistance. The amount you end up training with depends upon your goals. I call this VARIABLE INTENSITY TRAINING, as each person in class trains at his or her own level. Our rule is that when two people play together, the intensity is adjusted for whoever wants to go lighter. Some people lift weights to tone up, others train to be bodybuilders. Some people want to train martial arts for health and self-defense; others want to become cage fighting champions. The amount of resistance and the level of intensity will differ depending upon your goals. You may end up doing two sets of squats with 135 pounds. You stop when you start to feel the burn. A professional may build up to 400 pounds over six sets, taking many of the sets to the point where they cannot possibly do another rep. (Those are the guys screaming in the corner of the gym.) They add more resistance at a greater level of intensity. In our training, I can spar at full resistance, doing my best to defend each offensive attempt from my opponent, but without using full intensity. I can strike quickly, but without full power so that my partner is not overwhelmed. That way we all improve and have fun doing it.

There is one more very important aspect of this weight lifting analogy.

Whether you are in the gym to tone up or to become a competitive bodybuilder, THE BASIC TECHNIQUES YOU PERFORM ARE THE SAME! You do squats, bench press, curls, lat pulls, etc. The professional adds greater intensity and uses more variations of each technique, but the basics are the same. This holds true for fight training as well. The basics will be the same whether you are a hobbyist or a professional fighter. There is no need to have one curriculum for fighters and an entirely different curriculum for people who want to learn self-defense. The professional is just more skillful in the basics and has more variations. Nothing magic, just scientifically tested techniques and training methods performed using progressive resistance to build that skill.

I hope you can see why Progressive Resistance is an extremely important part of our training. This is what allows people of all ages, sizes, and goals to train in the same general manner as an "Ultimate Fighting Champion". Since the concept of progressively adding more and more Resistance is not widely understood, many martial arts systems simply don't include that all-important factor that triggers the Adaptive Response: RESISTANCE! They instead practice forms, drills, and techniques where neither person ever actually fights back. These drills and techniques are performed without any resistance of any kind. Bruce Lee used the term "aliveness" to talk about adding resistance. This is often misinterpreted. People will take a technique that is practiced without resistance and try to make it "alive". They do this by bouncing around like Muhammad Ali while doing the technique, but still without resistance. Bouncing around does not make it alive. Resistance makes it alive. Movement is part of resistance, and it is easy to confuse the two. If your partner is trying to keep you from performing your technique, then there is resistance and you are going to improve.

Intensity is also mistaken for resistance. A person can go through a technique routine with a well-trained, compliant partner at great intensity. This is wonderful in demonstrations. One person feeds and the other person flies into a fast, intense series of blocks, eye strikes, nerve hits, followed by a takedown. Very impressive. That guy was moving with unbelievable speed, precision, and power. If you were to watch the demonstration again, it is best to watch the feeder. What you will usually see is a person who throws a punch then stands there like a statue while the defender goes through the routine. No resistance. There is great intensity in this type of demonstration, but without resistance you won't be able to deal with a real attacker who will resist 100%.

Am I saying that it is useless to train without resistance? No. Training without resistance is important to memorize the various techniques. By memorize I mean that your body has to develop the coordination for the technique so that you have all the details in place. You can also use them for conditioning the body. Just like learning the squat, you need to learn each technique. But, again like the squat, it should only take a few minutes to learn most techniques. There are only two types of drills that martial artists do. Memorization drills or resistance drills. I call resistance drills Performance Games. We learn the technique, and then put it right into the Performance Game so that you develop the skill to utilize the technique while under pressure.

Is an attacker in the street going to resist you? Absolutely. If you don't practice with resistance you won't be able to handle the situation. I'm going to say it again.

"If you want to learn how to fight, you must practice fighting against someone who is fighting back!"

57. QUESTION THE ANSWERS

It is interesting to note that everything in our lives can be made better. There is always room for improvement in every facet of our lives, and in everything around us. This is very true of our martial arts training. It will continue to evolve and change for the better as long as we persevere in our quest for the truth, constantly looking for those techniques and training methods that yield favorable results under the stressful and unpredictable reality of combat. The only way to keep this upward spiral of growth alive is to constantly question the answers that we tend to take as gospel.

It is easy to fall into the trap of being what one of my friends calls a "true believer". This is someone who believes so much in his or her system that no actual thought is given as to whether or not the techniques or training methods are valid, i.e. actually functional in combat. A typical conversation can go like this. "Does that technique work?" "Of course!" "How do you know that?" "My sifu told me so." "How does he know that it works?" (This question is rarely asked because the sifu is supposedly beyond reproach, and can never be questioned!) "Sifu said that his sifu said that it worked." "And how did that sifu know that the technique worked?" "Because the great grandmaster of the system said so 400 years ago!" This is a common line of reasoning that is simply not reasonable. Krishnamurti referred to this kind of reliance on others for your information as being a second hand human being. If you really want to understand the martial arts, the information must come from first hand experience, or it is merely hearsay.

This is something I emphasize to my students. Learning the martial arts through the Jeet Kune Do approach should be experiential. The student must learn for him or herself. Instead of watching others or taking someone else's word, you should find out if it works for you. This is the path to developing true confidence in your art. If you have never tried to pull off your technique against an aggressive opponent, what is going to happen if you have to face a large aggressive foe in the street? The street is not the time to find out whether you have developed timing, power, and flow. Discover this in the school where you aren't going to be sent off to the hospital for making a mistake. Practicing in a more realistic environment will prepare you physically and mentally for the street.

This brings us back to questioning the answers. You must try to look at your training with the eyes of a child who has never seen your particular methods. After training for years it is easy to become so used to doing the same old things that you forget to analyze your art. If you want to be your best, it is imperative that you periodically analyze your training and see what you can do to improve yourself. Here are a few questions that you can ask yourself.

1. Is my current training method the end-all be-all, perfect martial art? If you truly believe that it is, growth is going to be difficult for you to sustain. No method is "perfect", because situations always change. There is always a new counter waiting to be discovered and another counter after that. Nobody knows it all. We all have partial truths. The only thing that really counts when under the stress of combat is whether or not you can apply some portion of your art that is appropriate at that particular time against that particular opponent.

2. Are my training methods as good as they can be? Spar with some of the top fighters in other arts and find out. If you have experience in your art, but are totally lost when sparring, there may be a problem. If you do well, you should still recognize that there are always new training methods to experience.

3. Am I really a complete fighter? It is very important to be a complete martial artist, because in the street you can't always dictate the range that the fight takes place in. Can you fight well in kicking

range? How about in punching, or trapping range? Can you keep someone from taking you to the ground? How are you in the clinch? On the ground? With weapons? Defending against weapons? Do you have sound tactics for multiple opponents? Have you tried them out? Competence in all ranges is a must.

4. If there is a range that I don't train in, why don't I? Is it because of fear of the unknown? Afraid that you might look silly? Afraid of what your students might think if they find out that you don't know everything? Just jump in there and practice and in a few years you will be comfortable in the new range, and you will have more to teach.

5. Are the techniques I am using actually battle tested? Techniques that work against a cooperative, slow moving opponent may not work well against an aggressive attacker. Speed, power, and unpredictable movement must be countered with strong basics, not flashy, complicated combos.

6. If I think my techniques are battle tested, am I getting this information through 2nd or 3rd hand knowledge, or by way of my own experience? If you haven't done it or seen in done under stress, you don't really know.

This is the scientific approach. We have to constantly ask ourselves tough questions if we want to get solid answers. It is very important to me that my students are receiving the best techniques and training methods that I can find. Sooner or later one of those students is going to get into a bad situation and if I have merely been entertaining that student with the fanciest techniques that I can find, there is a good chance that he or she is going to get hurt. I couldn't live with that. That is why I am so adamant about my research and development. Not just for my own training, but so I can make the road a little shorter and a bit straighter for my students.

Enjoy your training, and be happy each time you discover a weakness. That is the first step to massive improvement!

58. THE CHANGE THAT MADE ALL THE DIFFERENCE

In 1992 I was living in Long Beach, California, training and teaching a variety of martial arts. At that time, my emphasis was to research every art and instructor I could find. I would practice, and then pass as much of the new information along to my students as possible. I did this through my school and through seminars that I taught. Over time, I found myself teaching about three out of state or international seminars per month. I worked hard at my training and teaching, and with the help of my wonderful and extremely generous mentor Dan Inosanto, I was able teach seminars that were very popular. Little by little, something unexpected happened. I was being recognized for my hard work and attention to detail, but in that search for more and better ways, I began training with a different type of martial artist: the fighter.

These were guys who had no interest in uniforms, history, etiquette, or hierarchy. They just wanted to practice fighting to become better fighters. The main training method was sparring in all the ranges. As I engaged in sparring with a variety of fighters, from jiu-jitsu champions to kickboxing champions to wrestling champions, I discovered that I knew a huge amount of techniques, but could not apply much of it against a trained combat athlete. It didn't all present itself at once, but I had to admit an awful truth to myself; when matched against top competitors I couldn't stick fight well, kickbox well, or grapple well. That was extremely disheartening. What to do?

Well, I did something that I must admit that I am now very proud of. As I continued to train with professional NHB fighters I came to a decision. I would no longer teach the theoretical aspects of the martial arts that I loved so much to students in class or in my seminars. I was determined that my students would all be able to fight well. I also decided to stay with the concepts of Bruce Lee by making sure that everything we did was street applicable instead of being designed specifically for the rules of the ring or cage. I have nothing against teaching the traditional arts, or practicing the demonstration moves, but I decided that for myself, I would focus on only those training methods, techniques, and tactics that worked consistently against an aggressive, skilled opponent. I informed all my seminar hosts of my new direction. Guess what happened? My seminars dropped off precipitously. Most people were simply not interested in this type of training. They wanted the trapping drills and high speed multiple disarm techniques. And that is fine, but this severely impacted my income which was highly reliant on seminars. You might think I was tempted to go back to teaching the "art" portion, but I really wasn't. To feel good about myself, I needed to follow the most important, guiding principle in my life, which is to be true to myself and my beliefs while being open to trying new approaches. I went back to my academic roots (I graduated in biology from USC and worked in a Harbor UCLA research lab) and applied it to martial arts.

I tested everything through strict adherence to the scientific method to see if the results were favorable and could be duplicated by others consistently. My pledge was and is to avoid teaching anything that has not been tested and proven effective in rigorous sparring or in an actual fight. Until we can make it work under the high stress of combat, there is no sense in passing it along. Well, guess what happened then? A new type of student and seminar host began to emerge, one that was there all the time. These are the people who knew what fights looked like. Maybe they had done amateur boxing or did wrestling in college. Maybe they had been picked on in their youth and had to fight to survive. These students with great attitudes who were mainly interested in fighting proficiency started coming to class and hosting this new type of seminar. I am also proud to report that many of my students decided to change with me and have developed into formidable fighters who prepare their students to defend themselves against a aggressive attackers.

I can sum up what I have learned about effective self-defense training in my one sentence quote: "If you want to learn how to fight, you must practice fighting against someone who is fighting back." Very simple, and anyone in any style of martial arts can use this as a guideline. I still love doing weaponry work in the air and Silat dance. This type of training is highly functional for maintaining health and mental acuity, and, as Guro Inosanto says, "Fighting aging". And it just plain feels good. But if part of your martial arts goal is to be able to defend yourself, then you should regularly try your stuff out. Put on protective equipment, go against someone who is fighting back and see what happens. This is the essence of what I have done, and anybody in any style can do it. We can't help but learn and improve when we regularly put ourselves into the crucible of combat.

59. LOYALTY

In the martial arts world we often hear about the importance of loyalty to whichever style you happen to be training in. I believe that in the martial arts or any area of our lives, our first loyalty should be to the truth. We must always search for that which is true in our art and within ourselves. This way we can discover what really works and what is just cultural conditioning. There are hundreds of things in western society that are deemed unacceptable in other societies. Why? Cultural conditioning. It is illegal in the U.S. for a woman to bathe topless at the beach, but normal, without any sexual stigmas, in many other parts of the world. Why? Cultural conditioning. The same in martial arts. Students are conditioned to believe that their style's way is the very best, but without actually testing the methods. They rely on belief rather than experiencing truth.

Students are often conditioned to have "loyalty" to their instructor. This came from the village days when the military leader needed loyalty to ensure that all secrets were kept away from the enemy. Nowadays, this is partially a business tactic to retain students. I believe it should be the other way around. If a teacher is loyal to their students, that teacher will encourage his or her students to train with anyone who can improve them. This is what my main teacher Guro Dan Inosanto does and I do the same because it is best for the students. I even do it when it is not best for me, as when I sometimes direct a paying student to another school that is better for that student's particular goals. We want to avoid instilling blind loyalty. Blind loyalty is what causes a county of good people to support an inhumane dictator. A similar fervor exists in many martial arts due to instructor influence and the fact that we humans always want to believe that whatever group we are associated with is the very best.

First, be loyal to the truth. Be loyal to honesty. Nobody knows it all. If my students are so "loyal" that they just do what I do, I will never learn from them and we will all stagnate. I want them to train with the truth in mind so that they can show me where I can improve. Guro Dan Inosanto always emphasizes that no two people are going to have the exact same view, and that everyone should express their own "way" in the arts. He is loyal to his students, and therefore receives loyalty in return. The truth is outside any particular style, and can be found living and changing within us every moment. If we embrace that truth, we will be better off for it.

60. MY LAST OFFERING

Twelve years ago I turned in my first Inside Kung Fu column. It was a piece on the Indonesian art of pentjak silat, an art which was rarely heard of at that time. The article was also a sort of "try out" to see if could handle a monthly column slot. I still remember what IKF editor said to me on the phone. "If you keep writing like this you will be here a long time." Twelve years is a long time, and this will mark my last column for the magazine. IKF is moving toward further representation and emphasis of traditional Chinese martial arts, along with features on other arts. This is not what I tend to write about, and therefore the column no longer fits. So to finish up a good run, I would like to go through a few of the most important things that I have learned through my martial studies in the last dozen years.

For me, the most important aspect of the physical art that I have understood is summed up with the following saying. "Knowledge is not power, the ability to apply your knowledge under pressure is true power." As much as I loved teaching and practicing the wide myriad of drills and amazing techniques that the martial arts of the world have to offer, I eventually directed myself toward the purely self-defense aspects of the arts. In this quest I found that there are two main points that we should all adhere to develop practical martial arts skills.

WE MUST PRACTICE FIGHTING IN ALL THE RANGES. Fights happen in all distances. They just do. No amount of training can keep a surprise attack from putting you on the ground. If we want to really be prepared, we must practice in all the distances, regardless of your style.

WE MUST TRAIN AGAINST AN UNCOOPERATIVE PARTNER. We can make any technique look plausible against a partner who stands just right and feeds the perfect energy. A real attacker will fight you 100%. Training with resistance doesn't mean all-out sparring, but training at a safe intensity against a partner who does not give you any breaks.

These are the two most important aspects of self-defense training. Regardless of style, your self-defense training should embrace both of these aspects if you want to be well prepared for an all-out street attack. Some people are more focused on the artistic expression of the martial arts and I respect that. But we must realize that preparing for a fight is different than preparing for an exhibition. I have written about the details at length, but my advice is always the same. Don't just believe me and my experience. Get in there and do your sparring. If possible, do what I do and spar with every top fighter you can. We can't help but learn and improve when we put ourselves in the crucible of combat. As BJJ great John Machado once told me, "No sparring, no miracles."

Probably the greatest personal directive that I have learned through martial arts training is that we need to get out there and do the things we wish to do. Time passes quickly, especially when you don't take action towards your goals. Set a goal, make a good plan, get good training, and make it happen. Learn to take quality actions and you will reach your goal. Part of doing what you wish to do also involves your personal relationships. In this I have been indeed fortunate. I live in Honolulu, Hawaii with my lovely and loving wife Sarah. She is an amazing person, and has greatly enhanced the quality of my life. I am also blessed to be surrounded by many, many wonderful friends who are really more than friends. We are part of a family. This includes my amazing friends all over the U.S., South Africa, Italy, and in many other countries. Each and every one of these people has encouraged me and inspired me to become a better fighter, coach, and person. I am indeed very fortunate, and I am exceedingly thankful for each of you.

I want to sincerely thank Dave Cater for taking a chance on me so many years ago, and for being such a great guide since then. He is a good friend and has always been ready to help. I want to thank Curtis Wong also, as he pushed to get me started. Thanks also to everyone at Unique Publications. If you want to see what I am up to, I will continue to write on my website. Check in at www.jkdunlimited.com to see my latest work. I am very happy with my current research and am eager to share it with all who want to improve along with me.

So much can be done if we just do a little each day. In the last twelve years I have put out 28 videos, countless articles, a book, and have traveled to the Philippines, Brazil, all over South Africa, Reunion Island, France, Spain, all over Italy, England, Japan, Switzerland, and more. I have appeared in 15 Hollywood films as a stunt man, actor, and fight choreographer. I have produced 12 instructional videos for other instructors, and am now producing short films. I have also written six screenplays which I hope to produce in the coming years. I even moved from Los Angeles to this paradise called Hawaii. A little each day makes a lot! Just be true to yourself and strive to enjoy each moment of each day. Focus on the positive, because even when prospects look bleak there is always so much more to be thankful for. Develop an attitude of gratitude and it will take you a long way toward finding happiness.

BURTON RICHARDSON: AN UNLIMITED JOURNEY

By Jose M. Fraguas

Burton Richardson started training martial arts in 1979 and he has never stopped. He was lucky to take his first lessons at the original Kali Academy, home of martial arts greats Sifu Richard Bustillo and Guro Dan Inosanto. He also became a senior full instructor under Sifu Larry Hartsell.

Richardson traveled the world extensively to pursue his passion. He trained in Manila under Grandmaster Antonio Ilustrisimo, Master Tony Diego, and Master Christopher Ricketts. He's visited Brazil to practice Brazilian Jiu Jitsu. He earned his Black Belt in 2006 under the first non-Brazilian BJJ world champion Egan Inoue and has trained extensively with many top Brazilian Jiu Jitsu exponents, including the Machado Brothers, Carlson Gracie, Baret Yoshida, Charuto Verissimo, and Marcelo Garcia. Burton has even journeyed to South Africa several times to train with Zulu warriors in their method of stick fighting.

His constant quest for self-improvement and continued research has most recently led him to earn the rank of black belt in the art of Krav Maga and is an instructor in the South African Piper knife fighting system.

This broad spectrum of experience gives him a unique perspective on the arts. Civilians as well as Law Enforcement Officers (LEOs) seek his courses for training and practical combat knowledge.

He is the author of several books and was elected self-defense instructor of the year by "Black Belt" Magazine and inducted into their "Hall of Fame".

How long have you been practicing the martial arts and who are your teachers?

I started my training and studying in 1979, so it has been 44 years. Does that make me old?

I was extremely fortunate to start at the original Kali Academy under Sifu/Guro Dan Inosanto and Sifu Richard Bustillo. I've trained with many great instructors, but I will just list the ones that I actually have spent a significant amount of time training with. Out of respect, I will not count people I trained with on seminars or in just a few classes. I will list the instructors in chronological order of when I started training with them. I am so grateful for each of their influences.

In JKD, I trained under Sifu Dan Inosanto, Sifu Richard Bustillo, Sifu Chris Kent, Sifu Mark Mikita, Sifu Larry Hartsell, Sifu Tim Tackett, Sifu Taky Kimura and Sifu Leo Fong.

In Filipino Martial Arts under Guro Dan Inosanto, Guro Richard Bustillo, Guro Chris Kent, Guro Mark Mikita, Guro Ted Lucaylucay, Guro Eric "Top Dog" Knaus, Punong Guro Edgar Sulite, Master Roberto Labaniego, Grandmaster Antonio "Tatang" Ilustrisimo, Master Tony Diego and Master Christopher Ricketts.

In Silat under Guru Dan Inosanto, Pak Herman Suwanda and Pendeker Paul DeThouars. I also trained with a man from Laos, but he prefers not to have his name mentioned.

In Muay Thai under Kru Dan Inosanto and Master Chai Sirisute.

In Brazilian Jiu Jitsu under Master Rigan Machado, Chris Haueter, Egan Inoue, Baret Yoshida, Charuto Verissimo and Marcelo Garcia.

In MMA under Egan Inoue, Enson Inoue, Randy Couture, Robert Follis.

I have many friends in South Africa and for Zulu Martial Arts. I want to especially nthank to Barry Leitch, Blessing, Star, and Skei.

In Krav Maga, I trained with Nir Maman and in Piper Knife System under the guidance of Lloyd DeJongh.

How many styles or systems of Martial Arts have you trained in?

In addition to the ones listed above, I have studied other arts or sub-systems of those previously mentioned. It is a daily passion [more like an obsession] with me to constantly study, grow, and improve.

Did training in different arts at the same time create some kind of "problem" for you from the perspective of assimilating techniques from very different styles?

I have found that studying different styles gives me more perspectives and points of reference from which to learn new styles. For example, when I was learning the Ilustrisimo system in Manila, all my years of training in various other Filipino martial arts through Guro Dan gave me a base from which to work. I just had to make minor adjustments and add details or certain movements to what I already knew. That helped me to learn very quickly.

This also helps tremendously when training in entirely different arts. My Kali experience helped tremendously with my MMA training, as many tactics carried over. I believe that as long as you do your sparring, you won't get confused.

Would you tell us some interesting stories of your early days in Kali and some anecdotes during that time?

It was Kali that caught me hook line and sinker and really pulled me into the martial arts. The first night I got to watch a class at the original Kali Academy in 1979, I was enthralled. The students were training in a very athletic way which appealed to me since I was a baseball player. They were shadow boxing, skipping rope, hitting mitts, and then they put the gloves on and sparred. One student got a bloody nose right in front of me! That was pretty exciting for the 17-year-old version of myself!

I was having a very good time watching when Guro Dan signaled to the students to get out the weapons. There were aluminum training swords hanging on the wall and there were sticks and other implements in a wicker basket. The students went over, grabbed the training weapons, and Guro Dan started to play the drums. The students began to move in a way that absolutely mesmerized me. (I later learned that first drill is called "Numerada"). It was pure magic. That was it. I was hooked!

I remember having a distinct thought as I watched it all. My thought was "I will never be able to move like that, but I am sure going to try to learn as much as I can." I am so thankful that I was later accepted into the Academy and was able to train with Guro Dan, and later with many of those students I watched the first night.

How hard did you find the training at those early stages of your development as a martial artist?

Let me tell you, it was a work out! I would literally ring my shirt out after class, as it was so absolutely soaked with sweat. We trained very hard with each other and on the equipment. Once sparring started, we sparred quite hard too. The environment was much closer to a Boxing gym than to a standard martial arts school. All the students were there to learn how to fight, and part of that training was serious conditioning.

Were you a 'natural' at Martial Arts – did the movements come easily to you?

As far as being "natural", I can give you another story.

The very first day in class Sifu Richard Bustillo was teaching. He had us go over and put one hand against the wall for balance, extend a side kick, then raise it as high as we could. I raised my foot slightly above knee level which was as far as my foot would go. I glanced around the room and, to my surprise, every other student had his foot close to head level! I was aghast. It was clear that I had some sort of physical defect that I wasn't aware of that didn't allow me to bring my leg up as high as the others. It was a disheartening feeling. I later found out that every other student already had a black belt in another art! That made me feel a little better, but I had a long way to go!

So no, I was certainly not a "natural". There were a few things that came easy, such as footwork and generating power, but other than those, I struggled with most of the learning. It was all so foreign to me.

How has your personal Martial Arts journey changed and developed over the years with extensive practice and training?

I have had many changes as I have evolved. The most visible one is that a great majority of my training is sparring-based, just like at the original Kali Academy. I train, then put the techniques (and myself) to the test in almost every training session.

I am also very aware of training with the greatest efficiency possible. The number of techniques is basically infinite, but our training time is limited. I prefer prioritizing my time to training in a functional manner that will give me favorable results in a fighting situation.

I am also very aware of training in a way that promotes longevity. As Guro Dan has pointed out, the biggest fight we all face is aging. So I train my solo "sinawali" every day which helps promote fluidity and movement in my whole body, and am careful now about overdoing the impact training in order to prolong the functionality of my joints.

I also focus on helping others who have trained in martial arts for a long time to make sure they can functionalize what they've learned. This comes down to the fact that I want people to prevail in a serious self-defense situation. Imagine someone training for years in Kali, but not being able to apply any of it in a real situation because they have never trained in a functional manner. To me, that's the very "worst case" scenario. It's not that the art is bad or the techniques are useless; it's just that the functional training methods are often lacking.

I would say that almost all instructors in the Filipino Martial Arts know a plethora of counters for an angle one stick strike, including blocks, counters, disarms, and throws. But many of those instructors have never experienced a "real" angle one. A real angle one is not a partner holding his arm outstretched so that you can do a variety of beautiful techniques. An angle one is someone hitting full speed, full power, at your head and following through to prepare another vicious strike. How do you think an attacker in the real world is going to strike you with an impact weapon? All out. If we are to apply our art in the real world, we must get experience dealing with real strikes, safely, in training.

And that should happen often.

I like to help people so that they have both sides, both the martial and the art. But the martial comes first. If you make a mistake at a public demonstration, you might just be embarrassed. If you make a mistake in a self-defense situation, you and your loved ones will pay dearly for it.

The word "martial" comes before the word "art" in "martial art". I think we should train in that order.

What are the most important points in your teaching methods today?

I break my Filipino Martial Arts (FMA) and other training into three categories: fighting proficiency (training against a resisting partner), technical precision (knowing how to apply techniques in a precise manner), and power generation (being able to hit hard and accurately). I first devised this categorization due to my stick fighting experience with the original Dog Brothers (my nickname is Lucky Dog) as it became clear to me that these were the three areas that, when developed, produce a formidable fighting when going against a highly skilled opponent.

Every Kali class I teach has all three elements. We work on technique, developing power, and sparring as these three elements create a synergy that allows the student to develop at a very rapid pace. Without the sparring, you won't have the ability to read an opponent's intentions and the timing to take advantage of momentary opportunities. Without precise technique, your application will be ineffective. Without power, your opponent will not be in danger and can walk right through your blows. All three are very important to practice.

With all the technical changes during the last 40 years when the art started to spread around the world, do you think there are still 'pure' styles or systems of Kali?

I think the "pure" system is the one that you develop yourself which is specifically for you. Any system made by a particular fighter was a blend of what he learned and what his experiences taught him. As soon as you teach that system to someone else it is going to change. The numbering system may be retained along with certain terminology and a general look or signature movement. But if you really get down to purity, it is a "moment to moment" thing in combat. Actual fighting, which is what Kali is about, is spontaneously making great choices in the midst of life and death combat. There is no style that gives you all the answers. They are all part of the whole. A great style can give you excellent tools, but then you have to be able to apply them your own way. Just as we all learned to write the letters of the alphabet by looking at a particular template, nobody actually writes the letters like that. We have our own individual way of writing that is as unique as our individual fingerprints. So I don't believe that there is any "pure" styles other than that you express for yourself.

Do you think different 'styles' are truly important in the art of Kali/Escrima and why?

I do think styles are important in the Filipino martial arts because each style is a part of the whole. By studying different styles we can understand more facets of the complete approach. If you only have a "long range" style, what happens when you end up at close range? Or what if you get stuck in middle range where someone is about to die but you've only learned close range techniques and tactics? Studying many styles will help you to find what works best for you.

Again, we then have to pressure test the elements of these styles to find out what works best for us.

What is your opinion of sport Full Contact Escrima/Arnis tournaments and MMA events?

I believe competition is extremely important. That is where you go up against someone who is trying to totally shut down all of your techniques while imposing his technique on you. That's what a fight is, and if we want to really learn how to fight, experience through competition is a great venue to improve ourselves.

That said, there are many FMA tournaments that are so far from reality that it actually makes the competitors worse fighters than if they hadn't competed at all. I'm talking about the tournaments where there is continuous hitting and points are only scored for offense. In these tournaments, if I hit you 100 times and you hit me 101 times, you win. But in reality, we're both dead. In these tournaments we typically see fighters trading blows to the head over and over again in a bid to outscore the opponent. Imagine if that was a sword fight. As one of my instructors says, "Kali is the art of hitting your opponent without getting hit." Pretty simple.

The closer we get to a realistic tournament, the more danger is involved. As one of the original Dog Brothers, we fought using headgear, light hand protection, and heavy sticks. We went all out, hitting as hard as we possibly could. Dangerous? Yes. But that is the environment where you must rely on your technique to save you instead of protective equipment.

Now there are some who fight Dog Brother style and rely on the headgear to protect their brains while they get in strong leg shots, but I'd like you to think back to the competitions of old where combatants went in with rattan sticks and no protection whatsoever. Those competitions were how the art was tested at a very high level. Clearly, there was very little trading and only the best techniques survived.

Besides technique, competing will help you to respond well when under pressure. You will also be able to check your conditioning. The last thing you want is to be out of gas in an actual self-defense situation. I had a severe wake-up call in one of my first tournaments when half-way through the first round I was already feeling exhausted. That made me work a lot more on my conditioning.

So yes, whether it's stick fighting, MMA, or any other combat competition, there is a great deal to be learned by entering and testing yourself. The closer to reality the event is, the more danger there is, but the more you will learn. I highly recommend competing.

What are the most important qualities for a student to become proficient in Kali?

The first attribute necessary to become proficient in anything is perseverance. You have to stick it out for the long term, practicing consistently overtime. That said, we have to ask what proficient means when talking about Kali. Does it mean being able to demonstrate well with a cooperative partner? Does it mean being able to move the sticks in a fluid manner? Or does it mean being able to fight well against someone who's fighting back? Maybe it means having all of the above.

Certainly, previous generations of FMA masters actually fought sword against sword versus invaders. For them, proficiency meant being able to save the village from a raiding enemy. Nowadays, I think proficiency has taken on a lot of different connotations.

If we're talking about fighting ability, then I would say you need to get your resistance training in. Notice I didn't just say sparring there. As much as I love sparring and as beneficial as it is, dueling with sticks or training knives is not everything. Scenario training against a resisting partner is equally important. That's where you don't start at a convenient distance at long range. Instead, you may start at close range with your partner directly in front of you or at your side. You might start with an extreme disadvantage, such as being on the ground. The key element is you are practicing against a partner who is fighting back. I don't think we can call someone proficient in a warrior art unless they can actually show that they can fight effectively.

Being fluid and demonstrating techniques with great precision helps your fighting. But there is no substitute for fighting experience.

Do you think that Kali and Escrima in the West is in the same technical level that you can find in the Philipines?

I've been to the Philippines to train at least 12 times and I've been able to see Filipino martial arts practitioners all over the world. So I think I have a good perspective to answer this from.

There are a lot of great practitioners in the Philippines. I find that many there have this extra edge as they really feel the life and death warrior roots as they practice their art. Very intense. That said, I have also seen Instructors in the Philippines who are of a subpar level who make up for their lack of skill by playing the part of the grandmaster to fool inexperienced practitioners. But that is human nature, isn't it? This happens in all fields, including martial arts in America and other countries. There are some extremely high-level *practitioners and there are some who are not so good but have a knack for marketing. That's never going to change. This is why I suggest everybody spar. The truth comes out when the choreography ends and the battle begins.*

How would you describe Dan Inosanto's influence in your overall Martial Arts training?

Guro Dan influences every single aspect of my training and teaching. He is the most generous instructor, tirelessly researching and training, then making his hard earned insights available to anyone who is willing to undertake the training.

I strive to emulate him by researching and developing the arts and then making my research available. I find this way very gratifying. I am so grateful for his tutelage and mentorship.

Again, literally everything I do (not just in training but in my entire life) is impacted by Guro Dan. I am so much better off because of his influence.

Martial Arts are nowadays often referred to as a sport. Would you agree with this definition?

No. There are combat sports and there are true combat arts that are for life and death situations. The problem is that most combat arts no longer train with resistance like combat sport athletes do. They used to. Don't you think you would want to get sparring time in before going into the field to fight an enemy sword to sword? The battlefield is not where you want to get your first fighting experience!

I use the training methods of combat sports to ingrain the techniques and tactics of the combat arts. We wear protection and we do train safely, but that is how we develop high levels of self-defense specific fighting proficiency in our students.

Do you feel that you still have further to go in your studies of the arts?

So far to go! I really feel like I am in my first year of training. I'm excited about my own training and about all the discoveries that are ahead of me. On top of that, I'm very excited about improving the techniques that I already know. Constant progress. The future is bright and exciting!

How do you see the art of Kali in the world at the present time?

As you can tell by my previous answers, I'm very interested in training in a manner that produces effectiveness in real situations. As a teacher, my assumption is that someday, one of my students is going to need to use the art for real. I want to make sure that I did my best to prepare the student for that situation instead of just entertaining them with the flowery parts of the art.

The traditional Filipino martial art is based on fighting– all of the masters of old spent lots of time sparring and fighting. That's how they got so, so good and gained a profound understanding of the art.

Today, I am happy to say that more and more people are including sparring in their training. But the flash portion of the art will always attract more people than getting in there and learning that it takes a lot of hard work and humility to deal with the rigors of sparring. I'm happy that there are more options available than ever to train. That is a wonderful benefit of living in our times of easy access to information.

Does the weaponry aspect of Kali enhance the student's empty hands ability or are those two completely non-related skills?

This is a very interesting concept. Training Kali can definitely enhance aspects of empty hand skills. But fighting with a weapon is different than fighting empty-handed. A great fencer, for example, will have amazing footwork, reaction time, and a fine sense of distance that can enhance empty hand fighting. But he or she is not going to do well in a kickboxing setting without spending a lot of time dealing with actual punches, kicks, elbows, knees, and head butts. So yes, training with the weapons to see the speed of the stick and improve your visual sensitivity, to feel the distance and to have a good footwork will definitely add to your attributes when going empty-handed. But just because you are proficient with weaponry technique does not mean it's going to relate directly to empty hand application.

Weaponry movements can be translated into empty handed movements, but please remember that a technique originally meant to work with a knife in your hand is not going to be nearly as effective as when going empty handed. Please discern between which techniques can be effectively translated and which are weapon-specific.

How important is sparring in the skill development of the student?

Sparring? What's sparring? Just kidding! If we are talking about making someone a proficient fighter, then sparring is absolutely essential. It is not everything, and it will not take the place of learning good technique and having sound fundamentals, but without trying your techniques consistently against resisting partners, you simply will not have the timing or the ability to read an incoming attack as well as you would if you spend a significant amount of time sparring.

When teaching the Martial Arts – what is the most important element; self-defense, health or tradition?

I would definitely put health first. As one of my friends told me decades ago, martial art is simply the art of staying healthy. If someone attacks, you use your art to stay healthy.

Part of martial arts is staying in excellent condition and observing a healthy diet that improves your performance. That's practical self-defense we can apply every single day!

From my point of view, some traditions can be good for people and others can actually hold people back. If you are in a tradition where you are subservient to a glorified master, I don't think that's healthy. Anyone who wants to be that kind of master is unhealthy as well.

I think tradition should push us forward to be our very best. Traditions of strong moral values, and traditions of respect. I find those very beneficial to healthy living.

Teaching is different than personal training and development. Where are you these days as far as your 'personal' training goes? How do you train yourself at this point in your life?

I train more than I teach. Back when I first became an instructor and started teaching some of the classes at the Inosanto Academy, I had the realization that I was not longer training as much as I did before becoming an instructor. I changed that in a hurry!

In the late 80s, Guro Dan taught 18 classes per week in Los Angeles. I was in every single class. Living in a tiny camper trailer in the parking lot of a dog and cat hospital near downtown L.A., I would go home after class and spend more time practicing in that parking lot. I love learning and practicing.

I also really, truly love to teach. It's a great joy in my life to see students improve and have a better quality of life because of their training. But I started martial arts because I loved the training. And certainly I found that the more I train the more I have to offer my students.

Now, my own personal training consists of sessions with my family (my wife Sarah is a JKD Unlimited instructor and a black belt in Jiu-jitsu, and my daughter Talina loves jiu-jitsu, kali sparring, and JKD kickboxing) training with my JKDU students and instructors, and have sessions with my martial arts friends and training partners.

I also do a lot of solo training. Almost every morning I walk down to the beach and swing the double sticks to warm up and get a nice groove going for the day. I do other solo training at various times including impact training on equipment. Did I mention that I absolutely love my training?

Do you have any general advice you would care to pass on the practitioners in general?

The first thing that comes to mind is this: don't be afraid of looking "bad". The whole idea of training is to improve, and we improve quickest through negative feedback. We need to try things and look at the results. I think a lot of people avoid sparring because they don't want to show that they are fallible. Somehow, probably through martial arts movies, the martial artist is not supposed to ever make a mistake. But when you do rounds of stick sparring, guess what? You get hit sometimes! If you're never getting hit, then you need to handicap yourself a bit so your partner has a better chance of scoring on you. That's how you are going to continue to improve.

Do you want to know how to avoid making any mistakes in sparring? Don't spar! But that is the biggest mistake if you're interested in functional training and you really want to improve.

The second advice is to make the training as fun as possible. There are times where you have to grind and utilize your discipline to push yourself if you want to be your very best. But for the most part, it should be a very enjoyable adventure. Often, combat athletes come to the end of their career and they quit training altogether. Why? Because their training was so brutal that they just don't want to have to ever go through that again. So make it as fun as you possibly can, but also intersperse the hard stuff and put yourself in positions to make mistakes. That is how you will optimize your growth.

Some people think going to Southeast Asia to train is necessary, do you share this point of view?

It isn't necessary, but there is nothing like being in the homeland to get a feel of not just the art, but also of the surroundings it was developed in. Let me tell you, the feeling of a swinging a Moro Kris on a mountaintop in the middle of Mindanao cannot be replicated. You have to be there to get the full sensation.

The trips I made to learn Zulu stick, spear, and axe fighting in the hills of QuaZulu Natal gave me priceless insights into the culture, history, and current usage of the arts. Not to mention making wonderful friends in a very different world.

We are fortunate to have so many great instructors in the West. If you only want the technical skill and the moral guidance, you can definitely get it here. But an even deeper understanding can be absorbed by going to the birthplace of the art. Again, not absolutely necessary, but I would highly recommend it.

What do you consider to be the major changes in the arts since you began training?

When I started in 1979 nobody knew what the Filipino martial arts were. It had been in America for a long time, but hidden. All these years later, thanks to Guro Dan's constant promotion of the art and making it available to so many, the Filipino martial arts has become a mainstay in the world. I think it is just fabulous that this art is not just alive, but thriving now. It was alive and well in the Philippines, but it was rather underground there as well. It's nice to have worldwide recognition of the beauty, culture, and incredible technology of these arts.

I want to mention something that happened during my first training trip in Manila with Grandmaster Tatang Ilustrisimo, Master Tony Diego, and Master Christopher Ricketts. At the end of a long day of training, I was chatting with the three luminaries. They asked me to please thank Guro Dan for all he had done for the Filipino martial arts. They said that if it wasn't for Guro Dan, the FMA would still be obscure. I wholeheartedly agree.

Who would you like to have trained with that you have not (dead or alive)?

I would like to have actually trained with Floro Villabrille. I was fortunate to meet him a few times, but he was already on in years and was not very physically active. I would have loved to have trained with him in his prime when he was the stick fighting champion of the Philippines in the days of fighting with no armor at all. Can you imagine the insights he had into stick fighting after 80 matches? That would have been amazing.

I would have loved to train with John LaCoste as well. He blended central Philippines weaponry and empty handed methods with Kuntao Silat of the Southern Philippines. He moved incredibly well. Since I was a kid growing up in Carson, California, I have enjoyed the cultural dances of the Philippines, and LaCoste taught Filipino dance. Those are the two main masters that I would love to have trained with.

What would you say to someone who is interested in starting to learn Martial Arts?

Start right away! I can't tell you how many people I've spoken with who say that wish they had started training 10 years earlier. Well, what are you going to think in 10 years if you don't start today? Find a school that you like the vibe, and begin. You don't have to get in shape first. Just start. That's always the biggest obstacle.

Once you start, make those class times "hard appointments" in your schedule and vow not to miss them. If something comes up, you say, "I have an appointment" and go train. So just start and commit to being consistent. You will be so, so happy that you began the journey.

What is it that keeps you motivated after all these years?

I really love the training and I love personal development in myself and my students worldwide.

If we go back further, it is clear that the deep initial motivation comes from a horrible incident I endured when I was abducted by a predator when I was 9 years old. I don't ever want to feel that kind of helpless and terror in the face of evil again, and I don't want my students to ever feel that either. You can see how that incident pushes me to ensure that we are practicing to develop effective self-defense skills rather than merely learning a curriculum of techniques with a cooperative partner.

Do you think it is necessary to engage in free-fighting to achieve good self-defense skills in the street?

Yes, definitely, but the street environment is very different than the sporting cage or ring. So for self-defense, you can't just do free-fighting and maintain all the rules of the sport.

When we do our free-fighting, the students have training weapons in their waistband or in a pocket. If it starts empty hand, anyone can pull the training weapon at any time and attack with it. That changes everything. You must be monitoring the hands at all times when at close range or you won't see the draw.

At long range you have to be ready to escape, arm yourself, or charge forward if you see your partner reaching for the weapon. This weapon awareness is one of the reasons that the Kali and Silat mentality is so important to infuse into self-defense training.

When I asked Tatang Ilustrisimo if he could show me some empty hand fighting, he said yes, dropped his stick, and told me to pick up a knife. For him, the attacker would always be armed. Empty hand versus empty hand was sport.

So yes, free-fighting is a very important part of our training, but since we are focused on self-defense and not competition, we do our resistance training with self-defense elements included.

What is your opinion about mixing different styles? Does the practice of one nullify the effectiveness of the other or on the contrary, can it be beneficial to the student?

All of the martial arts are a mixture of different influences. You might have a style that seems to be of itself, but whoever created it certainly had various influences that they used to put that style together. So yes, mixing styles can be very beneficial to have a more compete approach.

Problems arise when two styles have a contradictory approach. One says to fight with the sword in the front hand but the other says to fight with your sword hand in the rear hand. How do you reconcile those differences? This conundrum is actually good for us because it brings us beyond the question, "which technique is best?" and leads us to a much more empowering question- "When in a fight is each approach most appropriate?"

If fighting at long range, it is usually advantageous to fight with your sword in the front hand as you keep your head and body as far from the adversary as possible. But what if you were able to pick up a shield with your free hand? Now you want your shield in front and your sword in the rear hand. There are several other reasons for each stance, but you get the idea.

Mixing styles, when you understand the reasons for the differences, can give you more effective options for the myriad of situations that can occur in real life, fluid combat.

What is your philosophical basis for your Martial Arts training?

I sum it up in a phrase I use often: "Be Your Best!" I want to continually develop into a better and better version of myself. To do that, I have to train as well as I can. My best self has no time to gossip about others as I am too busy trying to improve myself. I have compassion for others who are on the path but not so far along because I myself am still learning and understand the struggle. I can best help these students through kindness and compassion instead of harsh ridicule.

In the end, I want myself and my students to develop such confidence in ourselves that when we encounter people we don't know, we can greet them with a kind smile instead of fearful disdain. That is the power of a confident martial artist.

Do you have a particularly memorable experience that has remained as an inspiration for your training until this day?

I'm thankful that I have had many, many memorable and inspirational experiences. If I were to pick one, it would be when Guro Dan Inosanto came up to me (a shy, unsure 24 year old kid) before a morning class at the IMB Academy. He said, "Are you going to keep training?" This caught me off guard. "Yes" I stammered. He replied. "Good. I'm making you an apprentice instructor" and walked away and started class. I was dumbfounded. I never dreamed that I could someday be any level of instructor. But as it sunk in, it was clear that he saw something in me that I couldn't see in myself. He believed in me. That moment has made all the difference in my life. And I pay that forward as I know, from personal experience, that we all have vast reservoirs of untapped potential. We can all do great things, but many of us don't have enough belief in ourselves to do them. I'm here to encourage everyone to go in the direction of your dreams. If that kid living in a parking lot could do it, so can you.

After all these years of training and experience, could you explain the meaning of the practice of Martial Arts?

I will say that the greatest meaning of martial arts is that they bring meaning to our lives. It is a quest, full of obstacles to overcome. It is a true hero's journey where we start with a feeling that we know something about martial arts, then we enter into the practice and realize that we know nothing. Then we build ourselves up through toil and facing adversity. It brings out the best qualities in ourselves and reveals our worst. It is the hero's journey. Unlike sports, martial arts deal with life and death so with that as the background for all that we do, our training becomes more serious and precision in execution is absolutely vital.

When we transpose that mindset into our everyday lives, we perform better at our other tasks. Not perfect, but we can constantly be better than we were before and we know that we have what it takes to overcome obstacles.

Self-defense wise, we know we stand for something. We stand for doing what is right in the face of temptation. We stand for justice in the face of criminality. Martial arts gives our lives meaning.

If you had to choose one single art to practice at the expense of not training in any other styles, what method would you chose?

This is so hard. My overriding approach is called JKD Unlimited because I need freedom from styles. No art is complete in itself. But if I had to choose one art to practice the rest of my life it would be Kali. It is so vast, includes a myriad of weapons combinations and empty hand ranges, and is still effective as we get to our later years. I would not want to exclude all the other arts that I love so much, but if I had to choose one, then Kali would be it.

Is there anything lacking in the way martial arts are taught today compared to how they were in your beginnings?

I actually think that the martial arts are taught much better now than before. I was lucky to be training with Guro Dan and his vast repertoire of styles over 40 years ago. You had to go to him to get all of those approaches at an expert level.

Now, there is so much available all of the time through a variety of sources. Any teacher can have a very wide repertoire and understanding because they can easily study many different approaches whether in person or through online learning. So I think that the martial arts are taught even better today.

Of course you, you probably think I'm going to bring up sparring or lack of sparring, but I believe that more people are sparring fully today than ever before.

I would like to see combat sports schools incorporate a "For The Street" approach to self-defense in their gyms. Just because you can take somebody down and submit him does it mean you can deal with a knife or a pistol. It's a very different way of doing things which better equips students who aren't there to compete. But all in all, I believe today's teachers are much better than the average teachers of the past.

Could I ask you what you consider to be the most important qualities of a successful martial artist?

To be a successful martial artist I think the primary quality is to be in control of your ego and have confronted your fears. Do this and you can adopt a generous attitude with your art while not being too full of yourself. If you then develop students who are skilled and have that same attitude, I think you are quite a success as a martial artist.

What advice would you give to students on the question of supplementary training (running, weights, et cetera)?

I would definitely suggest weightlifting as it is the most efficient way to build healthy muscle that can keep you strong and well aligned.

For cardio, I subscribe to the advice of my University of Southern California baseball coach Rod Dedeaux. (Dedeaux was the winningest coach in collegiate baseball history.) He always said "play yourself in the shape." Instead of spending a lot of time running and doing calisthenics, which certainly build your stamina, he preferred to spend every moment possible working on skill development while naturally building the kind of cardio that you need.

Jiu-jitsu legend Marcelo Garcia, who I spend a lot of time with, does the same thing. The time and energy that would be used running is instead used to further sharpen his skills that create the small edge that means the difference between second place and multiple world championship titles.

Personally, instead of running as I did many years ago, I'd rather do a solo workout honing my martial arts skills. That can be hitting the bag, weapons "karenza", Silat forms, or any other aspect of the martial arts that get my heart rate up.

What do you enjoy the most about the practice of Martial Arts?

I most enjoy that feel of constant improvement. I'm a little better or understand a little more than yesterday. That feeds into my passion for teaching which means I have a little better insights to pass on to my students.

I want to be able to train my students at the highest level possible, and martial arts is always evolving and progressing. I need to stay on the cutting edge and I do that through a high volume of study and training. The personal practice and teaching feed each other. Whether I am working on a better way to set up a hand hit with the stick, exploring how I can better apply Silat in an MMA environment, or any of my study, I do so to improve myself and my students. It's really fun to share.

I hope everybody can experience the level of enjoyment that I get out of martial arts.

In your opinion, why is it that a lot of students start falling away after two to three years of training?

I think there are many reasons that come up. Life can change in two or three years. Families get bigger, people move, other interests come up. But I will tell you that when people are really enjoying their training and the camaraderie of the group, they tend to stick around. There are just so many benefits that the martial arts have to offer, from fitness to socializing to learning to better protect yourself and your loved ones.

Also, as teachers, I think we need to do whatever we can to set goals for the students and help them achieve those goals, while making sure that they're having a great time on the journey. Passing a level test is a big deal. It is a real accomplishment. Earning instructor credentials is huge! Gigantic accomplishment! I have found that it is an important part of the entire picture, and helps students to see that they really are progressing.

Have there been times when you felt fear in your training?

Oh yes! I felt fear of initially joining the Kali Academy class (fear of the unknown) and I felt the fear that I wasn't talented enough when I first started. I became an instructor and felt the fear of doing something to let down Guro Dan. I feared looking bad. I competed and faced the fear of losing. Each time I would fight Eric Knaus as a Dog Brother, I felt the fear of being seriously injured by that heavy stick.

I think the worst fear is the fear of failing and looking bad. That's the one that can keep us from pushing ourselves and stretching to become the best we can be. We can become very comfortable in our current position or condition, but that comfort can make us stagnate.

I watched Guro Dan Inosanto put on a white belt and start Brazilian jiu-jitsu at the age of 60. When you start jiu-jitsu, you look bad. You don't move well, you don't know the moves, etc. After many years of rigorous training, once you are a black belt, when you roll with good partners you will still look bad at times. That's just the way it is, but that didn't stop Guro Dan from starting a new art. His was such a good example for everyone.

I think that dealing with our fears in the martial arts helps us to realize that many of the fears we have in our everyday lives are just imaginary. We imagine a bad outcome before it even happens. We suffer from fear over and over again by imagining that bad outcome. But so often, the event we fear doesn't come to pass or it ultimately ends up being a blessing. We need to control our negative imagination and see things for what they actually are. Once again, a great lesson from martial arts that we can use to enhance our everyday lives.

What are your thoughts on the future of the art?

I think the future of the martial arts is very bright. We have the entire continent of Africa that is full of amazing martial arts yet to be fully enjoyed in the west. I've made several trips to South Africa to study Zulu stick, spear, and axe fighting with the Zulus. It is phenomenal. That is just the tip of a very large iceberg.

Imagine all of the arts in Southeast Asia that have yet to be discovered or those in India. As we are better and better connected we have more access to all of these amazing approaches.

As technology leaps forward, we will have even better ways of learning and training as well. Imagine being able to learn from and spar with one of my friends in South Africa but without actually having to travel all the way there. I'm sure as virtual or augmented reality and artificial intelligence improves, we will be able to do just that, where we can actually feel like our partner and/or teacher is right in front of us. It's going to be amazing!

Let's talk about your Jeet Kune Do journey. When did you meet Dan Inosanto for the first time and when did you start training under him?

I went to watch a class at the original Kali Academy space in 1979. Sifu Dan (we usually referred to him as Sifu at that time) was teaching and it was absolutely amazing. I had seen karate before and was certainly intrigued, but here we had a group of people moving smoothly and athletically, wearing T-shirts and sweat pants while they hit the mitts and then each other (during the sparring phase of the class). I was an athlete, and that feeling of high level athletic performance really resonated with me. I had no idea that my visit would change my entire life path.

I filled out an application and waited for a slot to open up. I got the call in early 1980 just after my 18th birthday. A new class was starting and I was invited to sign up for that class. I did so immediately. I was thrilled.

What attracted you to the training then?

I had a strong inner desire to gain the ability to protect myself since enduring a terrible incident when I was 9. The predator was a large adult and the ordeal of being absolutely helpless while he continually threatened to kill me if I didn't do what he wanted created that desire for self-defense skills. I didn't ever want to be in that helpless situation again.

When I was able to start training, it was the athletic feel and reality of the Kali/Jun Fan Academy training that was so appealing. Plus the weapons just mesmerized me. I was hooked.

How was the JKD training philosophy those days?

The basic training philosophy was that we were all preparing for a fight. A few fought in combat sports, but the main emphasis was training to win a street fight. It wasn't about exploring different martial arts for artistic expression, but was about enhancing our combat athleticism, working the basics hard, and testing it all in sparring.

Carson and the surrounding areas in Los Angeles could be rough. Some coming in to train were thinking of looking like Bruce Lee, but the majority were just there to dominate a street self-defense situation.

From a philosophical perspective, wasn't the JKD philosophy confusing to you?

Not at all. It actually made perfect sense to me because I was already a successful athlete. By the time I started my martial arts training, I already knew what it took to excel in sports. JKD is all about excelling in combat which, like sports, is an athletic endeavor. Here's a story which I think will illustrate why the philosophy was very easy for me to understand.

When I was 13 years old, I played on three different baseball teams in separate leagues at the same time. That meant that I had six main coaches. Each one of them would give me advice on how to be a better hitter, and a lot of that advice was contradictory. Some wanted me to have an open stance while some wanted my stance closed. Some wanted my feet far apart, some said close together, others said medium. I was told to hold the bat on my shoulder, another said extend my arms back, and one liked having the bat up above my head, and so on. This was very confusing.

I asked my dad (who was an accomplished athlete in High School and became a professional motorcycle racer) what I should do. He said matter-of-factly, "Listen to all of them, try out all the different ways, and then use what works best for you." A very rational approach that ended up giving me great results in sports.

When I started JKD there was the famous plaque on the wall that said:

The truth in combat is different for each individual in this style.

1. Research your own experience.

2. Absorb what is useful.

3. Reject what is useless.

4. Add what is specifically your own.

That was basically the advice my father gave me about all those different styles of hitting. I got different points of view, I tried each one out, and ultimately used what worked best for me. And of course, I would naturally add my own flavor as every hitter does. So the JKD philosophy made perfect sense to me and I still follow that methodology to this day.

What do you think are the most important principles in the art of JKD?

JKD had the nickname of "scientific street fighting". Besides being an athlete, I happen to be have a great love of science. I won the Science Award my senior year at Carson High School and I went on to work in research labs at Harbor UCLA Medical Center while I was studying biology at USC. So I was a scientist.

The basis for research and development is the scientific method. The scientific method is to create a hypothesis, test that hypothesis in a realistic environment, and then observe the results of the test. The results are the results. It's not about how you would like the world to be, it is about what it actually is.

If you don't get favorable results, you change your hypothesis and repeat the *process until you get results that you want. That is the methodology that Bruce Lee used to create the art of JKD. He used the scientific method by taking his techniques into the lab of hard sparring against martial artists of various styles to find out what worked and didn't work.*

Today, I use the phrase "pressure testing". Beyond particular techniques or tactics, it is the training methods, that include pressure testing, that are most important in developing a formidable fighter. And that is what JKD is about.

JKD is not a cultural art; it is a fighting method that requires rigorous testing by every single individual. "Research your own experience ". That's why Bruce Lee said that JKD was not for everyone. The majority of people in a relatively peaceful society don't see the need to endure that kind of training.

I have a vivid memory of Sifu Inosanto at the first Marina Del Rey Academy lecturing at the whiteboard. He said, "What is the most important aspect of JKD?" We all had different responses, such as strong side forward, intercepting, etc. After several answers, Sifu Dan said emphatically, "Training methods!" and wrote it on the board. That made such an impression on me as it changed my view of what must be prioritized. Just as an athlete must spend a lot of time playing the game to get experience and find their own way, JKD practitioners must spend a lot of time "playing the game" (sparring or competing) to find out what works best for them under pressure.

If you have to 'describe" what Jeet Kune Do is, how would you do it?

That depends on whether we're talking about "Jun Fan JKD", the moves and methodology that Bruce Lee used himself, or JKD as a personal expression of an individual. As far as describing the approach, it's best done in person because it's about interaction in the moment with a live opponent. But let me say a few things.

Jun Fan JKD Is based on training yourself to be able to fight very effectively in the street environment where there are virtually no rules. Not just learning the techniques and theories, but actually engaging in the type of training that prepares you to fight well. Bruce Lee developed a method that was brilliantly simple yet highly tactical. Blending the principles of Western Fencing with empty hand martial arts was sheer genius. You may think differently, but I believe if someone is using the term JKD as their personal expression, then their approach should be based upon street specific self-defense fighting that encompasses all of the ranges and draws heavily from the principles of Jun Fan JKD. Sparring regularly is an absolute must. No sparring, no JKD!

I will also mention that many people mistake "Jun Fan Gung Fu" for "Jun Fan JKD". There are many aspects of the former that Bruce Lee realized were not so functional when he started sparring hard and therefore discarded them. Many truths were revealed once the scientific method was applied to Jun Fan Gung Fu.

It is written that Bruce Lee's JKD was essentially Wing Chun, Boxing and Western Fencing? Would you please elaborate how these methods became the foundation for Lee's art of JKD?

I believe we should also add Northern Chinese kicking styles and French Savate as they were very influential in Lee's kicking repertoire.

Bruce Lee started with Wing Chun, and was familiar with a few other methods. After he moved to Seattle, he began to evolve, changing the Wing Chun structure and adding techniques, thus creating Jun Fan Gung Fu. When he started sparring hard in Los Angeles, he found that he "had a lot of prejudices, but those ideas were wrong". This is when he changed the name to Jeet Kune Do. It was a new direction based on evidence gleaned from sparring many types of opponents.

Lee was also fencing at this time and the efficiency and high-level tactics of Fencing became imbued in Bruce Lee's approach. He discarded more of the Wing Chun approach and added the fencing principles of strong side forward, efficient foot work, various ways of attack, and other tactics. Jeet Kune Do was, as Bruce Lee called it, "fencing without a sword". Blend this with the upper body movement, curved punches, and circular footwork of boxing, add the kicks, and you have the foundation of Jun Fan JKD.

How has the JKD philosophy influenced your training in other arts?

Everything I do is imbued with the JKD philosophy. I am interested primarily in street self-defense. Although I have become proficient in various combat sports, I modify them using JKD street-specific principles. My works "BJJ For The Street" and "MMA For The Street" are perfect examples. I simply "JKDized" these combat sports. Similarly, my "Silat For The Street", "Battlefield Kali", "High Performance Krav Maga", and other programs are highly efficient because of using the JKD mindset and training methods. The thread that runs through all these programs, derived from JKD, is to develop martial arts character and skills through consistent street-oriented pressure testing.

How do you reconcile the idea of training in different martial arts with the idea of perfecting a "few tools" to be really effective in real combat?

We certainly need a small collection of tools that are honed to a very sharp edge. That is essential and it comes naturally out of sparring. You will find something that works well for you, your mindset, and your physical attributes, so you will naturally use it over and over again. It becomes one of your "go to" tools. But we also need contingency techniques for when our main stays are not working or if we end up in a position where they are not applicable.

Bruce Lee was doing just fine with his Jun Fan Gung Fu. Then he ran into Wong Jak Man. That fight showed him that his normal go to techniques were not enough. Guess what he did? Bruce Lee added boxing techniques to his repertoire. According to Sifu Leo Fong, he did that the very next morning! He later added principles from fencing and even explored grappling techniques in his practice sessions. He expanded the scope of his training to account for situations where his fundamentals were not effective.

Here's something for all JKD people to think about. Yes, we want simplicity. But in high-level fighting against a skillful opponent, we must employ a level of complexity that can overcome the high-level defense of the opponent. While maintaining simplicity, Bruce Lee added higher levels of complexity in order to have tools, approaches, and tactics that foiled the defenses of skillful opponents.

Setting up an opponent with footwork variations, applying a proper stop kick, closing the distance to trap to open up a strike, then using head movement to avoid a counterstrike is not simple. It is many simple movements strung together purposely in order to outthink a cunning adversary. Simple attacks work great on fighters you outclass. A level of practical complexity is necessary for the higher level opponents.

As long as you are sparring to test them out, training in various arts can enhance your understanding while filling-in portions of your training that are lacking. This aids greatly in our quest to be complete fighters. Just look at groundwork. Bruce Lee dabbled in it, but he didn't have the benefit of being exposed to many high-level grapplers like we have access to today. I'm sure he would have added some important elements to his ground fighting if he had access to the current set of grapplers.

How do you think the practitioners should "divide" their time between the self-perfection and the self-preservation aspects?

I don't believe there should be a division between self-perfection and self-preservation. You don't see basketball players spending a lot of time on fancy movements that would be ineffective in actual game situations. I believe in self-perfection through the practice of self-preservation. I work on precision and detail of movement and technique while I'm sparring or drilling with a partner, and when I am training solo. There is so much functional material to work on that I don't see a need to practice techniques that are extremely low percentage moves. The "caveat" is that if you are in the entertainment industry, then you need the super impressive techniques because that is functional for film and TV where the point is to impress an audience.

I definitely spend time on mind/body/spirit aspects of martial arts that develop relaxation and flow. I train sinawali (double stick flowing) nearly every day. I also do Southeast Asian and some Polynesian dance which have martial roots. I find it very beneficial to do these movements for my mind and body connection and to keep my body moving fluidly. And it just feels good to me. Some people might consider that training to be self-perfection. To me it is more the total health aspect, both physical and mental. If my mind and body are not functional, I will certainly have no chance at self-preservation in a severe self-defense situation.

What I don't like is drilling techniques with a cooperative partner that look combative when in reality they're extremely low percentage moves. This tends to develop dangerous false confidence in a student. It's so easy to get pulled into the drills that make you look cool. That's another reason for consistent sparring. It keeps you in touch with reality as to what works and what doesn't work under fight conditions.

You started with Sifu Dan Inosanto at the old Kali Academy. Then in the mid-80s the seminars came along and Sifu Inosanto was extremely busy traveling. These seminars were a turning point in the spread of JKD Apprenticeships around the world. How would you describe this evolution from the Kali Academy and a small group of die-hards to what JKD has turned out to be these days?

I believe that this was a fantastic evolution for JKD and other arts that Sifu Dan teaches. Of that original die-hard group of the early days, there are just a handful that are still actively teaching. Of those, most just teach a few students. Imagine if those were all the instructors available. JKD would be close to extinction. Because of Sifu Dan's extreme dedication to make these arts available through seminars, we have hundreds (if not thousands) of highly qualified instructors worldwide who are keeping these arts not just alive, but thriving. That is an incredible accomplishment.

This was such a sacrifice. Can you imagine getting on a plane 48 Fridays out of the year, flying out to destinations to teach all day Saturday and Sunday just to turn around and fly back home Monday morning? Then teaching all week and doing it again the following weekend. That is dedication. Did he get paid for the seminars? Yes, but in my opinion, not nearly enough, especially in early days. This was and still is a labor of love.

Some think it must be wonderful to visit all these places. But Sifu Dan never gets to actually see the places he is traveling to. He sees the airport, the hotel, the seminar location, and a restaurant or two before heading back to the airport to go home. It really is a sacrifice.

Personally, because of Sifu Inosanto's pioneering efforts in the seminar industry, I have friends all over the world and I am able to teach seminars myself abroad which is always a wonderful experience.

Going back to the early group, I would say that the majority of the students then were more hard-core. The sparring was pretty heavy and it was a big focus of the training. The original Kali Academy felt more like a boxing gym than a martial arts dojo, so imagine 25 really tough fighters in that advanced class. But what has happened since? You can't have hard sparring on seminars, but the result of exposing so many to the art has paid great dividends on the fighter side as well. There are now many, many more hard-core JKD-based martial artists out there than there would have been otherwise. Many of the top UFC coaches have connections to JKD through the Inosanto Academy. That is all thanks to Sifu Dan.

In the early 80s at the Kali Academy the art was called "Jeet Kune Do" with no other word attached to it. Then the "JKD Concepts" appeared". Why do you think that happened and didn't that create a lot of confusion for the masses?

That "concepts" tag started because of the confusion in the JKD world. Some people thought that JKD was exactly what Bruce Lee did himself and nothing else. They would include all the training that he did before he started sparring hard, discarded many techniques and training methods, then changed the name to Jeet Kune Do.

Then there was another group who thought that JKD was the process of personal development through the martial arts and therefore included many different arts to create an individual, personal expression. It got to where combining elements of different arts was the key principle that guided JKD. So which one is the real JKD?

It was Shannon Lee who had the brilliant suggestion to call the art that Bruce Lee did himself after moving to Los Angeles "Jun Fan JKD" or Bruce Lee's (personal) Jeet Kune Do. The era before would be described as Jun Fan Gung Fu. What a simple, easy to understand way of delineating between the approaches. But in the magazines, it was divided differently. There was original

JKD, which included only what Bruce Lee did in his lifetime, and JKD concepts which included the study of a variety of other arts beyond what Bruce Lee used.

Although I learned straight Jun Fan JKD from Sifu Dan, (with some throwbacks to Jun Fan Gung Fu) I also studied Filipino and other Southeast Asian arts from him. There is so much valuable information available to improve our fighting skills and understanding of the arts. Sticking only to what Bruce Lee did was actually against his philosophy. Just look at what his symbol says "Using no way as way, having no limitation as limitation." It doesn't say, "Only using Bruce Lee's way, and limiting yourself to what Bruce Lee did." Clearly, if you limit yourself only to what Bruce Lee did in his lifetime, you are going in the opposite direction of the basic philosophy that is the foundation of his symbol and art.

Which camp do you consider yourself to be in?

Actually, neither one. The majority (not all) of the "Original JKD" crowd are extremely limited, following a set curriculum. Instead of doing the hard work to better their approach, they stay within the safety of what has become a style. As mentioned before, this is not what Bruce Lee advocated.

The problem I found with many (definitely not all) of the JKD Concepts teachers is that while they have open minds and an open approach, but stray far from the foundational JKD principle of "pressure testing". Pressure testing is what allows each individual to determine what works for him or her. They tend to teach as though everything works all of the time. There is no discernment as to what is practical and what isn't.

I consider myself a JKD practitioner, pressure testing everything in my life long quest for constant, practical improvement, but without limiting myself to what Bruce Lee did in his lifetime. I follow the decree of "Using no way as way, having no limitation as limitation." That is why I call my approach "JKD Unlimited". I am keenly aware that there are always many things to improve and that the evolution will never stop unless I stop evolving myself. I pass my findings on to my students, but more importantly, I pass on the JKD principles so that they can engage in their own research and development to better themselves. They can then share their findings so we are all better off.

Dan Inosanto, Ted Wong, Larry Hartsell, Dan Lee, Richard Bustillo, Bob Bremer, etc—all were Bruce Lee's students but their "product" seems to be very different one from each other. Why do you think is that?

I think that's exactly what the JKD idea is. All of us learned to write the letters of the alphabet by following a model in a textbook of how each letter should look. But none of us write the letters exactly like the template because we are all different. Each individual in JKD should have a different approach. You should end up doing, as Sifu Richard Bustillo would say often, "your own JKD".

When we are talking about Jun Fan JKD, what Bruce Lee did himself towards the end of his life, each of the aforementioned teachers displayed their own way of teaching it, meaning each approach is different. But, there are far more similarities than many think.

Sifu Inosanto is often thought of as being primarily a Kali and Silat man. People who haven't trained extensively with him think that he is calling all that he does JKD, but that is not true. Those people were not in the JKD class at the original Kali Academy, IMB Academy, or Marina Del Ray Academy. There was no Southeast Asian martial art taught when Sifu Dan was teaching "JKD". They were a mix of Jun Fan Gung Fu and Jun Fan JKD methodologies. And his progression and teaching priority was different than all the other first generation instructors I learned from.

So yes, each individual taught JKD in their own way, but they were teaching very similar principles and techniques.

According to Bruce's notes, the idea of JKD is to simplify. But training in Kali, Silat, Thai boxing, Jiu-Jitsu, Savate, etc, seems to people – from the outside – more an endless accumulation process instead of a simplification. How can those two be reconciled?

I hear this all the time. JKD is definitely about simplification. But you must start with something to simplify. If you only have one art to draw from, you are severely limited.

Bruce Lee started with Wing Chun, then ADDED techniques as he created

Jun Fan Gung Fu. As Bruce Lee evolved to Jeet Kune Do, guess what he did. He ADDED strikes, head movement, and footwork of boxing. He ADDED tactics, footwork, and efficiency principles of Western Fencing. He ADDED kicking methods of Savate. He didn't teach it, but he ADDED weaponry work of Eskrima/Kali. He ADDED judo throws and ground work. Then, after studying and trying out these various arts, he absorbed what was useful for him, rejected what was useless for him, and ADDED what was specifically his own.

I think you get my point. Yes, much of the art is hacking away at the inessentials. That is refinement. But if you want to create a magnificent sculpture like Michelangelo's David, you must start with a very large piece of marble.

How has your personal "JKD journey" evolved throughout the years?

What an evolution it has been! It's a good example of what we were just discussing. It's also a very long story, over forty three years at this point, but I'll give a brief synopsis.

I started at the original Kali/Jun Fan Gung Fu Academy learning primarily JKD and Filipino martial arts. Later, Sifu Inosanto added various styles of Filipino martial arts along with Thai Boxing and Silat. I didn't just study at the Academy, but, thanks to Sifu Dan Inosanto's encouragement and help, I was able to study with other instructors like master Chai Siriute, Pak Herman Suwanda, and Pendekar Paul DeThouars. Later I started on my Brazilian jiu-jitsu journey with many of the very best, primarily Rigan Machado, Christ Hauter, Egan Inoue, Enson Inoue, Charuto Verissimo, Baret Yoshida, and Marcelo Garcia. I studied Kali in the Philippines with Grandmaster Roberto Labaniego and later with Grandmaster Antonio "Tatang" Ilustrisimo. I made four trips to South Africa to study Zulu stick, spear, and axe fighting with the Zulus. In recent years I have become a black belt instructor in Krav Maga under Nir Maman and an instructor in the South African Piper knife fighting system through Lloyd DeJongh.

Many will say that you don't need to become an instructor or Black Belt in a system to glean the most important elements of it to enhance your own JKD.

I agree with that to a point, as you can get many of the major principles early on. But I have found that when you go very deep into an art, you eventually get many insights into fighting that you wouldn't have otherwise.

Here's another thing to consider - all I do is martial arts. I spend hours each day training, studying, pondering, and on some days, teaching. I train and study much more than I teach. That allows me the luxury of going very deep into various arts, continuing to study and improve long after I have become considered (by my instructors) an expert in a particular art.

Brazilian jujitsu is a good example. After 12 years of training, I was awarded my black belt by Egan Inoue (The first non-Brazilian to win a BJJ world championship) in 2006. Currently, I have been a black belt for 16 years, but I continue to study every single day. I became an instructor in JKD in the late 80s. And yes, nearly 40 years later, I train and study JKD every day. I love it.

The most important evolution for me, though, concerns the principle of pressure testing. Bruce Lee changed from Jun Fan Gung Fu to Jeet Kune Do because of what he discovered once he started sparring hard. Namely, many of the elements that he believed were functional actually were not. If you don't believe me, you may want to believe what Bruce Lee wrote in a letter to his Wing Chun classmate and oftentimes instructor Wong Shun Leong.

"*Since I started to practice realistically in 1966 (body protectors, gloves, headgear, etc.), I feel that I had many prejudices before, but they were wrong. So I changed the name of the gist of my study to Jeet Kune Do.*"

I wasn't aware of this letter as I went through my evolution. I had learned a lot of great information and had become an instructor when I decided to enter some combat sports competitions. I found that I could not apply many of my most practiced techniques against an adversary who was actually fighting back. To make a very long story short, I realized through combat sports that it wasn't my technique that was lacking, but rather my method of practicing. I was not doing enough sparring to develop the ability to read an opponent and to properly time my attacks or counterattacks.

We sparred in the JKD class at the Inosanto Academy, and sometimes we did knife sparring in the Kali class. But I didn't really understand the importance of it as I was so infatuated with learning absolutely everything. When I decided to make sparring a primary focus after doing poorly in combat sports competitions, I first started sparring under the rules of combat sports. I later had a revelation; my main goal was practical self-defense, not sport. What I did was to simply put on proper protective equipment and spar kickboxing, clinch, and ground while including the street aspects that were not allowed in sport fighting. Strikes to all targets, suddenly inserting training with knives, and training with pistols into the sparring, and dealing with multiple attackers. Adding these elements radically changed the basic structure and directives in all of the ranges. It was simply running martial arts through the scientific method filter in the environment that I was actually training for.

I came up with a phrase that sums it all up for myself and my JKD Unlimited students. "If you want to learn how to fight, you must practice fighting, against someone who is fighting back!" That is exactly what Bruce Lee did. What changed Jun Fan Gung Fu to Jeet Kune Do was not an evolution of technique; it was an evolution of training methods, i.e. pressure testing through sparring, that necessitated an evolution of technique. Training for self-defense in the same manner that a boxer, fencer, or MMA athlete prepares for a fight is what makes JKD so functional. It illustrates how Bruce Lee was so far ahead of his time. Dry land swimming just can't prepare you for the realities of the ocean.

Why do JKD practitioners get stuck in only doing with Bruce Lee did?

Isn't that an interesting phenomenon? They train in JKD yet many will say that there is absolutely no use for Silat, BJJ, Kali, Krav Maga, or other approaches. This all comes down to bias. Bias is an unsubstantiated prejudice for or against something. Some Jeet Kune Do practitioners (like other martial artists) become biased toward their own art, and then get to a point that their bias is also against all other arts. It's not just "My way is a good way", but it becomes "My way is only way!" In my mind, that is either very shallow or plain dishonest.

The curious thing is that Bruce Lee also addressed bias in his letter to Wong Shun Leong when writing about his prejudices being wrong. He wrote, "Jeet Kune Do is only a name. The most important thing is to avoid having bias in the training."

If you get beyond the name of your art and just immerse yourself in fighting (including sparring against people of other styles, as Bruce Lee did), you can overcome our human tendency towards bias. And you will be much better for it because you will be open to other ways of improving.

You moved to Hawaii and pursued your life there. How has this affected your Martial Arts training since you left Sifu Inosanto's school?

Many people have asked me over the years, "Don't you miss Los Angeles?" I always say that the main things I miss are my extended family, Sifu Inosanto, my friends, and some restaurants. But life here in Hawaii is better than I could've ever imagined.

Luckily, thanks to technology, I'm able to keep in touch with Sifu Inosanto and I see him each time I go to Los Angeles. I've had him here for seminars as well. So I'm glad that connection is still strong. We really have a great time together, with lots of laughing and joking.

My own training has been amazing as well. Hawaii is a warrior place. Fighting is highly respected, and almost everyone raised here has trained martial arts at some point in their life. For a small state, we have produced an inordinately high number of professional MMA fighters. So there are many opportunities to cross train with very high-level athletes.

What do you consider the correct way and protocols to put a student on the JKD path to self-discovery?

You used the key phrase there – self-discovery. Remember "research your own experience"? There are many paths to get a student to be able to express him or herself, but the key is them having personal experience which means sparring. Have I mentioned sparring before? (Laughs)

There are many ways to train a basketball player but they're not going to be any good in a game unless they have actually played a lot of games, whether those are scrimmages or actual contests. To be good at the game, you have to play the game.

I think a big reason that many schools avoid sparring is because people mistake sparring with fighting. Very few people want to go to a class they're paying to get beaten up. That is destructive. We need to understand that sparring and fighting are quite different. In sparring, we are both doing our best to avoid any injury to our partners. In fighting, you are doing your best to dominate an attacker and you inflict as much damage as necessary to end the engagement. Sparring is not fighting, and should be safe and usually enjoyable.

In my classes, new students, even those without any experience at all, spar on the very first night (and in every subsequent class). Does that sound irresponsible? It would be if I had them fighting, but we're talking about sparring.

Bruce Lee introduced what we now call isolated sparring, which is limiting the students to just a few tools and sparring only with those. New students play what I called the "open hand game". Notice it's not the "open hand fight", or "open hand combat"; it is a game. Both people have their hands open and they try to touch the top of their partner's head with control. I sometimes start with only the lead hand allowed. It looks a bit like Western Fencing, but they're just trying to touch the top of the head and guess what happens? The students have a blast! They start smiling and laughing and having fun as they play in a safe environment.

From the very beginning they learn about keeping their hands up, head movement, blocking, and timing their attacks. This is the environment in which I want them to be able to apply their techniques, so this should be introduced daily from day one. Again, imagine learning how to swim for five years without ever getting in the water. We need to experience the environment to function well in that environment.

We start very light and add tools and intensity over time. I borrowed a term from Bodybuilding and call it "progressive resistance". Nobody has to spar hard ever. That is a personal choice. Just keep in mind that while sparring hard is more dangerous, it also gives us more realistic feedback.

So instead of teaching techniques for years and then finally having the student spar once in a while, we just get at it right away so they know that the goal is to apply the techniques they are learning against an uncooperative partner.

When I started at the Kali Academy in 1980, we learned fundamentals for two months and then were instructed to buy boxing gloves and a mouthpiece for the following week. That's when we started sparring. Unfortunately, that first night was quite wild and we lost a lot of students from the class after that first night of sparring. It was a good lesson for everyone.

I introduce sparring from the beginning, but very lightly and slowly build up to more vigorous sparring for those who wish to do so. Those who wish to be instructors must log many, many rounds of sparring. Anyone who does enough moderate intensity, safe sparring can become proficient in it. They don't have to be world champion caliber and nobody is going to be Bruce Lee. But they must be fluent in the language of sparring. In my eyes, if an instructor candidate cannot spar well, then he or she doesn't have a deep understanding of how to apply the art. They shouldn't teach until they are competent in sparring. Jeet Kune Do is a fighting art, so every instructor must be able to fight. That's why the physical test is predominantly moderate intensity sparring. No sparring, no JKD. Pretty simple.

The art of JKD is about 'self-expression'—if we follow that conceptual part of the art and our personal expression ends up being something totally different from what Bruce Lee was doing and teaching physically…should we call it Jeet Kune Do?

Are we talking about Jun Fan JKD, the fighting methods that Bruce Lee developed and actually used himself, or the philosophy of JKD which is research and development, using no way as way and having no limitation as limitation? It's an interesting debate. If someone is highly competent fighting in all the ranges, should they call it JKD?

I am inclined toward Sifu Inosanto's point of view on this. Discussing this many years ago, he told me that he thought someone must have a strong base in Bruce Lee's method in order to call their personal expression JKD. That seems reasonable to me. If you put a Ferrari looking body kit on a Chevrolet you shouldn't call it a Ferrari. But you can modify a Ferrari all you want and still call it a Ferrari. I also believe that a JKD-labeled practitioner should not be limited to those who only practice what Bruce Lee did in his tragically short lifetime. Start with Jun Fan JKD as a base and as you expand, be sure that the *principle of "street-specific pressure testing" remains front and center.*

UFC president Dana White has called Bruce Lee the "grandfather of MMA". Many JKD devotees refute this, saying that JKD has absolutely nothing to do with sport. It is purely for street self-defense. Do you have any thoughts on this?

I do. First off, I think it's absurd to say that JKD has nothing to do with sports. Wing Chun, Fencing, and Boxing are the foundations of JKD. Two of those are "combat sports". Only Wing Chun, which is less than a third of the foundation, is not a sport.

I have coached at the highest level of MMA both in the UFC and "Shooto" organizations. Training to win an actual fight is exactly what Bruce Lee intended. He mixed elements of various martial arts to fill in the gaps to become a complete fighter when sticking to one method was the norm. The majority of MMA champions and coaches were highly influenced by Bruce Lee's art and philosophy and often give him credit for much of their success. So I agree that if there is a grandfather of MMA, it is Bruce Lee.

When you are training a fighter to compete against another highly skilled athlete, there is no time for foolishness. Everything must be highly efficient, pressure tested, and modified for the individual fighter. This is exactly the mindset that Bruce Lee had in his JKD training; he just directed all of his energies toward preparing for a street altercation with no rules at all.

Where do you see the art of Jeet Kune Do going into the future with the first generation of Bruce Lee's student almost gone or retired from teaching?

My fear is that it just becomes another "paint-by-numbers" traditional art. That would be such a loss for the martial arts world and for the legacy of Bruce Lee. Jeet Kune Do must remain alive. Each individual practitioner must become a competent fighter, through fighting, instead of a master of memorization. Real fighting is about relating to an opponent in the moment. Not merely going through a routine of techniques, but feeling the situation, detecting or creating openings, and taking advantage of them with proper technique at the precisely correct moment. That is not easy. It takes great dedication and a lot of disappointment when sparring to find all of your weaknesses.

The beauty of taking this road is that it truly builds character. People often talk about martial arts as a character building activity. You don't build character when everything's going great. You build character through overcoming difficulties. This is another reason why Bruce Lee said that JKD is not for everyone. You have to fail, engage in serious self-reflection, then have the courage to go back and repeat the process over and over again until failure is minimized. Minimized, but never totally eliminated if you are doing it right.

For those who train in authentic Jun Fan JKD (where sparring is the most important training method) will eventually earn the right to have great confidence while remaining humble. Just as Bruce Lee found that a lot of his prejudices were wrong, we can discover the causes of our ignorance, change them, and become better people.

For me personally, I think the ultimate goal of training realistically in the martial arts is to build confidence in yourself so that you can display kindness, from strength, to people you do not know. You don't have to be afraid to ask a stranger if they need help. You can smile at strangers regardless of what their reaction might be. This actually takes a lot of strength and I'm glad I developed that through the practice of Jeet Kune Do and other arts. It has made my life much more peaceful, and that little boy who is so horribly abused at the hands of a bigger stronger predator can now walk the streets with a smile on his face, unafraid.

Would you like to say any closing words?

First, I have so much gratitude for all of my instructors. Many of them have now passed away but they live on through me, their other students, and through our students. Their generosity will never be forgotten.

I would like to revisit something I mentioned earlier. I believe it's a great goal to train to be so confident in your self-defense skills that you don't need to fear any stranger you happen to come across on the street. Instead of being fearful and putting up shields, you can be at peace, smile, and offer them kindness. That may sound sappy to you, but I really believe it does both parties so much good. And you will feel amazing.

I would like to thank especially to the man with the highest integrity I've ever known, who is also the most generous person I've ever known; Sifu Dan Inosanto. I can tell stories for hours about his integrity and generosity. I wish you could all know him as I do.

Let's not allow Jeet Kune Do to become a dead art. Let's actually play the game and develop ourselves and students, regardless of age, into JKD combat athletes who are exemplary martial artists. That's what Sigung Bruce Lee did and I am sure that would want this.

www.ingramcontent.com/pod-product-compliance
Lightning Source LLC
Chambersburg PA
CBHW081441070526
44586CB00019B/2191